The

Warren Family
of Philadelphia,
Pennsylvania

and their ancestors

The
Warren Family of Philadelphia, Pennsylvania

and their ancestors

Contents

To all those who came before us.
We would not be what we are without your work and sacrifice.
You are not forgotten.
– Kerry Gans

Preface

This book is the result of twenty years of genealogical research. In addition to full source citations as endnotes after each chapter, I have a name index in the back for ease of looking up individuals, and a place index that provides a good overview of where my ancestors lived and came from.

Most of the Warren lineages extend back all the way to the very earliest colonial America times. This can make it hard to make the connection "across the pond" to my roots in Europe.

In particular, I have had very little luck with the Warren trunk line—finding only back to James William Warren, Sr., born in Nova Scotia in 1811.

One wonderful resource that came into my possession recently was the Warren Family Bible, which belonged to Mary Hobson Warren Leinau, James' wife, and her second husband, Daniel Leinau. Daniel would have been the only father my ancestor James William Warren, III, ever knew, as his father, James, died before young James was even born.

The Warren Family Bible also contained pages torn from Mary Hobson Warren's Hobson Family Bible, delineating the Hobsons and the Kites. These combined family Bibles were a windfall of information, opening doors into many lineages.

This book is organized with the Warren and McFarlin Lineage chapters first, since they are the trunk lineages, and all the rest in alphabetical order. The Gans–specific chapters are at the end, because they are a subset of the overall Warren ancestry and do not apply to everyone. Lineages are arranged from oldest known ancestor to newest, set up in families with appropriate cross–references where applicable.

I hope you enjoy this family history, complete with lineage trees, nationality charts, and pictures. Anyone reading this book with further information to add, or evidence to prove or disprove information in this book, please contact me, so we can grow our family history together!

Kerry Gans
28 February 2014

The Warren Lineage

James W. Warren, Sr.
1811-1904
(emigrated from Nova Scotia, Canada)

Mary Sellars Hobson
1821-1904
(see Hobson Chapter)

James William Warren, III
1853-1920

Clara C. Godshall
1859-1925
(see Godshall Chapter)

Harold Stites Warren
1893-1961

Clara McFarlin
1891-1987
(see McFarlin Chapter)

Clara Andrina Warren
1918-2011

Nancy McFarlin Warren
1919-1992
(see Gans Chapter for marriage)

Marjorie Edith Warren
1922-2012

The Warren Lineage

James W. Warren (1811–1852) and Mary Sellars Hobson (1821–1904)
(see The Hobson Lineage chapter)

Not much is known about James W. Warren. According to the coroner's report, James W. was born in Halifax, Nova Scotia.[1] James W. Warren was born on 18 May 1811.[2] Mary Sellars Hobson was born 7 May 1821.[3] Although there is some indication that James W. might have been in Philadelphia as early as 1837 (in the City Directory there is a J.W. Warren, Cabinet maker)[4], our first positive documentation of him is his marriage to Mary Hobson.

James W. and Mary were married 18 September 1839 by the Rev. Mr. Grant, who was apparently an Episcopalian minister at Grace Church in Philadelphia.[5] Mary was 18 years old, James W. was 28, and they both lived in the Spring Garden District at the time.

James W. and Mary had 6 children. All were born in Pennsylvania:

Clara (b. 1841) – *married Lt. Frederick Valletto McNair, US Navy, 9 October*
    1862 in Philadelphia.[6]
Thomas Clifford (1844–1879) – *married Emma Matilda Spooner*
    (daughter of John Henry Spooner and Matilda Sexton) 23 May 1873 in Philadelphia.[7]
Benjamin Franklin (1845–1914) – *married Emma Frances Kinsey 29*
    June 1887 in Philadelphia.[8]
James William, Jr. (1848–1853)[9] – *He died at age 5 of typhoid fever. He is buried with*
    his father and mother in Laurel Hill Cemetery, Section Q, Lot 304.[10]
Henry Laws (b. 1850) – *married Mary L. Drew (daughter of William Drew) 12 January*
    1888 in Philadelphia and later moved to Lansdowne, PA.[11]
James William, III (1853–1920) – *married Clara C. Godshall.*

The 1840 census showed a James Warren in Spring Garden. Also in the household were 2 women between 15 and 20. Mary would be 19, so one would be her. The other? Could be a sister or even a friend.[12]

The City Directory showed James W. in 1852 as a conductor living at 209 Green,[13] and again in 1853 as a conductor living at 340 Green.[14]

James W. Warren died 5 October 1852 of "injuries sustained on the railroad," at age 41. He was a conductor on the Philadelphia, Wilmington and Baltimore Railroad. He fell off the roof of the train and was run over, severing his arm and killing him instantly when his chest was crushed. Prior to being a conductor, he worked as a clerk at Rockwell & Wilson, who were tailors and clothiers' of boys' and men's clothes.[15] James' brother–in–law Benjamin Hobson was a tailor, so this could be either how James got the tailor job or how he met Mary.

He lived at 340 Green Street at the time of his death. James was buried in Monument Cemetery, Philadelphia, PA, in a plot owned by Margaret Seward Hobson, his wife's sister–in–law.[16] Monument Cemetery is now closed. Notations on the records indicated he was moved to Laurel Hill Cemetery on 26 March 1869[17], and is buried there in Section Q, Lot 304.[18] His widow, Mary, was 31, left with 5 children and another on the way.

James W. Jr. (age 5 at death) died of typhoid fever on 31 January 1853[19] (cemetery records says 1 February 1853). He was buried with his father in Monument Cemetery. Like his father, his final resting place is in Laurel Hill.[20]

It is interesting to note that our ancestor, *James William Warren, III*, was born 3 months after his older brother died. It seems that his mother named him after both his deceased father and older brother. This is perhaps why he often used William rather than James.

After James W. Sr.'s death, the City Directory listed Mary Warren for several years:

In 1854, Mary Warren (33), a washer, lived at 12 Ralston.[21]
In 1855, Mary Warren (34), washer, at 12 Ronaldson[22]
In 1856, Mary Warren (35), widow, on Church below Reed[23]
In 1857, Mary Warren (36), 17 Federal[24]
In 1858 & 1859, Mary Warren (37–38), Christian Court[25]
In 1860, Mary Warren, seamstress, 910 S. 6th St. [26]

On 31 March 1857, Mary Hobson Warren was married to Daniel Leinau in Philadelphia, PA, by the Rev. J.Z. Ashton. Daniel was from Murfreesboro, TN.[27]

Mary Hobson Warren (aged 38) is on the 1860 Census as the wife of Daniel Leinau (aged 63). In 1860, Mary and the 5 Warren children (Clara, 18; Thomas, 16; Benjamin, 14; Henry, 9; and James William, 7) lived with Daniel Leinau in the 13th Ward of Philadelphia, PA. Daniel (25 years older than Mary) had real estate valued at $7,000, and a personal estate of $10,000. They also had 2 domestics from Ireland – Mary Henry and Rosa Madden.[28]

In 1870, Mary (48), Daniel (70), and the 4 Warren boys (Thomas, 27; Benjamin, 25; Henry, 18; and James William, 16) lived in the 45th District, 15th Ward of Philadelphia, PA. Daniel was a retired merchant, real estate valued at $1,600, personal estate valued at $2,000. Of the 4 boys, only Henry was working, as a clerk in a publishing house (he later owned his own publishing company). James William, at 16, was still in school.[29]

In the second Enumeration of the 1870 Census Mary (50) lived with second husband Daniel (75), her daughter, Clara McNair (25), and her husband, Frederick (30), and Mary's boys Thomas (25), Harry (20), and Willie (15). Also listed there were Elizabeth Friend (15) and Susan Smith (25). I don't know if they were servants or how they are related.[30]

In 1880, Mary (54), Daniel (83), Henry (30), and James William (28) still lived in Philadelphia (at 1017 Arch St.), but they seem to have fallen on harder times. All 4 were listed as Boarders, rather than owning their own house. Henry was a clerk in a bookstore and James William was a clerk in a tobacco store. [31]

Daniel died 9 March 1883 at age 87. His obituary mentions that he was a veteran of the War of 1812.[32] He was 16 years old when that war began. He is buried in Laurel Hill Cemetery, Section Q, Lot 304.[33]

Thomas Warren (aged 36 at death) and his wife, Emma (aged 79 at death), are buried in Laurel Hill Cemetery, Philadelphia, PA (Section T, Lot 78).[34] Four of their children are buried there with them.

Benjamin Franklin Warren (aged 69) and his wife, Emma Frances (aged 54), and her mother are buried in Laurel Hill Cemetery, Philadelphia, PA (Section T, Lot 380).[35]

In 1900, Mary Hobson Warren Leinau (79) lived with her son James William and his family at 53 W. Baltimore Ave., Lansdowne, PA.[36] Mary Sellars Leinau died 23 May 1904 at age 83.[37] She is buried in Laurel Hill Cemetery, Section Q, Lot 304. Altogether, Lot Q–304 contains Mary Sellars Hobson Warren Leinau; her first husband, James William Warren, Sr.; their young son, James William Warren, Jr.; Mary's grandsons Warren Leinau McNair (Clara's son, died aged almost 2) and Benjamin Franklin "Frank" Warren (James William, III's son, died age 2.5), and Mary's second husband, Daniel Leinau.

James William Warren, III, (1853–1920) and Clara C. Godshall (1859–1925)
(see the Godshall Lineage chapter)

James William Warren was born 22 May 1853.[38] After growing up in the Leinau household, James William married Clara C. Godshall (born November 1859) in 1884. He was 31; Clara was 25. They were married on 30 January 1884, [39] in St. Matthias Episcopal Church in Philadelphia, PA, by the Rev. Robert Edwards.[40]

James and Clara had 3 children, all born in Pennsylvania:

Ethel (1884–1967)[41] – *married Clifford E. Castle and moved to Connecticut.*[42]
Benjamin Franklin "Frank" (1887–1889)[43] – *He died at age 2.5 and is*
buried in Laurel Hill Cemetery Section Q, Lot 304, with his grandparents.[44]
Harold Stites (1893–1961)[45] – *married Clara McFarlin.*

From 1889 to 1893, the family lived at 611 North 18th Street, Philadelphia, PA.[46]

In 1900, the family lived in Lansdowne, Delaware County, PA. They lived in a rented house on Baltimore Avenue. James William (47) was a salesman. Also living with them was James' widowed mother, Mary Linaw (Leinau) (79). There were also 2 black servants from Virginia, Emma Drummond, who was married, and Nana C. Williams, who was single. Clara was 40, and children Ethel and Harold were 15 and 6.[47]

In 1910, James William (56) and family lived at 1229 South 59th Street in Philadelphia, PA. With him were wife Clara (47) and son Harold (16). This Census lists birthplaces of the parents of the people, and this one does state that James William's father was born in Nova Scotia. James William was a coal salesman, and they lived in a rented house.[48]

In 1917, the family lived at 5836 Ashland Ave., Philadelphia, PA. James was a clerk.[49]

James William Warren, III, died 6 December 1920, at age 67. At that time, he lived at 4042 Walnut St., Philadelphia, PA. His cause of death was senility, which caused a fall at home and a fractured femur.[50] He is buried in Laurel Hill Cemetery, Philadelphia, PA (Section T, Lot 380).[51]

Clara Godshall Warren died in March 1925, at age 65. She still lived at 4042 Walnut St., and was buried in Laurel Hill Cemetery, Philadelphia, PA (Section T, Lot 380) on 18 March 1925.[52]

Harold Stites Warren (1893–1961) and Clara McFarlin (1891–1987)
(see McFarlin Lineage chapter)

Harold Stites Warren was born at 611 N. 18th St., Philadelphia, PA, on 11 December 1893.[53]

Harold Stites married Clara McFarlin on 9 April 1917 in Philadelphia, PA. He was 24; she was 26. At the time of their marriage application in 1917, Harold Stites lived at 5836 Ashland Ave., West Philadelphia, and his occupation was listed as Insurance. Clara McFarlin was a school teacher residing at 5303 Catharine St., West Philadelphia.[54] After their marriage, they lived at 1027 South 54th Street, Philadelphia, PA.[55]

They had 3 children, all born in Pennsylvania:

Clara Andrina (1918–2011)[56] – *married William Bright. They had 4 children.*[57]
Nancy McFarlin (1919–1992)[58] – *married William Thomas Gans.*
Marjorie Edith (1922–2012)[59] – *married Edward Gondolf. They had 2 children.*[60]

In 1920, the family still lived at 1027 54th St. Harold was 27, Clara was 28. They owned this house free and clear, and Harold was an accountant with Birkley Knitting Mills. Daughters Clara (2) and Nancy (3 months) lived with them.[61]

In 1930, the family lived at 409 Strathmore Rd., Haverford, Delaware County, PA. This is the house that came to be known as "Warawee" to the Warren family. Harold (38) owned this house free and clear, and its value was $2,500. They also owned a radio set. His occupation at the time was salesman. He worked for the Janzen Knitting Company as their northeastern rep.[62] Wife Clara was 39. Daughters Clara (12), Nancy (10), and Marjorie (7) lived with them, and attended school.[63]

In 1940, Harold (48) lived there with wife, Clara (49), and youngest daughter, Marjorie (17). They owned the house, at a value of $ 5,000. Harold was a traveling salesman for a knitting company (Janzen), and he made $4,000 per year.[64]

Harold Stites and Clara continued to live at Warawee. Harold Stites Warren died 30 May 1961 at home, at age 67. Cause of death was stroke due to hypertension/heart disease. He is buried in West Laurel Hill Cemetery, Philadelphia, PA, in Everglade 516.[65] [66]

Clara McFarlin Warren continued to live at Warawee until 1975, when she moved to Devon Manor in Devon, PA.[67] As her health declined, she moved into Tenacre, a Christian Science nursing facility in Princeton, NJ. She moved into Tenacre 27 March 1981, and stayed there until her death on 7 March 1987, at age 95.[68] She is also buried in West Laurel Hill Cemetery, Everglade 516.[69] [70]

Nancy McFarlin Warren married William Thomas Gans, Sr. in 1939. He was 23; she was 19. *(See The Gans Lineage chapter.)*

---

[1] Cemetery Return 1852 Roll 606, Frame 1126. Coroner's entry Oct. 5, 1852, Thomas Oliver Goldsmith. Originals housed at Philadelphia City Archives, 3101 Market Street, Philadelphia, PA 19104.
[2] Warren-Leinau Family Bible. Original in possession of Kerry Gans Douglas.
[3] Kite-Tunis-Sellars-Hobson Family Bible. Original in possession of Kerry Gans Douglas.
[4] *DeSilver's Philadelphia City Directory 1837*. Philadelphia: DeSilver's, 1837, p. 246.
[5] Marriage announcement of James W. Warren and Mary S. Hobson. *Philadelphia Public Ledger* 20 September 1839.
[6] Warren-Leinau Family Bible. Original in possession of Kerry Gans Douglas.
[7] Warren-Leinau Family Bible. Original in possession of Kerry Gans Douglas.
[8] Warren-Leinau Family Bible. Original in possession of Kerry Gans Douglas.
[9] Warren-Leinau Family Bible. Original in possession of Kerry Gans Douglas.
[10] Laurel Hill Cemetery Records. Original housed at Laurel Hill Cemetery, 3822 Ridge Ave., Philadelphia, PA 19132.
[11] Warren-Leinau Family Bible. Original in possession of Kerry Gans Douglas.

[12] *1840 United States Census*, Spring Garden District, Philadelphia, PA: Year: 1840; Census Place: Spring Garden Ward 1, Philadelphia, Pennsylvania; Roll: 487; Page: 364; Image: 1218; Family History Library Film: 0020555

[13] *McElroy's Philadelphia City Directory 1852*. Philadelphia: A. McElroy & Co., 1852, p. 460.

[14] *McElroy's Philadelphia City Directory 1853*. Philadelphia: A. McElroy & Co., 1853, p. 432.

[15] Obituary and article of James W. Warren's death. *Philadelphia Public Ledger* 7 October 1852.

[16] Cemetery Return 1852 Roll 606, Frame 1112. Originals housed at Philadelphia City Archives, 3101 Market Street, Philadelphia, PA 19104.

[17] Monument Cemetery Lot Books B 880, Roll XR 967.2

[18] Laurel Hill Cemetery Records. Original housed at Laurel Hill Cemetery, 3822 Ridge Ave., Philadelphia, PA 19132.

[19] Warren-Leinau Family Bible. Original in possession of Kerry Gans Douglas.

[20] Monument Cemetery Lot Books B 880, Roll XR 967.2

[21] *McElroy's Philadelphia City Directory 1854*. Philadelphia: A. McElroy & Co., 1854, p. 550.

[22] *McElroy's Philadelphia City Directory 1855*. Philadelphia: A. McElroy & Co., 1855, p. 582.

[23] *McElroy's Philadelphia City Directory 1856*. Philadelphia: A. McElroy & Co., 1856, p. 673.

[24] *McElroy's Philadelphia City Directory 1857*. Philadelphia: A. McElroy & Co., 1857, p. 705.

[25] *McElroy's Philadelphia City Directory 1858*. Philadelphia: A. McElroy & Co., 1858, p. 712; *McElroy's Philadelphia City Directory 1859*. Philadelphia: A. McElroy & Co., 1859, p. 743.

[26] *McElroy's Philadelphia City Directory 1860*. Philadelphia: A. McElroy & Co., 1860, p. 938.

[27] Marriage Certificate, and Warren-Leinau Family Bible. Original in possession of Kerry Gans Douglas.

[28] *1860 United States Census*, 13th Ward, Philadelphia, PA. Year: 1860; Census Place: Philadelphia Ward 13, Philadelphia, Pennsylvania; Roll: M653_1163; Page: 484; Image: 70; Family History Library Film: 805163.

[29] *1870 United States Census*, Dist. 45, 15th Ward, Philadelphia, PA Post Office: 1509 Ogden Street. Year: 1870; Census Place: Philadelphia Ward 15 District 45, Philadelphia, Pennsylvania; Roll: M593_1399; Page: 672A; Image: 775; Family History Library Film: 552898.

[30] *1870 United States Census*: Year: 1870; Census Place: Philadelphia Ward 15 Dist 45 (2nd Enum), Philadelphia, Pennsylvania; Roll: M593_1427; Page: 253A; Image: 517; Family History Library Film: 552926.

[31] *1880 United States Census*, Arch St., Philadelphia, PA. Year: 1880; Census Place: Philadelphia, Philadelphia, Pennsylvania; Roll: 1172; Family History Film: 1255172; Page: 190B; Enumeration District: 171; Image: 0186.

[32] Obituary of Daniel Leinau. *Philadelphia Inquirer* 13 March 1883.

[33] Laurel Hill Cemetery Records. Original housed at Laurel Hill Cemetery, 3822 Ridge Ave., Philadelphia, PA 19132.

[34] Laurel Hill Cemetery Records. Original housed at Laurel Hill Cemetery, 3822 Ridge Ave., Philadelphia, PA 19132.

[35] Laurel Hill Cemetery Records. Original housed at Laurel Hill Cemetery, 3822 Ridge Ave., Philadelphia, PA 19132.

[36] *1900 United States Census*. Lansdowne, PA. Year: 1900; Census Place: Lansdowne, Delaware, Pennsylvania; Roll: 1406; Page: 16B; Enumeration District: 192; FHL microfilm: 1241406.

[37] Obituary of Mary Hobson Warren Leinau. *Philadelphia Inquirer* 25 May 1904.

[38] Warren-Leinau Family Bible. Original in possession of Kerry Gans Douglas.

[39] Return of Marriages, Philadelphia, PA, Jan 1-June 31, 1884. Originals housed at Philadelphia City Archives, 3101 Market Street, Philadelphia, PA 19104.

[40] An email to the Episcopal Church revealed that Rev. Edwards was assigned to St. Matthias Church in Philadelphia in 1884, so I made the assumption that this is where they married. St. Matthias no longer exists and the records have disappeared.

[41] Warren-Leinau Family Bible. Original in possession of Kerry Gans Douglas.

[42] Daughters of the American Revolution Lineage – Thomas Waugh, submitted by Ethel Warren Castle. Originals housed with National Society Daughters of the American Revolution, 1776 D Street, NW, Washington, DC, 20006-5303.

[43] Warren-Leinau Family Bible. Original in possession of Kerry Gans Douglas.

[44] Laurel Hill Cemetery Records. Original housed at Laurel Hill Cemetery, 3822 Ridge Ave., Philadelphia, PA 19132.

[45] Warren-Leinau Family Bible. Original in possession of Kerry Gans Douglas.

[46] Death Certificate of Benjamin Franklin "Frank" Warren (1889); Birth Certificate of Harold Stites Warren (1893). Originals housed at Philadelphia City Archives, 3101 Market Street, Philadelphia, PA 19104.

[47] *1900 United States Census*, Lansdowne Borough, Delware County, PA. Year: 1900; Census Place: Lansdowne, Delaware, Pennsylvania; Roll: 1406; Page: 16B; Enumeration District: 192; FHL microfilm: 1241406.

[48] *1910 United States Census*, 5th Dist., 40th Ward, Philadelphia, PA. Year: 1910; Census Place: Philadelphia Ward 40, Philadelphia, Pennsylvania; Roll: T624_1410; Page: 5A; Enumeration District: 1011; Image: 122; FHL microfilm: 1375423.

[49] Marriage Application & Certificate of Harold Stites Warren & Clara McFarlin. Originals housed at Philadelphia City Archives, 3101 Market Street, Philadelphia, PA 19104.

[50] Death Certificate of James William Warren. Original housed at PA Department of Health, Division of Vital records, PO Box 1528, New Castle, PA 16103.

[51] Laurel Hill Cemetery Records. Original housed at cemetery, 3822 Ridge Ave., Philadelphia, PA 19132.

[52] Laurel Hill Cemetery Records. Original housed at Laurel Hill Cemetery, 3822 Ridge Ave., Philadelphia, PA 19132.

[53] Birth Certificate of Harold Stites Warren. Originals housed at Philadelphia City Archives, 3101 Market Street, Philadelphia, PA 19104.

[54] Marriage Application & Certificate of Harold Stites Warren & Clara McFarlin #360 900. Originals housed at Philadelphia City Archives, 3101 Market Street, Philadelphia, PA 19104.

[55] Marriage Announcement of Harold Stites Warren & Clara McFarlin. Original in possession of Kerry Gans Douglas.

[56] Personal Witness – author Kerry Gans Douglas attended Clare's memorial service

[57] Personal recollection of Clare Warren Bright

[58] Personal Witness – author Kerry Gans Douglas attended Nancy's memorial service

[59] Personal Witness – author Kerry Gans Douglas attended Marge's memorial service

[60] Personal recollection of Marge Warren Gondolf

[61] *1920 United States Census*, Ward 40, Philadelphia, PA. Year: 1920; Census Place: Philadelphia Ward 40, Philadelphia, Pennsylvania; Roll: T625_1642; Page: 1B; Enumeration District: 1514; Image: 559.

[62] Personal Witness: Harold Stites Warren's daughter Marjorie Warren Gondolf told author Kerry Gans.

[63] *1930 United States Census*, Haverford Township, Delaware County, PA. Year: 1930; Census Place: Haverford, Delaware, Pennsylvania; Roll: 2031; Page: 31A; Enumeration District: 73; Image: 766.0; FHL microfilm: 2341765.

[64] 1940 United States Census, Haverford, PA. Year: 1940; Census Place: New York, Queens, New York; Roll: T627_2721; Page: 3B; Enumeration District: 41-99.

[65] Death Certificate of Harold Stites Warren. Original housed at PA Department of Health, Division of Vital records, PO Box 1528, New Castle, PA 16103.

[66] West Laurel Hill Cemetery Records. Original housed at West Laurel Hill Cemetery, 215 Belmont Ave., Bala Cynwyd, PA 19004.

[67] Personal Witness: told to author Kerry Gans Douglas by 4 of Clara's grandchildren.

[68] Records of Tenacre nursing home.

[69] Social Security Death Index. Found online at: http://www.deathindexes.com/ssdi.html

[70] West Laurel Hill Cemetery Records. Original housed at West Laurel Hill Cemetery, 215 Belmont Ave., Bala Cynwyd, PA 19004.

THE WARREN FAMILY BIBLE

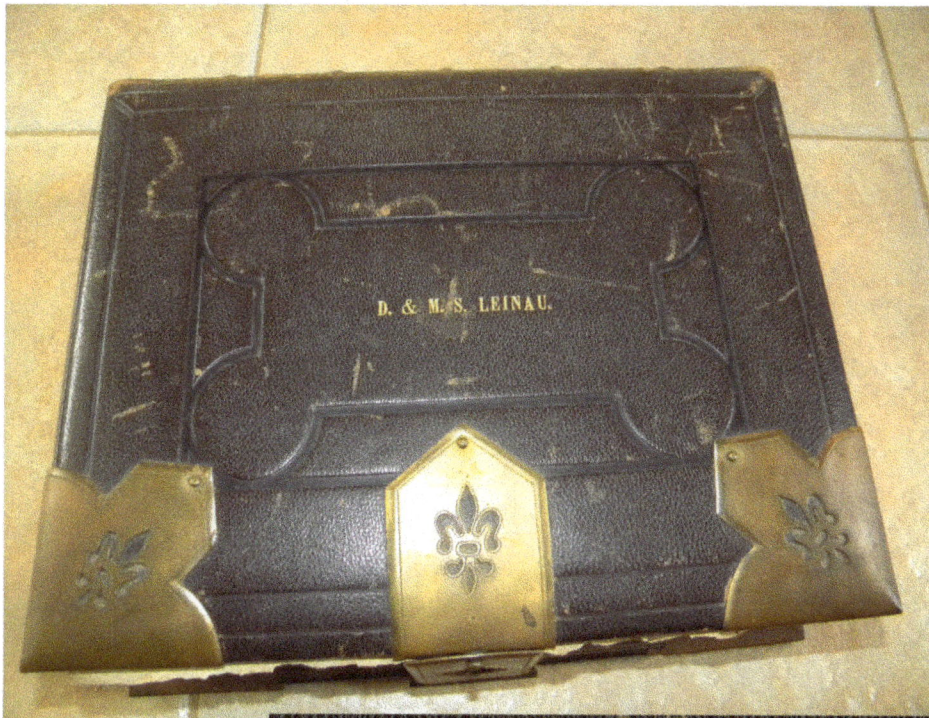

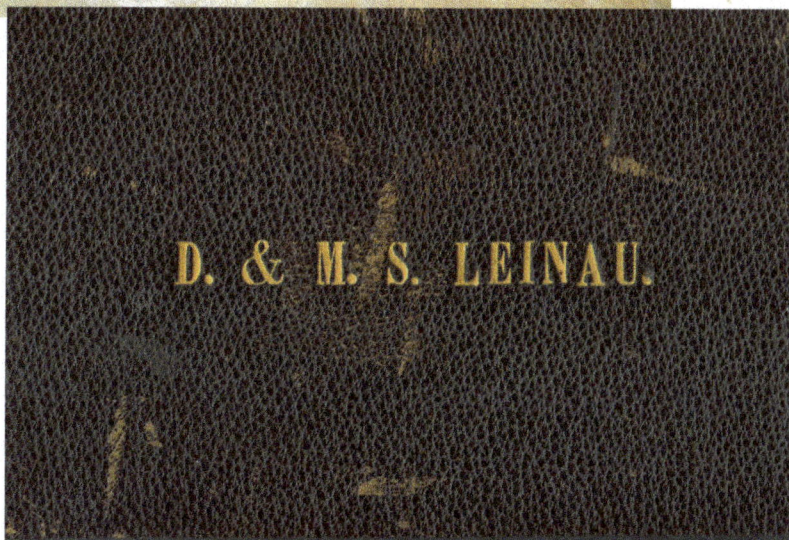

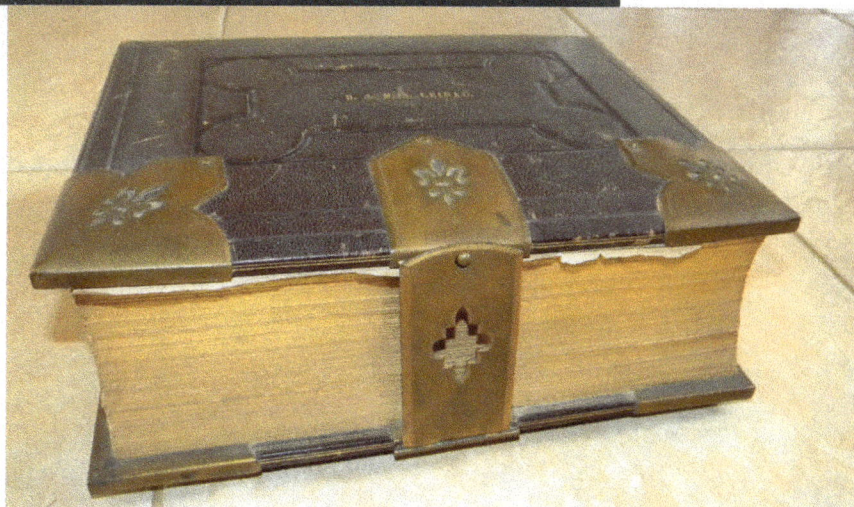

WARREN FAMILY BIBLE ENTRIES

MARRIED ON THE 18TH OF SEPTEMBER 1839
JAMES WM. WARREN TO MARY SELLARS HOBSON

JAMES WM. WARREN DIED
OCTOBER 6TH, 1852
AGED 41 YRS 4 M 17 D

JAMES WILLIAM WARREN
BORN MAY 22ND 1853
AT 7 AM

DANIEL LEINAU & MARY S. WARREN
WERE MARRIED ON THE
31ST DAY OF MARCH 1857
IN PHILADELPHIA, PENN.
AT 8 O'CLOCK AM BY J.Z. ASHTON

DANIEL LEINAU DIED
MARCH THE 9TH 1883
IN THE 87TH YEAR OF HIS AGE

Warren Family Bible Entries (Cont.)

married in Philadelphia
on Wednesday Jan 30th 1884
by Rev. Robt. A. Edwards
Jas Wm. Warren to
Clara C. Godshall, daughter of
Henry S. Godshall

**MARRIED IN PHILADELPHIA
ON WEDNESDAY JAN 30TH 1884
BY REV. ROBT. A. EDWARDS
JAS WM. WARREN TO
CLARA C. GODSHALL, DAUGHTER OF
HENRY S. GODSHALL**

Harold Stites Warren
Son of Jas Warren & Clara
Godshall Warren was born
Dec 11th 1893 at 12.30 M
Phila. Pa

**HAROLD STITES WARREN
SON OF JAS WM WARREN &
CLARA GODSHALL WARREN
WAS BORN DEC 11TH, 1893
AT 12:30, PHILADELPHIA, PA**

Mary Sellers Leinau
Died May 23rd 1904
Aged 83 years

**MARY SELLERS LEINAU
DIED MAY 23RD, 1904
AGED 83 YEARS**

MARRIAGE CERTIFICATE OF MARY HOBSON WARREN
AND SECOND HUSBAND DANIEL LEINAU, 1857

LAUREL HILL CEMETERY
PHILADELPHIA, PA

MARKER OF
BENJ. FRANK.
WARREN, SON
OF OUR
JAMES W., III

MARY HOBSON WARREN
LEINAU & 2ND
HUSBAND DANIEL

JAMES WILLIAM WARREN, SR.
& SON
JAMES WILLIAM WARREN, JR.

(PHOTOS TAKEN 30 APRIL 2011)

CLARA GODSHALL WARREN (1859-1925)

JAMES WILLIAM WARREN, III (1853-1920)

(DATE OF PHOTOS UNKNOWN)

LAUREL HILL CEMETERY
PHILADELPHIA, PA

PLOT OF JAMES WILLIAM WARREN, III, & CLARA GODSHALL WARREN
THEY HAVE NO HEADSTONES. THE HEADSTONES ARE FOR JAMES'
BROTHER, BENJAMIN FRANKLIN WARREN & HIS FAMILY.

WARREN PLOT MARKER

LAUREL HILL CEMETERY

Founded in 1836 and designed by Scottish architect John Notman, this was the nation's second major rural cemetery. With its rolling landscape, horticultural plantings, and eclectic architecture, it offered a romantic alternative to the crowded urban environment. Overlooking the Schuylkill River, 3.5 miles north of center-city, it had grown by 1861 to 78 acres. This cemetery was designated a National Historic Landmark in 1998.

PENNSYLVANIA HISTORICAL AND MUSEUM COMMISSION 2000

(PHOTOS TAKEN 30 APRIL 2011)

HAROLD STITES
WARREN
1921

(DATE UNKNOWN)

Mr. and Mrs. Edward Arthur McFarlin

announce the marriage of their daughter

Clara

to

Mr. Harold Stites Warren

on Monday April the ninth

nineteen hundred and seventeen

Philadelphia

At Home

after the fifteenth of May

Ten twenty seven South Fifty fourth Street

Philadelphia

CHAPEL OF THE EPIPHANY
380 BALTIMORE AVE., W PHILA
WEDDING OF HAROLD STITES WARREN & CLARA McFARLIN
9 APRIL 1917

CLARA MCFARLIN WARREN
CHRISTMAS 1937

Bachrach

WEDDING
9 APRIL 1917

HAROLD STITES WARREN
CHRISTMAS 1937

WARAWEE
(HAROLD STITES WARREN & CLARA MCFARLIN WARREN
IN FRONT OF HOUSE IN BOTTOM PHOTO)

"Warawee"
Harold Stites Warren & Clara McFarlin Warren's Home
409 Strathmore Ave., Havertown, PA

(photos: January 2006)

Harold Stites Warren's
Cigarette Case & Pocketwatch

HAROLD STITES & CLARA MCFARLIN WARREN

WARAWEE IN THE SNOW

HAROLD STITES & CLARA MCFARLIN WARREN

(PHOTOS COURTESY OF WARREN GONDOLF, TAKEN BY ED GONDOLF)

FROM LEFT: BILL BRIGHT, BILL GANS, SR., ED GONDOLF & HAROLD STITES WARREN

BABY MARGE, CLARE AND NANCY

WARREN SISTERS
c. 1926

The Warren Sisters

Marge, Nancy, Clare
c. 1928

Nancy, Marge, Clare
c. 1934

Nancy, Clare, Harold, Clara, Marge

March 1937 - Warren Family

Clare, "Gran," Marge, Nancy

Nov. 1973 -
at Bill & Clare Bright's
Huntsville, AL

Nancy, Marge, Clare
c. 1987

WEST LAUREL HILL CEMETERY
PHILADELPHIA, PA

WARREN

HAROLD S. WARREN
1893 ✝ 1961
CLARA McFARLIN WARREN
1891 ✝ 1987
WILLIAM T. GANS
1915 ✝ 1974
NANCY W. GANS
1919 ✝ 1992
WILLIAM JAY BRIGHT
1914 ✝ 1990
CLARE ANDRINA WARREN BRIGHT
1918 ✝ 2011

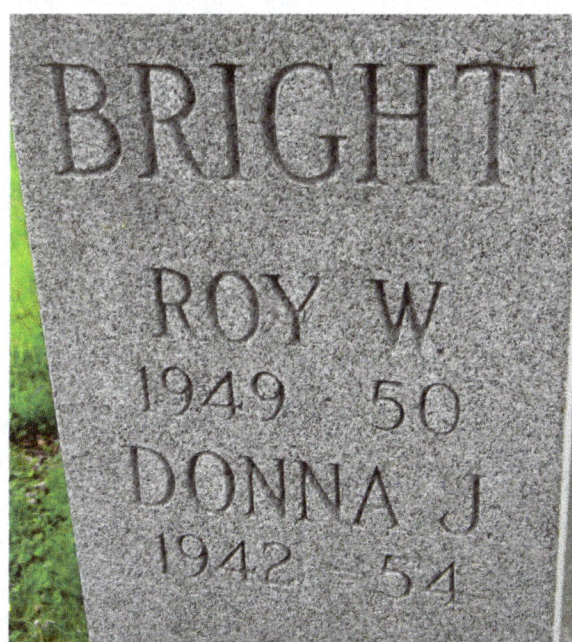

BRIGHT

ROY W.
1949 50
DONNA J.
1942 54

**WARREN-McFARLIN
FAMILY PLOT**

HAROLD S. WARREN &
CLARA McFARLIN WARREN

NANCY WARREN GANS
& WILLIAM T. GANS, SR.

CLARE ANDRINA WARREN BRIGHT
& WILLIAM JAY BRIGHT
& CHILDREN
ROY W. & DONNA J.

MARGERY WARREN GONDOLF
& EDWARD GONDOLF

(PHOTOS TAKEN 30 APRIL 2011 & 20 FEBRUARY 2013)

The McFarlin Lineage

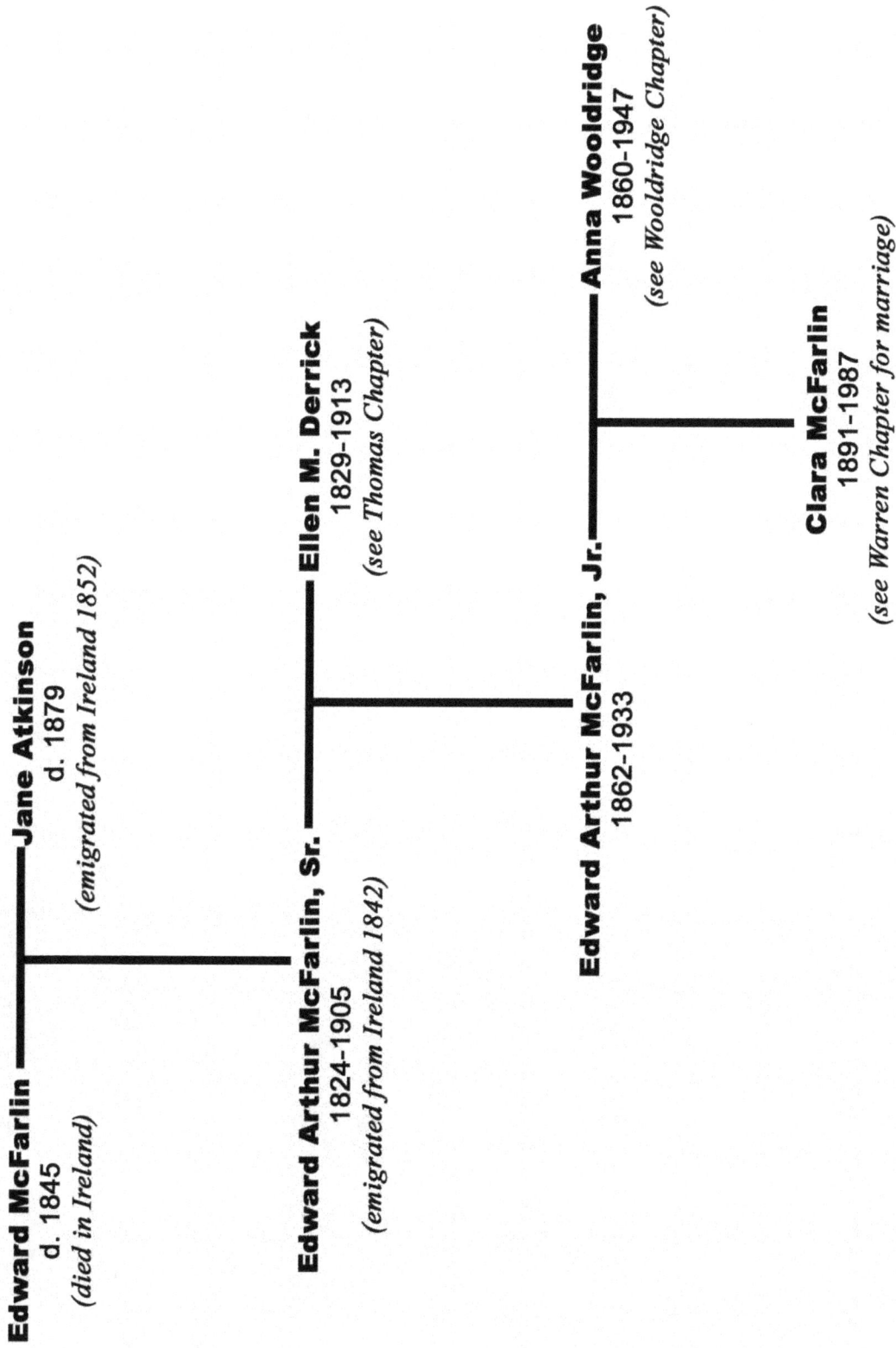

Edward McFarlin
d. 1845
(died in Ireland)

Jane Atkinson
d. 1879
(emigrated from Ireland 1852)

Edward Arthur McFarlin, Sr.
1824-1905
(emigrated from Ireland 1842)

Ellen M. Derrick
1829-1913
(see Thomas Chapter)

Edward Arthur McFarlin, Jr.
1862-1933

Anna Wooldridge
1860-1947
(see Wooldridge Chapter)

Clara McFarlin
1891-1987
(see Warren Chapter for marriage)

The McFarlin Lineage

Edward McFarlin (d. 1845) and Jane Atkinson (c. 1800-1879)[1]

All of the below (except where noted) was compiled by Robert D. Stuart, grandson of Edward McFarlin and Jane Atkinson, in January 1930. He would have been 16 at the time of Jane's death, and 67 when he compiled his report.

Not much is known about this couple. Edward McFarlin died in Ireland in 1845. His wife, Jane, immigrated to Delaware with her children. From the two United States Censuses she appears on, her birth date is circa 1800.[2]

Edward and Jane had 7 children, 6 of whom lived past 70 years old – quite a feat in those days! I believe Ellen was the one who did not live into her 70s, as her death date is a full 32 years (or more) before the rest. All were born in Ireland, as were their parents:

Robert (died 1895) – *married Jane Morrow, had no children. Is buried in Greenhill Presbyterian Churchyard, DE.*

Mary Jane (died 1900) – *married William Banks, reared 4 children to maturity. Is buried in Methodist Churchyard, New Castle, DE.*

Edward Arthur (1824–1905) – *married Ellen Derrick, reared 7 children to maturity. Is buried in Wilmington & Brandywine Cemetery, DE.*

Ellen (died 1863) – *married James Wright, reared 2 children to maturity. Is buried in Methodist Churchyard, Salem, DE.*

John (died 1906) – *married Margaret McCarter, reared 3 children to maturity. Is buried next to his mother in Episcopal Churchyard, New Castle, DE.*

Eliza Ann (died 1904) – *married Robert Stuart, reared 4 children to maturity. Is buried Riverview Cemetery, Wilmington, DE.*

Isabel (died 1910) – *married James McCarter, reared 4 children to maturity. Is buried in St. Peter's Cemetery, Smyrna, DE.*

The McFarlin family came to America in spurts. John H. McFarlin, a first cousin of the McFarlin family, was born in Delaware, 10 March 1814. He visited Ireland twice and was the cause of them coming to America. He was most likely the John McFarlin who sponsored Edward Arthur in his citizenship. John died 24 February 1881.

Edward Arthur was the first to come to the United States, immigrating in 1842. He applied for citizenship in 1847[3], and took the oath in 1850.[4] Mary Jane, Ellen, and John came in 1848. Robert, Eliza Ann, Isabel, and their mother, Jane, came in 1852, leaving none of the family behind in Ireland.

In 1860, Jane (60) lived with her daughter, Eliza Ann (25), and her husband, Robert Stuart (30). Jane's son John (Eliza's brother, age 28) also lived there. They resided in Christiana, White Clay Creek Hundred (a Hundred is like a township), New Castle, DE.[5]

In 1870, Jane (75) lived with daughter Eliza (35); her husband Robert Stewart (42); their children, Jane (9) and Robert D. (7); a laborer Joseph Livingston (28); a boy listed as "at home" William Levy (15); and domestic servant Eliza Hope (26). Robert was a farmer, and the family lived in Rockland, Wilmington, Christiana Hundred, New Castle, DE.[6]

Jane Atkinson McFarlin died in 1879, and is buried next to her son John in the Immanuel on the Green Episcopal Churchyard in New Castle, DE, in plot 37.[7]

Edward Arthur McFarlin, Sr., (1824–1905) and Ellen M. Derrick (1829–1913)
(see Thomas Lineage chapter)

Edward Arthur McFarlin, Sr., was born in Ireland in December 1824. He immigrated to Delaware in 1842 at age 17, [8] applied for U.S. citizenship in 1847,[9] and became a U.S. citizen 30 November 1850, at age 25.[10] Here he met and married Ellen Derrick (born 10 June 1829), tying the knot 6 January 1851 in New Castle, DE. They were married by Andrew Manship.[11] Edward was 26; Ellen was 21.

Edward and Ellen had 10 children, all born in Delaware:

Eliza Jane (1853–1855)
Mary (1855–1886) – *married a man named Springer.*
Elizabeth (b. 1858) – *married a man named Jordan.*
William (1859 – 1909)
Edward Arthur, Jr. (1862–1933) – *married Anna Wooldridge.*
John (b. 1864)
Maude (1866–1894) – *married a man named Ewing.*
Clara (1868–1903) – *married a man named Calhoun.*
Rebecca Jane (Mar 1871 – Jul 1871)
Alice (1873–1875)

In 1850, Edward (28) lived in the First District of New Castle County, DE. He was a clerk, and lived in a boarding house with his brother John (20), who was a laborer.[12]

On 7 February 1855, Edward (30) and his wife bought their burial plots in the Wilmington & Brandywine Cemetery in Wilmington. He paid $30 for 200 feet of land.[13]

Edward (34) is listed in the 1859–1860 Wilmington (Delaware) Directory as one of the owners of Morrow & McFarlin grocery store, located at 230 Market St. The family resided at 228 King St.[14]

In 1860, Edward (35); his wife Ellen (30); their three children, Mary (4), Lizzie (2), and William (8 months), and Ellen's mother, Ellen Derrick (63), lived in Wilmington, Delaware. Here Edward was a merchant working with a lumber mill the name of which was not quite legible, but seemed to be Larson or Landon or something close. The value of his real estate was $2,000, and his personal estate was $1,200. Also listed in their dwelling is Frederick Herting (36), a gunsmith.[15]

In the 1862–63 Wilmington Directory, Edward was still an owner of Morrow & McFarlin grocers, which is still at 230 Market. His family lived at 230 King St. – which could be a typo, considering that he had formerly lived one door down, at 228 King St. Since he still owned the grocery, it seems his Merchant status at the lumber mill was a sideline business.[16]

By 1870, the McFarlin family had moved away from the big city of Wilmington, and settled in the farmlands of the New Castle Hundred. Edward, now 45, did well for himself. Although listed as a Farmer, his real estate was worth $12,000, and his personal estate $2,500. Wife Ellen (40) and daughter Mary (14) kept the house running, while Elizabeth (12), William (10), and Edward, Jr. (8), went to school. John (6), Maud (4), and

Clara (2) were not in school yet. To help with the little ones, mother–in–law Ellen Derrick (75) still lived with them. Helping on the farm was William Young, a 13–year–old black male.[17]

1880 found the McFarlins in a new state – Pennsylvania. They moved to Ridley, PA, sometime between 1870 and 1880. Edward (54) was still a farmer. Wife Ellen was 50, and Lizzie (22), William (20), and Edward, Jr. (18), were done with school and "at home." John (16), Maude (13), and Clara (11) were now in school. Returning to the state of her birth was Ellen's mother, Ellen Derrick, still going strong at 84. Also living there was Thomas Lauley, a 60–year–old English white male listed as a laborer.[18]

The new millennium, 1900, saw a much depleted McFarlin residence. Still in Ridley, PA, in the Prospect Park Borough, 75–year–old Edward was once again a grocer, although they lived on a farm. Ellen (71) and Edward had been married 49 years, having borne 11 children, with only 5 still living in 1900. Among the living was son William, a 43–year–old bachelor making his living as a carpenter.[19]

Edward Arthur McFarlin, Sr., died of pneumonia in 1905, and is buried in the Wilmington & Brandywine Cemetery, DE, Section D, Lot 13.[20][21]

In 1910, Ellen (80) lived at 662 Chester Ave., Norwood, PA, with son John (45) and his family: wife Matilda (40) and daughter Martha (10). John was a merchant with his own business.[22]

Ellen Derrick McFarlin died 31 October 1913 in Norwood, PA. Cause of death was listed as apoplexy. She is buried with Edward in the Wilmington & Brandywine Cemetery, Section D, Lot 13.[23]

Edward Arthur McFarlin, Jr., (1862–1933) and Anna Wooldridge (1860–1947)
(see Wooldridge Lineage chapter)

Edward Arthur McFarlin, Jr., was born 2 March 1862 in Wilmington, DE.[24] Anna Wooldridge was born 22 April 1860, in Cincinnati, OH.[25][26] They married 19 November 1884, presumably in Pennsylvania, where they were both living at the time.[27][28] He was 22; she was 24.

Edward and Anna had 3 girls, all born in Pennsylvania:

Andrina H. (1888–1913)
Clara (1891–1987) – *married Harold Stites Warren.*
Anna C. (1893–1898)

In 1900, Edward (38) and Anna (40) had been married for 14 years. Edward owned (on a mortgage) the house in Philadelphia, PA, at 1422 McKean Street where they lived. Edward was an insurance adjuster. Andrina (11) and Clara (9) were both at school[29] – young Anna had already died, at age 5.[30]

In 1910, the McFarlins lived at 5303 Catharine St., Philadelphia, PA, in a house owned (but mortgaged) by Edward (48). He was an insurance adjustor with his own company, Superior Life Insurance Co., located at 7th and Pine in Philadelphia, PA. Wife Anna (50) and daughters Andrina (21) and Clara (19) all resided there as well. Both daughters were still attending school, so higher education was given to them.[31]

On 19 November 1910, Edward and Anna celebrated 25 years of marriage at a party in their house on Catharine Street in Philadelphia, PA.[32]

In 1920 they still live at 5303 Catherine St. On the Census, their name is misspelled as McParland, and Anna's name does not appear – it just says "McParland" and the designation "Wife." Edward (59) and Anna (54) were alone – 2 of their 3 daughters had died, the other had married. Edward was still an insurance broker.[33]

On 27 June 1926, Edward and Anna made an appearance in a photo in the *Philadelphia Record*, in an article about Ocean City, NJ.[34]

In 1930, Edward and Anna rented a house on Walnut Street in Philadelphia, PA. Their monthly rent was $70, and they owned a radio set. Edward (67) was still at work in the life insurance business, and his wife, Anna (69), still held the fort at home.[35]

Edward Arthur McFarlin, Jr., died 23 August 1933 at Bryn Mawr Hospital, Lower Merion, PA. Edward and Anna both lived with Clara and her husband at 409 Strathmore Rd., Brookline, Lower Merion, PA. Edward was 71 at his death, and died of a coronary occlusion (heart attack), with a contributing factor of chronic myocarditis. He is buried in West Laurel Hill Cemetery, Philadelphia, PA, in Everglade 516.[36]

Anna Wooldridge McFarlin died 9 May 1947, at age 87. She had spent 343 days at the Marsh. Sq. Sanitarium in West Chester, PA, prior to her death there. Cause of death was cerebral thrombosis, with severe, generalized arteriosclerosis, with psychosis and senility. She also had Paget's disease of the bone. This is also known as osteitis deformans, and is a condition in which normal bone regrowth is replaced by bone regrowth that is soft and porous, causing fractures, bone bending, and deformed or enlarged bones. It can also lead to heart disease, as in Anna. She lived with her daughter's family at 409 Strathmore Rd., Haverford, PA. She is also buried in West Laurel Hill Cemetery, Everglade 516.[37]

Clara McFarlin married Harold Stites Warren in 1917.[38] He was 24; she was 26. *(See The Warren Lineage chapter.)*

[1] Stuart, Robert D. *Family Record of Edward and Jane Atkinson McFarlin*, January 1930. Copy in possession of Kerry Gans Douglas.

[2] *1860 United States Census*, New Castle, DE. Year: *1860*; Census Place: *White Clay Creek Hundred, New Castle, Delaware*; Roll: *M653_97*; Page: *546*; Image: *550*; Family History Library Film: *803097*; *1870 United States Census*, New Castle, DE. Year: *1870*; Census Place: *Christiana Hundred, New Castle, Delaware*; Roll: *M593_120*; Page: *507A*; Image: *237*; Family History Library Film: *545619*.

[3] Application for Naturalization of Edward A. McFarlin, Superior Court of Newcastle County, DE

[4] Naturalization papers of Edward A. McFarlin, Superior Court of Delaware

[5] *1860 United States Census*, New Castle, DE. Year: *1860*; Census Place: *White Clay Creek Hundred, New Castle, Delaware*; Roll: *M653_97*; Page: *546*; Image: *550*; Family History Library Film: *803097*.

[6] *1870 United States Census*, New Castle, DE. Year: *1870*; Census Place: *Christiana Hundred, New Castle, Delaware*; Roll: *M593_120*; Page: *507A*; Image: *237*; Family History Library Film: *545619*.

[7] Immanuel on the Green Cemetery Records. Originals located at the parish office at 100 Harmony Street, New Castle, Delaware, 19720.; Graveyard Headstone. Cemetery is located at The Strand and Harmony Streets, New Castle, Delaware, 19720.

[8] Stuart, Robert D. *Family Record of Edward and Jane Atkinson McFarlin*, January 1930. Copy in possession of Kerry Gans Douglas.

[9] Application for citizenship of Edward A. McFarlin, Superior Court of New Castle, DE

[10] Oath of Citizenship of Edward A. McFarlin, Superior Court of Newcastle, Delaware

[11] Marriage Returns of Newcastle County, Delaware, Vol. 68, p. 18.

[12] *1850 United States Census*, District 1, New Castle County, Delaware. Year: *1850*; Census Place: *Division 1, New Castle, Delaware*; Roll: *M432_53*; Page: *315B*; Image: *94*.

[13] Wilmington & Brandywine Cemetery plot deed, original in possession of Kerry Gans Douglas

[14] *Boyd's Delaware State Directory, 1859-1860*, Wilmington: Joshua T. Heald, 1860, pg 124 & 136.

[15] *1860 United States Census*, 2nd Ward City of Wilmington, Newcastle County, Delaware. Year: 1860; Census Place: Wilmington Ward 2, New Castle, Delaware; Roll: M653_98; Page: 747; Image: 114; Family History Library Film: 803098.

[16] *The Wilmington Directory, 1862-1863,* Wilmington: J.T. Heald, 1862, p. 105

[17] *1870 United States Census*, Newcastle Hundred, Newcastle County, Delaware. Year: 1870; Census Place: New Castle Hundred, New Castle, Delaware; Roll: M593_120; Page: 634B; Image: 494; Family History Library Film: 545619.

[18] *1880 United States Census*, Ridley Township, Delaware County, Pennsylvania. Year: 1880; Census Place: Ridley, Delaware, Pennsylvania; Roll: 1125; Family History Film: 1255125; Page: 125B; Enumeration District: 007; Image: 0349.

[19] *1900 United States Census*, Prospect Park Borough, Ridley Township, Delaware County, Pennsylvania. Year: 1900; Census Place: Ridley, Delaware, Pennsylvania; Roll: 1406; Page: 10B; Enumeration District: 189; FHL microfilm: 1241406.

[20] Stuart, Robert D. *Family Record of Edward and Jane Atkinson McFarlin*, January 1930. Copy in possession of Kerry Gans Douglas.

[21] Wilmington & Brandywine Cemetery records, originals housed at the cemetery, 701 Delaware Ave, Wilmington, DE 19801.

[22] *1910 United States Census*, Norwood Borough, Delaware County, Pennsylvania. Year: 1910; Census Place: Norwood, Delaware, Pennsylvania; Roll: T624_1340; Page: 13B; Enumeration District: 0151; Image: 379; FHL microfilm: 1375353.

[23] Death Certificate of Ellen Derrick McFarlin, File # 107047; Registered # 26. Original housed at PA Department of Health, Division of Vital records, PO Box 1528, New Castle, PA 16103.; Wilmington & Brandywine Cemetery Records. Originals housed at the cemetery, 701 Delaware Ave, Wilmington, DE 19801.

[24] Death Certificate of Edward A. McFarlin, Jr. File #: 72871-33; Registered #: 242. Original housed at PA Department of Health, Division of Vital records, PO Box 1528, New Castle, PA 16103.

[25] Daughters of the American Revolution Lineage for Patriot Philip Strubing - lineage history submitted by Anna Wooldridge McFarlin, national # 184244. Originals in possession of Kerry Gans Douglas.

[26] Death Certificate of Anna Wooldridge McFarlin File #: 42926; Registered #: 168. Original housed at PA Department of Health, Division of Vital records, PO Box 1528, New Castle, PA 16103.

[27] Daughters of the American Revolution Lineage for Patriot Philip Strubing - lineage history submitted by Anna Wooldridge McFarlin, national # 184244. Originals in possession of Kerry Gans Douglas.

[28] 25th Wedding Anniversary invitation, original in possession of Kerry Gans Douglas.

[29] *1900 United States Census*, City of Philadelphia, Pennsylvania. Year: 1900; Census Place: Philadelphia Ward 26, Philadelphia, Pennsylvania; Roll: 1468; Page: 1A; Enumeration District: 639; FHL microfilm: 1241468.

[30] Gravestone of Anna McFarlin in West Laurel Hill Cemetery, 215 Belmont Ave., Bala Cynwyd, PA 19004.

[31] *1910 United States Census*, Ward 46, Philadelphia City, Pennsylvania. Year: 1910; Census Place: Philadelphia Ward 46, Philadelphia, Pennsylvania; Roll: T624_1413; Page: 9B; Enumeration District: 1184; Image: 758; FHL microfilm: 1375426.

[32] Anniversary Party Invitation, original in possession of Kerry Gans Douglas.

[33] *1920 United States Census*, 46th Ward of Philadelphia, Philadelphia County, PA. Year: 1920; Census Place: Philadelphia Ward 46, Philadelphia, Pennsylvania; Roll: T625_1646; Page: 4B; Enumeration District: 1741; Image: 1145.

[34] *Philadelphia Record*, June 27, 1926

[35] *1930 United States Census*, Ward 27, Philadelphia City, Philadelphia County, Pennsylvania. Year: 1930; Census Place: Philadelphia, Philadelphia, Pennsylvania; Roll: 2112; Page: 19A; Enumeration District: 415; Image: 120.0; FHL microfilm: 2341846.

[36] Death Certificate of Edward A. McFarlin, Jr. File #: 72871-33; Registered #: 242. Original housed at PA Department of Health, Division of Vital records, PO Box 1528, New Castle, PA 16103.

[37] Death Certificate of Anna Wooldridge McFarlin File #: 42926; Registered #: 168. Original housed at PA Department of Health, Division of Vital records, PO Box 1528, New Castle, PA 16103.

[38] Marriage Application & Certificate of Harold Stites Warren & Clara McFarlin #360 900. Originals housed at Philadelphia City Archives, 3101 Market Street, Philadelphia, PA 19104.

EDWARD & JANE ATKINSON McFARLIN FAMILY HISTORY

Family record of Edward and Jane Atkinson McFarlin
BY ROBERT D. STUART (GRANDSON), JANUARY 1930

Edward McFarlin died in Ireland in 1845

Jane, his widow, died in Wilmington Delaware in 1879 buried in New Castle Delaware.

Their family consisted of seven children, six of whom lived to be past seventy years

They are as follows

Robert – Married Jane Morrow he died in 1895. she in 1906

Mary Jane – Married William Banks he died in 1886 she in 1900

Edward A. – Married Ellen Derrick, he died in 1905 she in 1913

Ellen – Married James Wright, she died in 1863, he in 1905

John – Married Margaret McCarter, he died in 1906 she in 1909

Eliza Ann – Married Robert Stuart, he died in 1880 she in 1904

Isabel – Married James McCarter, she died in 1910 he in 1913

These are all buried in New Castle County, Delaware except Isabel who is buried in Kent County, Delaware

Robert is buried in Greenhill Presbyterian Churchyard, Dela.

Mary Jane is buried in Methodist Churchyard New Castle, Dela.

Edward A. is buried in Wilmington & Brandywine Cemetery, Dela.

Ellen is buried in Salem, Methodist Churchyard, Delaware

John is buried in Episcopal Churchyard New Castle, Delaware

Eliza Ann is buried in Riverview Cemetery Wilmington, Dela.

Isabel is buried in St. Peter's Cemetery, Smyrna, Delaware

John and his mother are buried side by side

Robert reard no children

Mary Jane reard four children to maturity

Edward A. reared seven children to maturity

Ellen two children were reared to maturity

John reared three children to maturity

Eliza Ann reared four children to maturity

Isabel reared four children to maturity

Edward A. was the first to emigrate to America he coming in 1842 then followed Mary Jane, Ellen and John he coming in 1848. Then followed Robert, Eliza Ann, Isabel and their mother in 1852 leaving none of the family in their native country.

The surviving grandchildren of Edward & Jane Atkinson McFarlin at this date are as follows.

Ellen Etchells, Elizabeth Mitchell, children of William and Mary Jane Banks

Elizabeth Jordan, Edward McFarlin, John McFarlin children of Edward A. and Ellen D. McFarlin

William E. Wright, Annie Whiteman, children of James and Ellen Wright

John Robert McFarlin, Francis Henry McFarlin, Bessie Bennett, children of John and Margaret McFarlin

Jane Stuart, Robert D. Stuart, Joseph Stuart children of Robert and Eliza Ann Stuart

Martha Tucker, John McCarter children of James and Isabel McCarter

PAGE 2

The deceased grandchildren of Edward and Jane Atkinson McFarlin as far as I could ascertain at this date are as follows

Thomas T. Banks died in 1906, Mary B. Stewart died in 1910. children of William and Mary Jane Banks.

Eliza J. died in 1855, Rebecca died in 1871 Alice died in 1875 Mary Springer died in 1886, Maud Ewing died in 1894 Clara Calhoun died in 1903, William D. McFarlin died in 1909 - children of Edward and Ellen D. Farlin

Laura died in 1894 child of John and Margaret McFarlin

Edward. McF. Stuart died in 1891 son of Robert and Eliza A. Stuart

Ellen J. Leevey died in 1897, Annie Tucker died in 1908 daughters of James & Isabel McCarter

John H. McFarlin, first cousin to the McFarlin family was born in Delaware March 10. 1814. he visited Ireland twice and was the cause of the McFarlin family emigrating to America. He died February 24th 1881. his wife Mary Ann born 1832 died July 30th 1889 buried in Wilmington and Brandywine Cemetery

Foregoing compiled by Robert D. Stuart, Grandson of Edward and Jane Atkinson McFarlin

Wilmington, Delaware

January 1930

Immanuel on the Green Episcopal Church
New Castle, DE

Church
of the
McFarlin
Family

(Photos taken
29 Aug 2012)

Immanuel
Protestant Episcopal
Church
Founded 1689
Erected 1703

Immanuel on the Green Episcopal Church
New Castle, DE
McFarlin Family Church

(Photos taken 29 August 2012)

Immanuel on the Green Cemetery
New Castle, DE

**McFarlin
Family
Plot**

**(Photos
taken
29 August 2012)**

JOHN McFARLIN
1828 — 1906

**JOHN McFARLIN
BROTHER OF
E.A. McFARLIN, SR.**

**JANE ATKINSON McFARLIN
MOTHER OF EDWARD A. McFARLIN, SR.**

**LAURA McFARLIN
DAUGHTER OF JOHN McFARLIN**

1847.

Be it Remembered that on the fifteenth day of May in the year of our Lord one thousand eight hundred and forty seven personally appeared in the Supreme Court of the State of Delaware for New Castle County Edward A McFarlan and did declare that it is his intention to become a citizen of the United States and to renounce forever all allegiance and fidelity to every foreign Potentate and State whatever and particularly to the Queen of the United Kingdom of Great Britain and Ireland of whom he was heretofore a subject.

Attest

Saml Bride Proy.

Edward A McFarlin

$1 ⁸⁰⁄₁₀₀ E Co D

EDWARD A. MCFARLIN, SR.
1850 - OATH OF CITIZENSHIP

BE IT REMEMBERED, THAT on the *thirtieth* day of *November* in the year of our LORD, one thousand eight hundred and *fifty* Personally appeared in open **Superior Court** of the State of Delaware, held at New-Castle, for New-Castle County, *Edward A. Mc Farlin* a native of *Ireland* and exhibited a Petition, praying to be admitted a **CITIZEN** of the **UNITED STATES:** and it appearing to said Court that he had declared on *Oath* before the *Prothonotary of this Court* that it was *bona fide* his intention to become a Citizen of the United States, and to renounce forever, all allegiance and fidelity to every foreign prince, potentate, state or sovereignty whatever, and particularly to the *Queen of the United Kingdom of Great Britain & Ireland,* of whom he was at that time a subject: And the said *Edward A. Mc Farlin* having on his solemn *Oath* declared, and also made proof thereof by the competent testimony of *John H. Mc Farlin* a citizen of the United States, that he hath resided upwards of **FIVE YEARS** in the United States of America, and **ONE YEAR** at least immediately preceding his application within the State of Delaware; and it appearing to the satisfaction of the Court, that during that time he had behaved himself as a man of good moral character, attached to the principles of the Constitution of the United States, and well disposed to the good order and happiness of the same; and having declared on his solemn *Oath* before the said Court, that he would support the **Constitution of the United States**, and that he did absolutely and entirely renounce and abjure all allegiance and fidelity to every foreign prince, potentate, state and sovereignty whatever, and particularly to the *Queen of the United Kingdom of Great Britain & Ireland* of whom he was before a subject: Thereupon the Court admitted the said *Edward A. Mc Farlin* to be a **Citizen of the United States of America**, pursuant to the provisions of the Acts of Congress of the United States, concerning Naturalization.

Attest.

Samuel Biddle

Prothonotary.

**EDWARD ARTHUR MCFARLIN, SR.
(1824-1905)**

**ELLEN DERRICK MCFARLIN
(1829-1913)**

(DATE OF PHOTOS UNKNOWN)

WILMINGTON & BRANDYWINE CEMETERY
WILMINGTON, DE

EDWARD A. MCFARLIN, SR,
ELLEN DERRICK MCFARLIN,
& CHILDREN
WILLIAM D. MCFARLIN,
MARY MCFARLIN SPRINGER,
MAUD MCFARLIN EWING,
CLARA MCFARLIN CALHOUN

MCFARLIN
FAMILY
PLOT

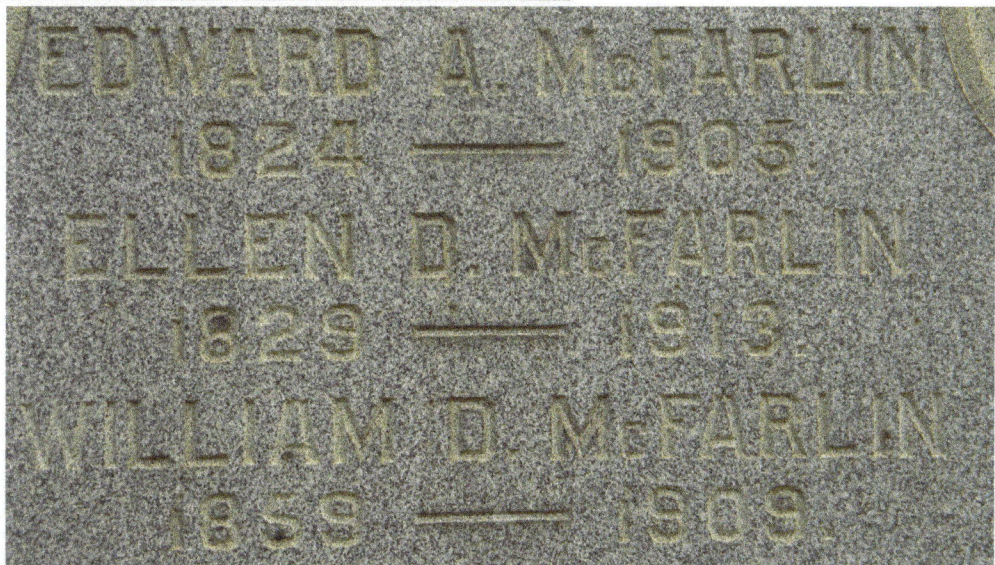

(PHOTOS TAKEN
1 SEPTEMBER 2012)

WILMINGTON & BRANDYWINE CEMETERY
WILMINGTON, DE

McFARLIN
FAMILY
PLOT

DIED AS CHILDREN:
ELIZA J.
REBECCA
ALICE

ELIZA J. McFARLIN
1853 — 1855.
REBECCA McFARLIN
1871 — 1871.
ALICE McFARLIN
1873 — 1875.

(PHOTOS TAKEN
29 AUGUST 2012)

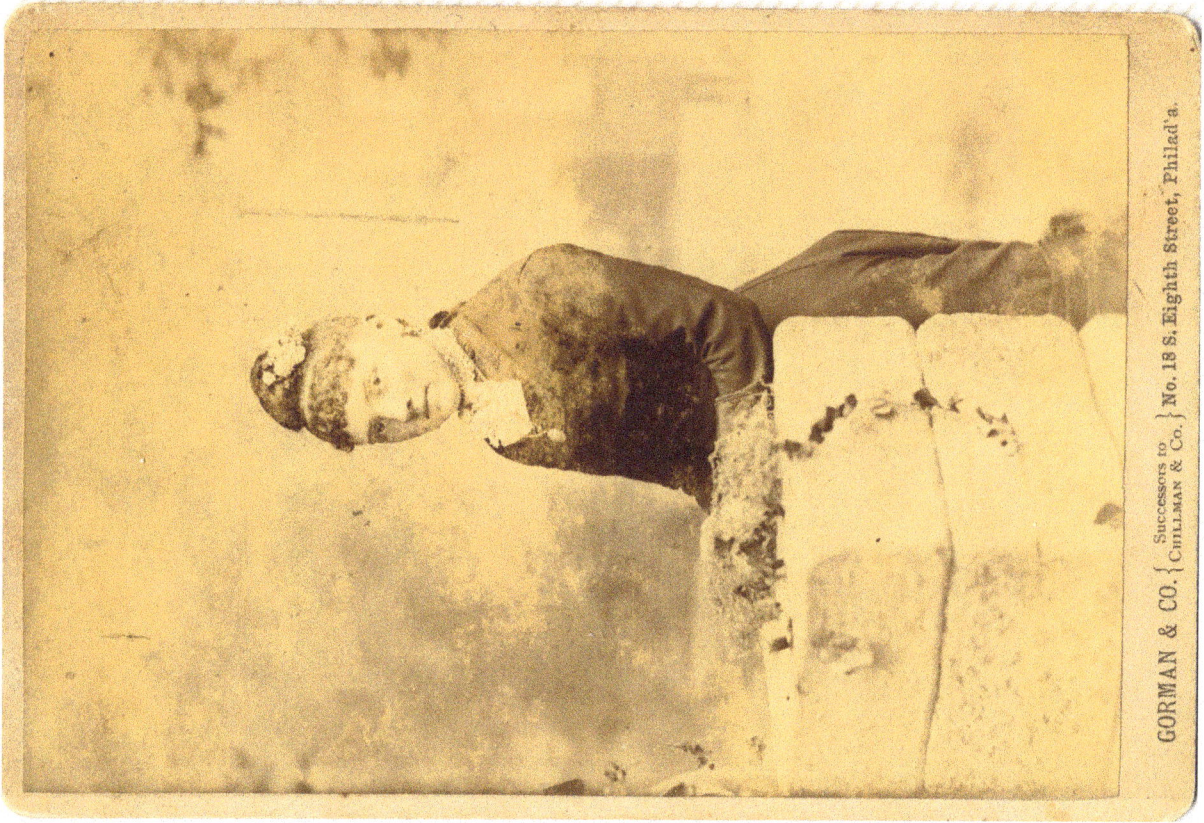

EDWARD ARTHUR MCFARLIN, JR.

(DATE OF PHOTO UNKNOWN)

GORMAN & CO. { Successors to } No. 18 S. Eighth Street, Philad'a.
{ CHILLMAN & Co. }

ANNA WOOLDRIDGE MCFARLIN

(DATE OF PHOTO UNKNOWN)

EDWARD ARTHUR MCFARLIN, JR. (THE UNIFORM IS THAT OF A MASON)

Edward A. McFarlin, Jr.
1910 - 25th Wedding Anniversary

1885   *1910*

Mr. and Mrs. Edward A. McFarlin

request the pleasure of your company at the

Twenty-fifth Anniversary of their marriage

Saturday evening November nineteenth

from eight until eleven o'clock

5303 Catherine Street

Philadelphia

R.S.V.P.

June 27, 1926 - Philadelphia Record
Edward A. & Anna McFarlin, Jr.

Mr. & Mrs Edward A McFarlin

THE PHILADELPHIA RECORD, SUNDAY, J

WATCHING THE STROLLERS AT OCEAN CITY, N. J.

way to their main depot at Eighth street.

Reading flyers enter the city at Fifty-first street, making their runs in 70 minutes, and after stopping at several stations along the way, they reach their main depot at Tenth street a few minutes later.

The "Pennsy" ferries from Market street, Philadelphia, connect with the steam and electric trains at the Terminal, Federal street, Camden.

The Reading ferries at Chestnut and South streets, Philadelphia, connect with the Reading trains at the new Terminal, Mechanic street, Camden. And, too, the Pennsylvania Railroad runs through Ocean City bridge trains via Broad street, thus connecting up with all the great and smaller cities. In addition to this excellent train service to Philadelphia connecting in that manner with all parts of the country, Ocean City has the added advantage of a trolley service every 30 minutes to Atlantic City.

Indulging in nature's cure-all—warm sunshine and cool ocean breezes, either relaxing or jauntily strolling along the famous boardwalk. Nothing compares to the rejuvenating effect of a sojourn at the seashore.

Superb Attractions Lure
Thousands to Ocean City

Bathing Big
Beach Off

Ocean City, N.
City is unique in
eight miles long an
America, bounded
beautiful Egg Harbo
mean much to the
for their beauty an
influence they exert

Of first interest
a change of residen
is the climate of
their attention, for
comfort and content
Ocean City. Ocean
its guests, offering
of accommodations
houses and apartm

The main streets
as the boardwalk
plied with high-class
al trolley line is a

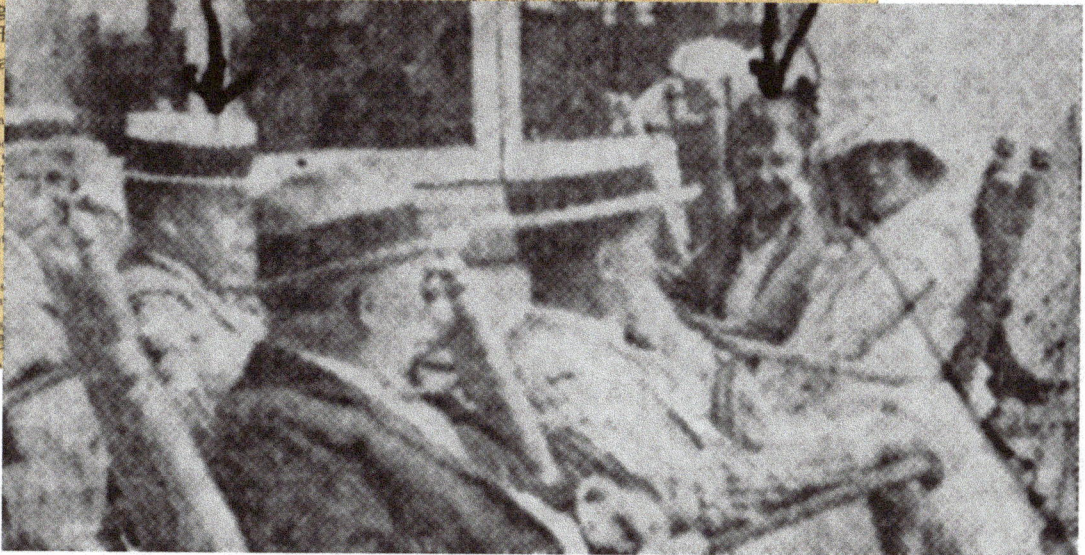

Ocean City's famous boardwalk, running from North street to Twenty-third street, gives opportunity for several miles of ocean front promenading.

If one likes to fish—and catch fish—Ocean City is the place he is seeking—the finest fishing grounds on the Jersey coast. Every foot of Ocean City's eight miles of ocean front is ideal for surf fishing.

nis may be finely enjoyed during the summer months. Twenty-two municipal courts in the centre of the city provide excellent amusement for the devotees of this favorite sport; courts are carefully kept and in active use by the resident experts and visiting players. A rest room, with shower ba hs is located in the centre of the group of courts.

On the occasion of an Honor Banquet for Edward Arthur McFarlin in 1926

My Dad

There's not a better man alive
   Than my Dad!
And I don't say it just because
   He's my Dad;
But I leave it up to you —
You who've known him long
      years through —
To answer, if I say what's true
   'Bout my Dad.

Did you ever see a humbler man
      Than my Dad?
Patient, kind, forgiving, true —
      My Dad
When criticism drags men down
Who holds his tongue — nor makes
      a sound?
Who'll stoop and help him from
      the ground?
      My Dad!

WRITTEN BY CLARA MCFARLIN WARREN
UNKNOWN IF SHE ALSO DID THE SKETCH
APPEARED IN THE HEART STRINGS BOOKLET
SHE MADE AND GAVE TO HER GRANDCHILDREN
IN 1978

WEST LAUREL HILL CEMETERY
PHILADELPHIA, PA

WARREN-McFARLIN
FAMILY PLOT

McFARLIN

ANNA WOOLDRIDGE
1860 ✠ 1947
EDWARD·A
1862 ✠ 1933
ANNA·C
1893 ✠ 1898
ANDRINA·H
1888 ✠ 1913

EDWARD
McFARLIN, JR.,
ANNA WOOLDRIDGE
McFARLIN,
& CHILDREN
ANNA C. &
ANDRINA H.

(PHOTOS TAKEN
30 APRIL 2011)

McFARLIN

ANNA WOOLDRIDGE
1860 ✠ 1947
EDWARD·A
1862 ✠ 1933
ANNA·C
1893 ✠ 1898
ANDRINA·H
1888 ✠ 1913

1910

CLARA McFARLIN

1914, ATLANTIC CITY

JULY 1914, ATLANTIC CITY

The Diemer Lineage

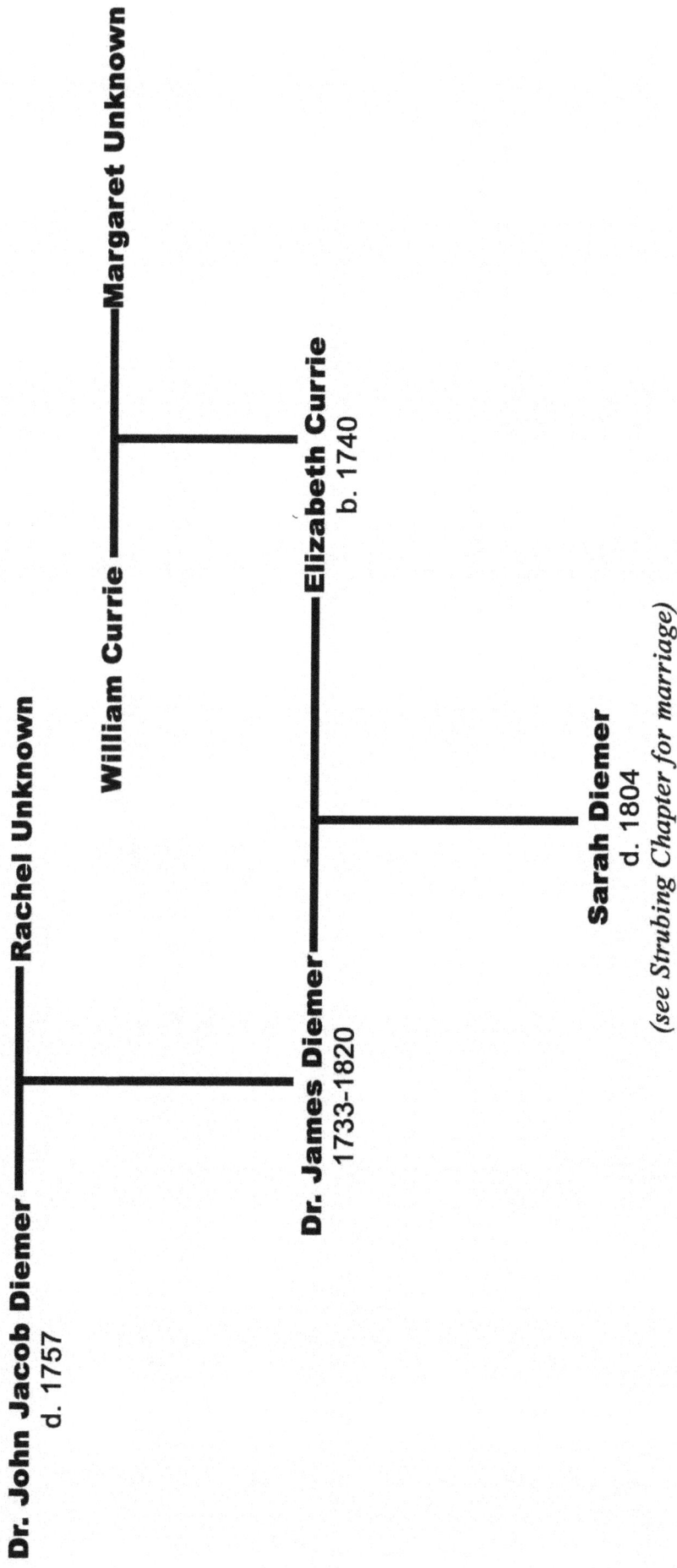

Dr. John Jacob Diemer
d. 1757

Rachel Unknown

William Currie

Margaret Unknown

Dr. James Diemer
1733-1820

Elizabeth Currie
b. 1740

Sarah Diemer
d. 1804

(see Strubing Chapter for marriage)

The Diemer Lineage

Dr. John Jacob Diemer (d. 1757) and Rachel Unknown

Dr. John Jacob Diemer was a medical doctor in Philadelphia, Pennsylvania. His wife's name was Rachel, and they had at least 4 children, although I only have the name of the eldest – *James*.[1]

On 16 March 1733, John Jacob bought a plantation of 161 acres in Providence, as well as 64 more acres also in Providence.[2] It is unclear to me if this is Providence, Rhode Island; Upper Providence Township, Delaware County, PA; Lower Providence Township, Montgomery County, PA; or some other area.

In January 1747, John Jacob was captain of 1 of the 4 military companies raised from Pennsylvania.[3][4][5]

John Jacob Diemer must have died around November 1757, because on 17 November 1757, his eldest son, James, was granted letters of administration to divide the estate of his father. The estate was settled 15 April 1760, divided among John Jacob's widow, Rachel, and 4 children.[6][7]

Dr. James Diemer (c. 1733–1820) and Elizabeth Currie (b. 1740)

Dr. James Diemer followed in his father's footsteps, becoming a doctor. He also became a judge in the Reading, PA, area. As expected of a man of those disciplines, James was literate. James gave the land for the Trinity (Episcopal) Church at Reading, PA, and at one time was a vestryman of the church.[8] He was born c. 1733, and died 21 June 1820.[9]

He married Elizabeth Currie (b. 1740), daughter of William and Margaret Currie on 5 December 1759 in Philadelphia, PA.[10] Elizabeth was christened at Christ Church and St. Peter's in Philadelphia, PA, on 22 January 1740.[11] At the time of their marriage, James was 26; Elizabeth was 19.

James and Elizabeth had only 2 known children:

Margaret – *married William Wilson.*
Sarah (d. 1804) – *married Philip Strubing.*

I suspect these are all the children he had who survived to adulthood and had children. In his will, he does recognize Sarah's children, even though she has died, so I would think if he had other children who pre–deceased him yet left grandchildren, he would have recognized those grandchildren in a similar way.

He was commissioned "Surgeon's Mate" in the Royal American Regiment, 5 April 1757. The regiment served against the French and Indians in the final wars with France, and was stationed in 1775 in West Florida.[12] For his services he received 2 grants of 500 acres of land each in West Florida from the English king. One grant was made 17 October 1774; the other 12 September 1775.[13] Both were located between the Mississippi and Perdido Rivers.[14] For more on this land claim, see *The Strubing Lineage* chapter, under James Strubing and Catherine Kromer.

James Diemer became a U.S. citizen in 1789.[15]

James appears on the 1790 Census in Reading, PA. His household contained 2 males over the age of 16, and 3 females over the age of 16.[16]

James also is on the 1800 Census in Reading, PA. It seems he and his wife were empty nesters at the time, because only 1 male and 1 female are listed in the household.[17]

James is also on the 1810 Census in Reading, PA. There seem to be at least 4 people in the household, but the columns do not match the printed version of the 1810 Census, so I cannot be completely sure what the markings mean. The male columns do match up, so it would seem to be James at age 45+, and a boy between 10 and 15. The female columns have one too many, so I am confused. The sixth and last column is undoubtedly his wife at 45+, and the female in the 2nd column from the left should be between 10 and 15, but with the mysterious extra column it is unclear. It is also unclear who these children are. However, I venture to guess that they could be grandson Diemer Strubing and granddaughter Elizabeth Strubing. Their mother, James' daughter, had died 6 years earlier, they would have been the right age, and it is possible that they came to live with the grandparents. Considering that James Diemer left land to both of these younger grandchildren, instead of just to his eldest grandson, James, it is possible they had a closer relationship.[18]

James Diemer's will was filed in Berks County, PA, on 18 March 1819, and proven on 24 June 1820. Everything was divided among his daughter, Margaret, three of his deceased daughter Sarah's children – Elizabeth (a tract of land in Columbia County), James (1,000 pounds), and Diemer Strubing (a tract of land in Columbia County)—and great–grandson James Strubing, Jr. (100 pounds when he turned 21). They had a long wait to inherit. Although the estate was inventoried on the 26th and 27th of June 1820, the final settlement and disbursement of money did not occur until 22 September 1828.[19]

Sarah Diemer married Philip Strubing around 1787. (*See The Strubing Lineage chapter.*)

---

[1] Research of Philip Henry Strubing, January 31, 1927. Originals housed with National Society Daughters of the American Revolution, 1776 D Street, NW, Washington, DC, 20006-5303.

[2] Research of Philip Henry Strubing, January 31, 1927. Originals housed with National Society Daughters of the American Revolution, 1776 D Street, NW, Washington, DC, 20006-5303.

[3] Research of Philip Henry Strubing, January 31, 1927. Originals housed with National Society Daughters of the American Revolution, 1776 D Street, NW, Washington, DC, 20006-5303.

[4] PA Archives, First Series, Vol. 1, pp. 724-730.

[5] Letter from Samuel Perry, Oct. 26, 1747, located in Colonial Records, Vol. V, p. 134 f

[6] Research of Philip Henry Strubing, January 31, 1927. Originals housed with National Society Daughters of the American Revolution, 1776 D Street, NW, Washington, DC, 20006-5303.

[7] Doetterer Manuscripts in the Historical Society of Pennsylvania, 1300 Locust Street Philadelphia, PA 19107.

[8] Research of Rush Strubing Whiteside, January 7, 1966. Originals housed with National Society Daughters of the American Revolution, 1776 D Street, NW, Washington, DC, 20006-5303.

[9] Obituary of James Diemer in the *Berks and Schuylkill Journal*, June 24, 1820, vol. 5, iss. 4, p. 3, Reading, PA.

[10] International Genealogical Index (LDS records), "International Genealogical Index (IGI)", database, FamilySearch (http://familysearch.org/pal:/MM9.2.1/MT3T-57W : accessed 2013-04-20), entry for James Diemer. batch number: 7004105 IGI Batch Type Code: 2 IGI Sheet Number: 58 IGI Serial Number: 00250 SourceDocType: CHURCHREC.

[11] International Genealogical Index (LDS records), "Pennsylvania, Births and Christenings, 1709-1950," index, FamilySearch (https://familysearch.org/pal:/MM9.1.1/V2FT-52C : accessed 20 Apr 2013), Elizabeth Currie, 22 Jan 1740. Indexing Project (Batch) Number: C72588-3 System Origin: Pennsylvania-ODM GS Film number: 1490580.

[12] Reports on Private Bills; Strubing, Catharine, heir of James Dreiner; CIS#: 808 H.rp.130; Document #: H.rp.130; Committee on Private Land Claims, House; February 23, 1855; Volume 808, p. 1. Found online at ProQuest. Permalink: http://congressional.proquest.com/congressional/docview/t05.d06.808_h.rp.130_index?accountid=63787

[13] Petition of Catharine Strubing, CIS#: 630 S.rp.193, Document #: S.rp.193, Committee on Private Land Claims, Senate, April 20, 1852, Volume: 630, p. 192. Found online at ProQuest: http://congressional.proquest.com

[14] Reports on Private Bills; Strubing, Catharine, heir of James Dreiner; CIS#: 808 H.rp.130; Document #: H.rp.130; Committee on Private Land Claims, House; February 23, 1855; Volume 808, p. 1. Found online at ProQuest. Permalink: http://congressional.proquest.com/congressional/docview/t05.d06.808_h.rp.130_index?accountid=63787

[15] Reports on Private Bills; Strubing, Catharine, heir of James Dreiner; CIS#: 808 H.rp.130; Document #: H.rp.130; Committee on Private Land Claims, House; February 23, 1855; Volume 808, p. 2. Found online at ProQuest. Permalink: http://congressional.proquest.com/congressional/docview/t05.d06.808_h.rp.130_index?accountid=63787

[16] *1790 United States Census*, Reading, Pennsylvania. Year: 1790; Census Place: Reading, Berks, Pennsylvania; Series: M637; Roll: 8; Page: 8; Image: 22; Family History Library Film: 0568148.

[17] *1800 United States Census*, Borough of Reading, Pennsylvania. Year: 1800; Census Place: Reading, Berks, Pennsylvania; Roll: 35; Page: 642; Image: 228; Family History Library Film: 363338.

[18] *1810 United States Census*, Reading Township Borough, Pennsylvania. Year: 1810; Census Place: Reading, Berks, Pennsylvania; Roll: 45; Page: 601; Image: 0193671; Family History Library Film: 00079.

[19] James Diemer's will, filed Berks County March 18, 1819, Proven June 24, 1820. Original housed in Berks County Register of Wills office, 633 Court Street, 2nd Floor
Reading, PA 19601.

James Diemer
1820 - Will, Berks County, PA

Third — I give bequeath & devise to my beloved Grand Son James Strubing One Thousand Dollars in Gold or Silver Money to be paid to my said Grand Son within twelve Months from the time of my decease

Fourth — I give devise & bequeath to my great Grand Son James Strubing One hundred Dollars to be paid to him when he attains the age of twenty one years and in the mean time to be put to Interest to accumulate for him by my Executors or the Survivor.

Fifth — I authorise request & direct my Executors or the Survivor to collect in my debts and convert my other Personal Property into Money as soon as convenient after my decease and also to dispose of my Real Estate within two years after my decease to the best advantage and after paying my Funeral Expences debts and the Legacies herein before bequeathed I give devise & bequeath the residue together with the residue of my Estate of whatever kind & wherever situated to my beloved Grand Children Elizabeth Good - Diemer Strubing & James Strubing their heirs and assigns to be equally divided between my said Grand Children share and share alike

And Lastly I do nominate Constitute and appoint my Trusty & esteemed friends Martin John Biddle Esquire & William Moore Merchant both of the Borough of Reading the Executors of this my Last Will & Testament hereby revoking & making null & Void all former Wills by me made & ratifying and confirming this & no other as my Last Will & Testament In Witness whereof I have hereunto set my hand & Seal this Eighteenth day of March Eighteen in the year of our Lord One Thousand Eight hundred & Nineteen

Signed Sealed & declared to be the Last Will of the said Testator in the Presence of us —

F. Miller
Thomas Moore

James Diemer (LS)

TO DAUGHTER MARGARET, WIFE OF WILLIAM WILSON:
LAND VALUED AT 1,000 POUNDS
TO GRANDDAUGHTER ELIZABETH, WIFE OF JACOB GOOD:
A TRACT OF LAND IN COLUMBIA COUNTY
TO GRANDSON DIEMER STRUBING:
A TRACT OF LAND IN COLUMBIA COUNTY
TO GRANDSON JAMES STRUBING:
1,000 POUNDS
TO GREAT-GRANDSON JAMES STRUBING:
100 POUNDS WHEN TURNS 21
REMAINDER DIVIDED BETWEEN ELIZABETH GOOD,
DIEMER STRUBING, & JAMES STRUBING

The Godshall Lineage

Frederick Godshall, Sr.
1761–1811

Ann Cummings
1771–1836

Frederick Godshall, Jr.
1800–1882

Prudence Stites
1800–1882
(see Stites Chapter)

Harold Stites Godshall
1829–1893

Elizabeth Huhn
1834–1916
(see Waugh Chapter)

Clara C. Godshall
1859–1925

(see Warren Chapter for marriage)

Godshall

The Godshall Lineage

Frederick Godshall (1761–1811) and Ann Cummings (1771–1836)

According to church records, Ann Cummings and Frederick Godshall, both of the Southwark district of Philadelphia, married at the Gloria Dei Church (now Old Swedes' Church) on 20 September 1800.[1] Frederick was 39; Ann was 29.

They had 2 known children:

Frederick Godshall, Jr. (1800–1882) – *married Prudence Stites.*
Andrew Godshall (1808–1868)

In 1790, Frederick Godshall (29) lived at 174 Swanson Street in Southwark, Philadelphia, PA. He was a laborer and the only male in the house. Two white females lived with him. I am guessing one is his mother, likely a widow since there is no other man in the house, and the other is perhaps a sister.[2]

In 1793, Frederick Godshall (32) lived at 174 Swanson St., Philadelphia, PA, and worked as a laborer.[3]

In 1794, Frederick (33) still lived at 174 Swanson St., but now worked as an Inspector of Lumber.[4]

The 1800 Census shows a Frederick Godshalk in Southwark, but the family composition does not match what the Godshall household should be. There is 1 male under 10, which could be Frederick, Jr., depending on the time of year this was taken. There is 1 male aged 26–44, which would be Frederick (39), and one female aged 26–44, which would be Ann (29). However, there are also a boy aged 10–15, 4 girls under 10, and a girl 10–15. These would not be their children, unless one of them was married previously and had children left in the house or if they had taken in the children of a relative. So I am suspicious of this being the right household, but it seems the most likely of any I could find.[5]

In 1804, Frederick (43) and Ann (33) lived at 37 Becks Alley in Philadelphia, PA. Frederick worked as a shingle and stave inspector.[6] Frederick, Jr., would have been 4.

In 1805–1808, they lived at Christian Street Wharf & 37 Becks Alley, Philadelphia, PA. Frederick worked in a shingle & staves yard.[7] Frederick, Jr., would have been 5–8.

In 1809 they still lived at 37 Becks Alley, but Frederick (48) was a corder.[8] Frederick, Jr., would have been 9, and younger brother Andrew would have been 1.

In 1810, they still call 37 Becks Alley home, and Frederick (49) was a stave inspector.[9] Frederick, Jr., was 10, Andrew 2.

On the 1810 Census, there is a Frederick Godshall living in East Southwark, Philadelphia, PA. His household includes 4 boys under 10, 1 male over 45, 1 girl 10–15, and 1 woman 26–44. While this still does not completely conform to what we know of the Godshall family, this is more likely than not to be them. Two of the 4 boys are Frederick (10) and Andrew (2) – the eldest and youngest of the 4. There is a 9 year gap between Frederick and Andrew, and it would be unlikely that no other siblings were born, so it is reasonable to assume that Frederick (49) and Ann (39) had other children who did not survive to adulthood. Therefore, the other 2 boys could easily be theirs. The girl 10–15 is something of a mystery – it could be one of the younger girls listed on the 1800 Census, if that is in fact the same family.[10]

According to their great–granddaughter, Frederick Godshall, Sr., died 10 June 1811, and is buried at the German Lutheran Church in Philadelphia, PA.[11] Frederick's death certificate states that he died of debility at age 50 on 11 June 1811.[12]

In 1814,[13] 1817,[14] 1818,[15] and 1819, the widowed Ann Godshall (43, 46, 47, & 48 years old) still lived at 37 Becks Alley. In 1819, Ann (48) was a teacher.[16] Frederick, Jr., would have been 14, 17, 18, and 19, while Andrew would have been 6, 9, 10, and 11.

In 1820, there is an Ann Godshall living in Southwark, Philadelphia, PA. The family composition is again not exact. There is 1 boy 10–15 (Andrew, 12), and 1 female over 45 (Ann, 49). Frederick, Jr., who is 20, is not listed, but it is probable that he is living elsewhere for work. The unknown girl under 10 could be a daughter who did not survive to adulthood born to Frederick and Ann in 1810 or 1811, before he passed away.[17]

In 1830, Ann Godshall (59) lived in East Southwark. A male 20–29 (Andrew, 22) lives with her.[18] Frederick, Jr., had married in 1823 and was living in Maryland in 1830.

A person believed to be Ann Cummings Godshall is buried in the same plot in Ebenezer ME Church Burying Ground (no longer there) as her son Frederick, Jr. Mrs. Ann Godshall died of bilious fever on 10 July 1836, at age 65.[19]

Frederick Godshall, Jr., (1800–1882) and Prudence Stites (1800–1882)
(see Stites Lineage chapter)

Frederick Godshall, Jr., was born 16 May 1800[20], in Delaware.[21] Family lore tells us that the first Godshall in America was a Mennonite preacher who came over from Europe in the early 1700s, possibly via Holland. There is a Mennonite Andrew Godshall who took the Oath of Citizenship in Pennsylvania in 1749[22], but we have not been able to tie him conclusively to our Frederick. However, Frederick's brother's name was Andrew, and names tended to pass down through families, so there is circumstantial evidence of a tie.

To further emphasize how family names were passed down, Frederick's wife, Prudence Stites, had a brother Henry Stites. She named her son Henry Stites Godshall, and she and Frederick had 7 grandsons named Henry Stites as well!

Prudence was born 20 July 1800 in Philadelphia, PA.[23] Her parents were Peter Stites and Hannah Wills.

Frederick and Prudence were married 18 September 1823 at Gloria Dei (now Old Swedes' Church), Philadelphia, PA, by the Rev. Nicholas Collins.[24] Both Frederick and Prudence were 23 years old.

Frederick and Prudence traveled quite a bit during their marriage. Their 5 children were born up and down the East Coast:

Samuel (1827–1866) – *born in Delaware. Married Aramathea Helon Webb in Tennessee.*
Henry Stites (1829–1893) – *born in Maryland. Married Elizabeth Huhn.*
Prudence Sophia (1832–1882) – *born in Maryland.*
Frederick, III (b. 1835) – *born in Pennsylvania. Married Maggie Unknown.*

George (b. 1844) – *born in Pennsylvania.*

In 1830, there was a Frederick Gadshee who lived in Millington, Kent County, Maryland.[25] This is presumed to be the Godshall family, although the vagueness of the 1830 Census makes it difficult to be certain. There are 2 girls, one 5–10, the other 10–15 who are unknown. If the marriage date is correct, only the 5–10-year-old could be from their marriage. These 2 girls make this family suspect, although the boys and adults match.

On 15 March 1840, Frederick and Prudence (both 40) had children Frederick, III, and Prudence Sophia baptized at the Ebenezer ME Church in Philadelphia, PA.[26]

In 1840, Frederick and his family lived in Philadelphia's Southwark, Ward 1. The household consisted of 1 boy under 5 (Frederick, III, 5), 2 boys 10–15 (Samuel, 13 and Henry Stites, 11), 1 man 30–40 (Frederick, Jr., 40), 1 girl 5–10 (Prudence Sophia, 8), and 2 women 40–50 (Prudence, 40, and perhaps a servant).[27]

In 1850, Frederick (49) and family still lived in Southwark, but now in Ward 5. The household consisted of wife Prudence (50), Henry (21), Sophia (17), Frederick, III (15), and George (6). Frederick, Sr., was a clerk, with son Henry as a broker.[28]

In 1860, Frederick (60) was a bookkeeper. Wife Prudence (59) and son George (16) lived with him in his Philadelphia home, located in the 2nd Ward of the city. George contributed to the household by working as a clerk. There was also a servant, Jane Shannon (23), in the house.[29]

In 1870, Frederick (70) and family lived in Philadelphia's 2nd Ward, 5th Division. He was still working as a bookkeeper, supporting wife Prudence, aged 69. Frederick had real estate valued at $2,000, and personal property valued at $600.[30]

In 1880, Frederick (79) and Prudence (79) lived at 914 Front St., Phildelphia, PA. It seems that Frederick finally retired, for his occupation was "Gentleman."[31]

Prudence Stites Godshall died at age 82 on 23 March 1882. Frederick Godshall, Jr., followed soon after, also at 82, on 29 April 1882. They were buried in the Godshall lot at Ebenezer ME Church Burying Ground in Southwark, Philadelphia, PA.[32] This burying ground was later closed and the bodies removed to Arlington Cemetery, Upper Darby, PA, in 1914. Unfortunately, the bodies were not tagged when moved, so their exact final resting place is unknown.[33]

Henry Stites Godshall (1829–1893) and Elizabeth "Lizzie" Huhn (1834–1916)
(see Waugh Lineage chapter)

Henry Stites Godshall, born on the Eastern Shore of Maryland about 1829[34], married Elizabeth "Lizzie" Huhn 17 July 1851 at the First Independent Presbyterian Church in Philadelphia, PA. This church became Chambers Church in 1873 and has since been demolished.[35] Henry was 22; Lizzie was 17.

Henry and Lizzie had 9 children, all born in Pennsylvania:

Norwell/Howell (1853–1870)
Charles F. (1855– bet 1910 & 1920)
Kate A. (1856–aft 1910) – *married Harry A. Nagle.*
Clara C. (1859–1925) – *married James William Warren, III.*

Mary L. (1860–aft 1920)
Henry (Harry) (1863–1932)
Lilly H. (1865–aft 1910) – *married George Woodside.*
Frederick (1869–aft 1900)
Louis (b. 1872)

Henry made his living variously as a coal dealer, bookkeeper, and accountant. He moved his family from house to house as circumstances allowed.

The 1855 Philaadelphia City Directory lists Henry (26) as a coal merchant at 11 Walnut Street. He resided at 107 Catharine Ave.[36]

The 1857 Philadelphia City Directory had Henry (28) still as a coal merchant, but now at 15 Walnut Street, residing at 649 Vine Street.[37]

1860 found Henry (30) and family living in the 15th Ward of Philadelphia, PA. He and Lizzie were well set. He was a coal dealer with a personal estate of $4,500, while Lizzie (26) had real estate valued at $3,000, and a personal estate worth $1,500. Norwell/Howell (8), Charles (6), Kate (4), and Clara (1) lived at home, looked after by domestic Margaret Blancy (25) and by Mary Huhn (24), Lizzie's sister.[38] Henry's coal business was located at 103 Walnut, and the family lived at 1635 Vine.[39]

In 1865, Henry (35) was listed as a bookkeeper at 201 Walnut, living at 1635 Vine.[40]

In 1870, Henry (40) was a coal shipper with real estate valued at $18,500 and a personal estate worth $11,500. The household, located at 1917 Mt. Vernon Street, consisted of Lizzie (34), Charles (15), Kate (13), Clara (11), Mary (9), Harry (7), Lilly (5), and Fred (1). Two Irish servants, Bell Kennedy (22) and Kate Diamond (21) helped with the large household. Henry worked at Hammett, Neill & Co. Son Norvell (Norwell) (18) (who no longer lived with his father) worked as a clerk at 217 Walnut St.[41 42]

In 1875, Henry (45) was still in coal, although now he and the family lived at 2105 Spring Garden St. Charles (20), still residing with his parents, worked as a bookkeeper at 135 South 2nd Street.[43]

1880 found Henry (50) and family still living at 2105 Spring Garden Street in Philadelphia, PA. He was an operator of coal and iron. It was still a very full house: wife Lizzie (45) and children Charles (26), Kate (22), Clara (20), Mary (18), Harry (17), Lilly (15), Fred (11), and Louis (8), as well as 2 Irish domestics, Margaret Clark (35) and Margaret McGuire (22).[44] Gopsill's Directory lists Henry as treasurer at 328 Walnut.[45]

The 1890 Philadelphia City Directory lists Henry (60) as an accountant residing at 2127 Arch St.[46]

The 1891 Philadelphia Blue Book, which listed all of the city's elite (thus the term "bluebloods"), lists Henry and his family.[47] It seems that all of Henry's expertise with math and his years of working with coal had pulled his family up into the crème of Philadelphia Society. He came complete with a spoiled rich heir. Son Harry married well, only to lose his wife and children because of his constant drinking.[48]

Henry Stites Godshall died 7 October 1893 at age 63, of meningitis. He lived at 1629 Vine Street at the time of his death, and had worked as an accountant for the Lehigh Railroad. He is buried in the Woodlands Cemetery[49] (Section F, Lot 663).[50]

In 1900, widow Lizzie (60) lived with daughter Lilly's family at 52 Garden St. in Mount Vernon, Westchester, NY. Lilly's husband, George Woodside (34), was head of household, with Lilly (32) and daughter Elizabeth (7). Also living there were Lilly's sister Mary (35), and 2 servants, Lizzie McGinnis (24, Ireland) and Albert King (19).[51]

In 1910, widow Lizzie (75) lived with her daughter Katherine and husband Harry Nagle at 4808 Warrington Ave., Philadelphia, PA.[52]

Elizabeth "Lizzie" Huhn Godshall died 21 May 1916, at age 81. Her death certificate is of poor quality, but the cause of death seems to be a cancer of some type – "carcinoma" was the only clear word. At the time of her death, she lived at 47th & Baltimore Ave. – her daughter Katherine Nagel's residence. Lizzie is also buried in the Woodlands Cemetery in Philadelphia, PA.[53]

Clara C. Godshall married James William Warren in 1884. Clara was 25; he was 31. (*See The Warren Lineage chapter.*)

---

[1] *Marriages Gloria Dei 1791-1856* film #0511808 at the Family History Library of the Latter-Day Saints in Salt Lake City, Utah.

[2] *1790 United States Census*, Swanson Street, Southwark, Philadelphia County, PA. Year: 1790; Census Place: Southwark, Philadelphia, Pennsylvania; Series: M637; Roll: 9; Page: 380; Image: 620; Family History Library Film: 0568149.

[3] *Hardie's Philadelphia City Directory, 1793.* James Hardie, ed., Philadelphia: T. Dobson, 1793; p. 53.

[4] *Hardie's Philadelphia City Directory, 1794.* James Hardie, ed., Philadelphia: Jacob Johnson & Co., 1794; p. 57.

[5] *1800 United States Census*, Southwark, Philadelphia County, PA. Year: 1800; Census Place: Southwark, Philadelphia, Pennsylvania; Roll: 42; Page: 19; Image: 27; Family History Library Film: 363345.

[6] *Robinson's Philadelphia City Directory, 1804.* Philadelphia: James Robinson, 1804; p. 94.

[7] *Robinson's Philadelphia City Directory*, Philadelphia: James Robinson, Year: 1805; p. 97; Year: 1806; p. 116; Year: 1807; p. 129; Year: 1808; p. 141.

[8] *Robinson's Philadelphia City Directory, 1809.* James Robinson, ed., Philadelphia: William Woodhouse, 1809; p. 118.

[9] *Robinson's Philadelphia City Directory, 1810.* James Robinson, ed., Philadelphia: William Woodhouse, 1810; p. 114.

[10] *1810 United States Census*, East Southwark, Philadelphia County, PA. Year: 1810; Census Place: East Southwark, Philadelphia, Pennsylvania; Roll: 56; Page: 92; Image: 0193682; Family History Library Film: 00110.

[11] Emma Holbrook Buzby Family History 1925

[12] Frederick Godshall Sr. death certificate. Philadelphia_City_Death_Certificates,_1803-1915_4009601_206

[13] *Kite's Philadelphia City Directory, 1814.* Philadelphia: B & T Kite, 1814; p. 187.

[14] *Robinson's Philadelphia City Directory, 1817.* Philadelphia: James Robinson, 1817; p. 190.

[15] *Paxton's Philadelphia City Directory, 1818.* John Adems Paxton, ed. Philadelphia: E & R Parker, 1818; p. 142.

[16] *Paxton's Philadelphia City Directory, 1819.* Philadelphia: John Adems Paxton, 1819; p. 178.

[17] *1820 United States Census*, Southwark, Philadelphia County, PA, enumeration date Aug 7, 1820. 1820 U S Census; Census Place: Southwark, Philadelphia, Pennsylvania; Page: 74; NARA Roll: M33_110; Image: 339.

[18] *1830 United States Census*, East Southwark, Philadelphia County, PA. *1830 United States Census*; Census Place: East Southwark, Philadelphia, Pennsylvania; Page: 233; NARA Series: M19; Roll Number: 158; Family History Film: 0020632.

[19] Ebenezer ME Church Cemetery Records. Originals housed at Historical Society of Pennsylvania, 1300 Locust Street Philadelphia, PA 19107.

[20] Death Notice of Frederick Godshall, Jr., *Philadelphia Public Ledger*, 2 May 1882.

[21] Emma Holbrook Buzby Family History 1925. Originals housed at Historical Society of Pennsylvania, 1300 Locust Street Philadelphia, PA 19107.

[22] Emma Holbrook Buzby Family History 1925. Originals housed at Historical Society of Pennsylvania, 1300 Locust Street Philadelphia, PA 19107.

[23] Death Notice of Prudence Stites Godshall, *Philadelphia Public Ledger*, 25 March 1882.

[24] Emma Holbrook Buzby Family History 1925. Originals housed at Historical Society of Pennsylvania, 1300 Locust Street Philadelphia, PA 19107.

[25] *1830 United States Census*, Millington, Kent County, Maryland. *1830 United States Census*; Census Place: Millington, Kent, Maryland; Page: 437; NARA Series: M19; Roll Number: 57; Family History Film: 0013180.

[26] Ebenezer ME Church, Philadelphia, Marriages 1833-1874; Baptisms 1826-1871. Originals housed at Historical Society of Pennsylvania, 1300 Locust Street Philadelphia, PA 19107.

[27] *1840 United States Census*, First Ward, Southwark, Philadelphia, PA. Year: 1840; Census Place: Southwark Ward 1, Philadelphia, Pennsylvania; Roll: 486; Page: 28; Image: 545; Family History Library Film: 0020555.

[28] *1850 United States Census*, Fifth Ward, Southwark, Philadelphia, PA. Year: 1850; Census Place: Southwark Ward 5, Philadelphia, Pennsylvania; Roll: M432_822; Page: 340A; Image: 206.

[29] *1860 United States Census*, Second Ward, City of Philadelphia, Philadelphia County, PA. Year: 1860; Census Place: Philadelphia Ward 2, Philadelphia, Pennsylvania; Roll: M653_1152; Page: 69; Image: 73; Family History Library Film: 805152.

[30] *1870 United States Census*, 5th Division, 2nd Ward, Philadelphia, PA. Year: 1870; Census Place: Philadelphia Ward 2 District 5, Philadelphia, Pennsylvania; Roll: M593_1388; Page: 134B; Image: 272; Family History Library Film: 552887.

[31] *1880 United States Census*, Philadelphia, PA. Year: 1880; Census Place: Philadelphia, Philadelphia, Pennsylvania; Roll: 1167; Family History Film: 1255167; Page: 25B; Enumeration District: 032; Image: 0430.

[32] Death Notices of Prudence Stites Godshall and Frederick Godshall, Jr., *Philadelphia Public Ledger*, 25 March 1882 & 2 May 1882.

[33] *Ebenezer ME Church Burying Ground in Southwark, Philadelphia*, p. 183. Originals housed at Historical Society of Pennsylvania, 1300 Locust Street Philadelphia, PA 19107.

[34] Henry Stites Godshall's Philadelphia *Public Ledger* Death Notice, 9 Oct 1893.

[35] *Marriages 1826-1875*, p. 54. Available Presbyterian Historical Society, 425 Lombard St Philadelphia, PA 19147.

[36] *McElroy's Philadelphia City Directory 1855*. Philadelphia: A. McElroy & Co., 1855; p. 202.

[37] *McElroy's Philadelphia City Directory 1857*. Philadelphia: A. McElroy & Co., 1857; p. 248.

[38] *1860 United States Census*, Ward 15, Philadelphia, PA. Year: 1860; Census Place: Philadelphia Ward 15, Philadelphia, Pennsylvania; Roll: M653_1165; Page: 535; Image: 541; Family History Library Film: 805165.

[39] *McElroy's Philadelphia City Directory 1860*. Philadelphia: A. McElroy & Co., 1860; p. 360.

[40] *McElroy's Philadelphia City Directory 1865*. Philadelphia: A. McElroy & Co.,1865; p. 268.

[41] *1870 United States Census*, 44 District, 15 Ward, Philadelphia, PA. Year: 1870; Census Place: Philadelphia Ward 15 District 44, Philadelphia, Pennsylvania; Roll: M593_1399; Page: 476B; Image: 384; Family History Library Film: 552898.

[42] Dittenhafer, Miriam Marcy. *Godshall Family History*,, p. 100; Original data: Gopsill's Philadelphia Directory 1870.

[43] Dittenhafer, Miriam Marcy. *Godshall Family History*,, p. 100; Original data: Gopsill's Philadelphia Directory 1875.

[44] *1880 United States Census*, Philadelphia, Philadelphia County, Philadelphia. Year: 1880; Census Place: Philadelphia, Philadelphia, Pennsylvania; Roll: 1175; Family History Film: 1255175; Page: 320C; Enumeration District: 272; Image: 0426.

[45] Dittenhafer, Miriam Marcy. *Godshall Family History*,, p. 101; Original data: Gopsill's Philadelphia Directory 1880.

[46] *Gopsill's Philadelphia City Directory, 1890*. Philadelphia: Gopsill's, 1890; p. 718.

[47] Dittenhafer, Miriam Marcy. *Godshall Family History*,, p. 99; Original data: Philadelphia Blue Book 1891.

[48] Dittenhafer, Miriam Marcy. *Godshall Family History*,, p. 99.

[49] Death certificates page # 7602 – Henry S. Godshall. Original housed at Philadelphia City Archives, 3101 Market Street, Philadelphia, PA 19104.

[50] Collections of the Genealogical Society of PA – Vol: Lot Holders of Woodlands Cemetery, Philadelphia, PA. Originals housed at Historical Society of Pennsylvania, 1300 Locust Street Philadelphia, PA 19107. Register p. 59.

[51] *1900 United States Census*, Mount Vernon, Westchester, NY. Year: 1900; Census Place: Mount Vernon Ward 1, Westchester, New York; Roll: 1175; Page: 19A; Enumeration District: 81; FHL microfilm: 1241175.

[52] *1910 United States Census*, Philadelphia City, Philadelphia County, PA. Year: 1910; Census Place: Philadelphia Ward 46, Philadelphia, Pennsylvania; Roll: T624_1413; Page: 5A; Enumeration District: 1189; Image: 883; FHL microfilm: 1375426.

[53] Death Certificate of Elizabeth W. Godshall. Philadelphia File # 58702, Registered # 12453 (last digit hard to read). Original housed at PA Department of Health, Division of Vital records, PO Box 1528, New Castle, PA 16103.

GLORIA DEI
(OLD SWEDES') CHURCH, PHILADELPHIA, PA

FREDERICK GODSHALL, SR.
& ANN CUMMINGS (1800)
AND
FREDERICK GODSHALL, JR.,
& PRUDENCE STITES (1823)
WERE MARRIED HERE,
AS WELL AS
PRUDENCE'S PARENTS,
PETER STITES &
HANNAH WILLS (1799)

(PHOTOS BY
THOMAS G.
HUMPHRIES, II,
GODSHALL RELATIVE)

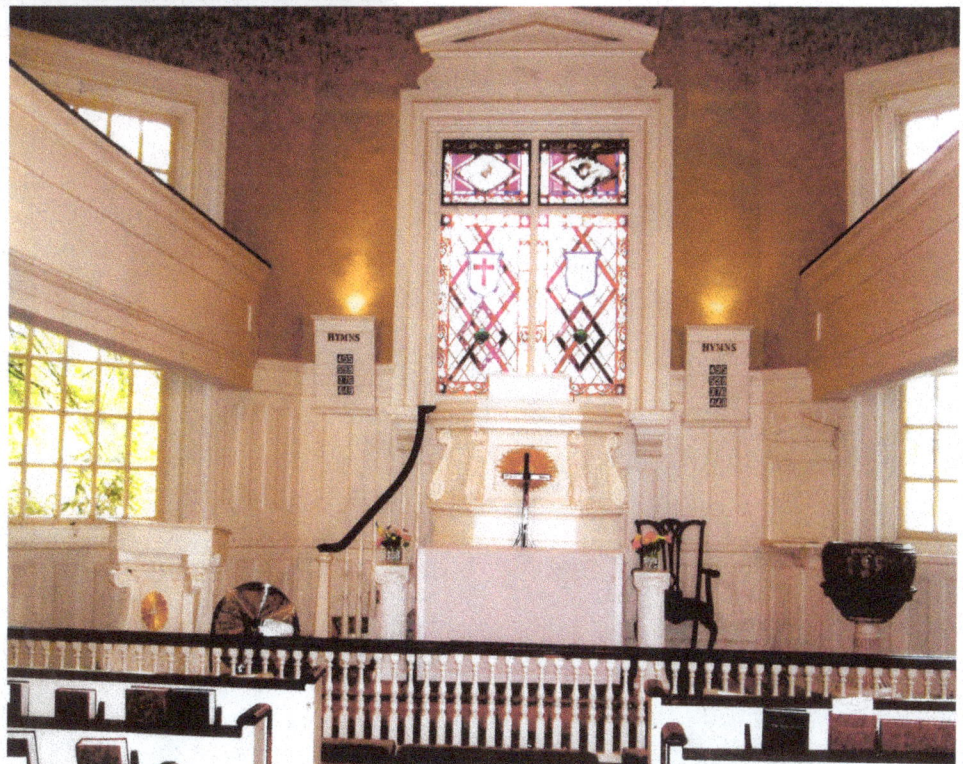

FREDERICK GODSHALL & WIFE PRUDENCE STITES GODSHALL
1863 - PHILADELPHIA - BOTH AGED 63

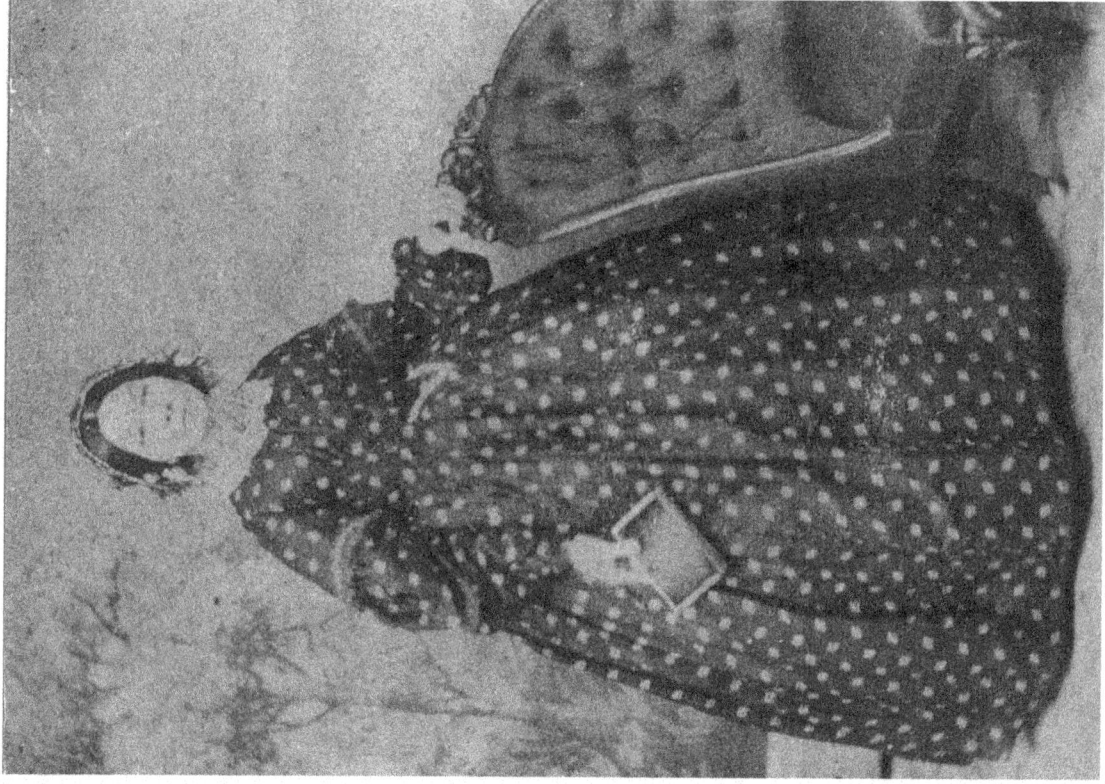

The Hobson Lineage

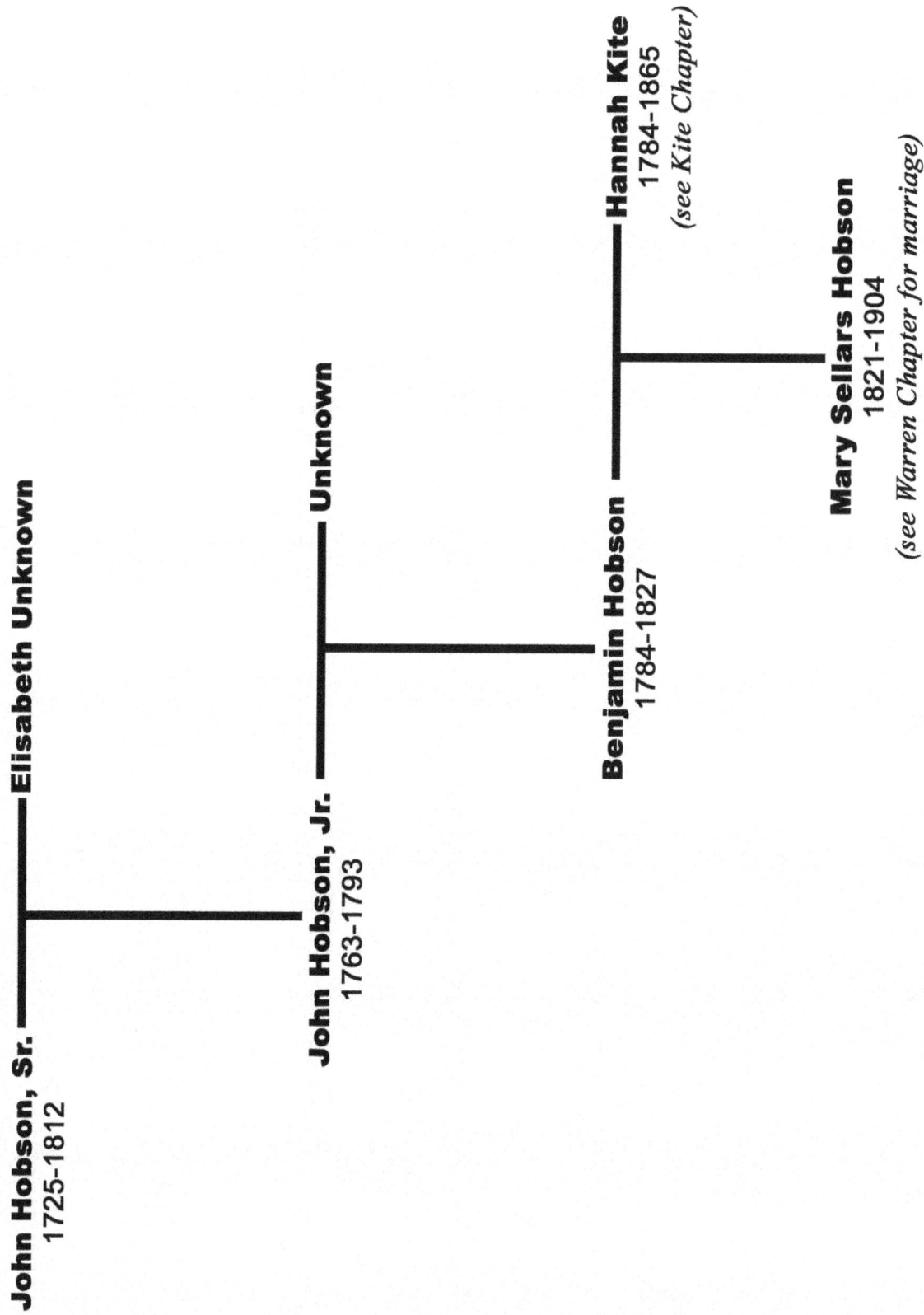

John Hobson, Sr.
1725-1812

Elisabeth Unknown

John Hobson, Jr.
1763-1793

Unknown

Benjamin Hobson
1784-1827

Hannah Kite
1784-1865
(see Kite Chapter)

Mary Sellars Hobson
1821-1904
(see Warren Chapter for marriage)

The Hobson Lineage

John Hobson, Sr., (1725–1812) and Elisabeth Unknown

This couple is known only through notations in a family Bible. The pages for the Kite–Tunis–Sellars–Hobson Family Bible were torn out of a much older Bible and tucked into the Warren–Leinau Family Bible, which belonged to Mary Sellars Hobson Warren Leinau. While the Warren–Leinau Bible had notations for Mary and her children, the pages from the Kite–Tunis–Sellars–Hobson Bible are all from her family tree.[1]

From the notations in the Kite–Tunis–Sellars–Hobson Bible, we know that John Hobson, Sr., died 14 October 1812, at the age of 87. From there we can extrapolate his birth year of 1725.

We know of his wife, Elisabeth, only because their son's birth and death was noted as "son of John and Elisabeth Hobson":

John, Jr. (1763–1793)[2]

If this couple had any other children, it is not noted in the Kite–Tunis–Sellars–Hobson Family Bible. There is also no information on Elisabeth's death.

John Hobson, Jr., (1763–1793) and Unknown

John Hobson, Jr., was born to John and Elisabeth Hobson 30 November 1763.[3] There is no notation in the Kite–Tunis–Sellars–Hobson Family Bible on whom he married, or the names of any of his children. But evidence points to the following being John, Jr.

On the 1790 United States Census, there is a John Hobson living at 19 Pewter–Platter Alley, Philadelphia, PA.[4] There are 3 males under 16, 3 males over 16, and 4 females. John was a sieve maker. One of the males over 16 is John, head of the household. None of the other males over 16 can be his children, as he would have been 11 years old or younger at their births. So who are they? Unknown. My guess (and it is only a guess) is that one might be his father, John, Sr., who would have been 65. The other might be a brother. The females are likely John, Jr.'s wife, perhaps his mother, and either daughters or sisters. The three young boys could be John, Jr.'s sons, or they could belong to any of the older people.

The reason I believe that this John Hobson is John, Jr., rather than John, Sr., is that in the Philadelphia City Directories for 1791,[5] 1793,[6] and 1794,[7] John Hobson, sieve maker, lives at 19 Pewter–Platter Alley. In 1793, he is described as a "junior sieve maker." John, Jr., would have been 30 that year, so possibly still in a junior stage of his career. John, Sr., would have been 68—definitely not of an age to be a junior anything.

John Hobson, Jr., died 7 November 1793.[8] The John Hobson, sieve maker, disappears from the Directories after a last appearance in 1794 (it often took a year for the Directories to catch up to people's deaths). So the evidence hints that this John Hobson is John, Jr.

John, Jr., and his unknown wife had at least 1 son:

Benjamin (1784–1827)[9] - *married Hannah Kite.*

Benjamin Hobson (1784–1827) and Hannah Kite (1784–1865)
(see Kite Lineage chapter)

I have no direct documentation that Benjamin Hobson is John Hobson, Jr.'s son. All I have is the Kite–Tunis–Sellars–Hobson Family Bible. The only 2 Hobsons in this Bible who could have fathered Benjamin are John, Sr., and John, Jr. In 1784, when Benjamin was born, John, Jr., would have been 21, and John, Sr., would have been 59. While John, Sr., might well have fathered a son at that age, his wife likely would have been past childbearing age, if she was even still alive. So I believe Benjamin to be John, Jr.'s son.

Benjamin Hobson died in 1827 at the age of 43,[10] which would put his birth in 1784. He married Hannah Kite (born 24 August 1784) on 8 August 1807 in Blockley Township, Philadelphia, PA. Benjamin was 23; Hannah was 22.

Benjamin and Hannah had 6 children:[11]

Sarah Ann (1808–1859) – *married Benjamin Plum.*
John (1811–1871) – *married Anna Kuhn.*
Benjamin (1812–1855) – *married Margaret Seward.*
Elizabeth L. (1815–1875) – *married William Henry Moore.*
Hannah Howell (1819–1819) – *died at age 3 months.*
Mary Sellars (1821–1904) – *married James William Warren, Sr.*

I believe the Kite–Tunis–Sellars–Hobson Family Bible to have been Benjamin and Hannah's Bible, as it details their children's and grandchildren's lives. Hannah's parents and grandparents have been entered meticulously. This is further evidence that Benjamin's father was John, Jr., and his grandfather John, Sr., as this is as far back as Hannah's line is entered as well.

In 1808 and 1810, Benjamin and Hannah lived at 29 N. Front Street, Philadelphia, PA. He was a brushmaker, as he was most of his adult life.[12] [13] In 1818 the family had moved to 124 N. Front Street.[14]

From 1819 through 1822, the family lived at 126 N. Front Street.[15]

On the 1820 Census[16], in the Upper Delaware Ward, Benjamin's family consisted of 2 males under 10 (John, 9, and Benjamin, Jr., 8); 2 males 16–26, 1 male 26–45 (himself, 36), 1 female under 10 (Elizabeth, 4), 1 female 10–26 (Sarah, 12); 1 female 26–45 (wife Hannah, 36); and 2 females 45+.

I do not know who the 2 males 16–26 are, or the 2 females over 45. By 1825 Benjamin and Hannah had a boardinghouse, so it is possible these people are boarders rather than family members.

In 1823 and 1824, Benjamin and family lived at 25 Coomb's Alley, Philadelphia, PA.[17] [18]

In 1825, they still lived at 25 Coomb's Alley, but Benjamin's occupation was running a boardinghouse, rather than working as a brushmaker. Hannah also had an occupation: Layer out of the dead.[19]

Benjamin Hobson died 22 February 1827.[20]

After her husband's death, Hannah maintained the boardinghouse. In 1829, the address was 20 Coomb's Alley.[21]

In 1830,[22] Hannah owned a boardinghouse at 374 N. Front Street. Her household consisted of 2 males 10–15, 2 males 15–20 (Benjamin, 18, and John, 19), 1 female 5–10 (Mary, 9), 1 female 10–15 (Elizabeth, 15), 2 females 20–30, 2 females 30–40, and 1 female 40–50 (herself, 46).

The 3 females 20–30, the 2 females 30–40, and the 2 males 10–15 were likely boarders of hers, as she ran a boardinghouse. The young boys are likely sons of the unknown women.

In 1831, Hannah still owned the 374 N. Front St. boardinghouse.[23] By 1833, she had moved her boardinghouse to SW Chancery Lane & Arch.[24]

In 1840,[25] she lived on Green, below 10th, in the Spring Garden District. Hannah lived with her daughter Sarah Ann and her husband, Benjamin Plum. The Plum household (misspelled Plumb) consisted of 1 male 5–10 (Lewis, 8), 1 male 30–40 (Benjamin, 40), 1 female under 5 (Julia Ann, 5), 1 female 30–40 (Sarah, 32), and 1 female 50–60 (Hannah, 56).

Hannah's occupation was listed as layer out of the dead. In 1841 she still lived with the Plums and had the same occupation.[26]

In 1850,[27] Hannah lived with daughter Elizabeth's family. The Moore household consisted of Elizabeth (31) and husband William Henry (35, clerk), children Anna (8) and Mary Elizabeth (5), nephew Lewis Plum (19, plumber), Hannah (64), and 2 women I assume were servants, Sophia Gray (51, from England) and Biddy McDonough (22, from Ireland).

In 1860,[28] Hannah was back with Sarah's family. The Plum household consists of Benjamin (57, plumber), Lewis (28, plumber), Julia (21), Hannah V. (12), and Hannah Hobson (74). Sarah had died the year before, so it is possible that Hannah moved in to help take care of the family, if she was still able–bodied.

Hannah Kite Hobson died 7 February 1865,[29] and was buried 11 February 1865 in Monument Cemetery.[30]

Hannah and Benjamin's daughter **Mary Sellars Hobson** married James William Warren, Sr., in 1839. Mary was 18; James was 28. (*See The Warren Lineage chapter.*)

---

[1] Kite-Tunis-Sellars-Hobson Family Bible. Original in possession of Kerry Gans Douglas.

[2] Kite-Tunis-Sellars-Hobson Family Bible. Original in possession of Kerry Gans Douglas.

[3] Kite-Tunis-Sellars-Hobson Family Bible. Original in possession of Kerry Gans Douglas.

[4] 1790 Census, Philadelphia, PA. Year: 1790; Census Place: Philadelphia City, Philadelphia, Pennsylvania; Series: M637; Roll: 9; Page: 223; Image: 519; Family History Library Film: 0568149.

[5] *Biddle's Philadelphia City Directory, 1791.* Clement Biddle, ed., Philadelphia: James & Johnson, 1791; p. 59.

[6] *Hardie's Philadelphia City Directory, 1793.* James Hardie, ed., Philadelphia: T. Dobson, 1793; p. 65.

[7] *Hardie's Philadelphia City Directory, 1794.* James Hardie, ed., Philadelphia: Jacob Johnson & Co., 1794; p. 70.

[8] Kite-Tunis-Sellars-Hobson Family Bible. Original in possession of Kerry Gans Douglas.

[9] Kite-Tunis-Sellars-Hobson Family Bible. Original in possession of Kerry Gans Douglas.

[10] Kite-Tunis-Sellars-Hobson Family Bible. Original in possession of Kerry Gans Douglas.

[11] Kite-Tunis-Sellars-Hobson Family Bible. Original in possession of Kerry Gans Douglas.

[12] *Robinson's Philadelphia City Directory, 1808.* James Robinson, ed., Philadelphia: William Woodhouse, 1808; p. 163.

[13] *Robinson's Philadelphia City Directory, 1810.* James Robinson, ed., Philadelphia: William Woodhouse, 1810; p. 137.

[14] *Paxton's Philadelphia City Directory, 1818.* John Adems Paxton, ed. Philadelphia: E & R Parker, 1818; p. 173.

[15] *Philadelphia City Directory.* Paxton's; Year: 1819; p. 207; Paxton's; Year: 1819; p. 207; McCarty & Davis; Year: 1821; p. 234; McCarty & Davis; Year: 1822; p. 264.

[16] *1820 United States Census*, Philadelphia, PA. 1820 U S Census; Census Place: Philadelphia Upper Delaware Ward, Philadelphia, Pennsylvania; Page: 204; NARA Roll: M33_108; Image: 222.

[17] *DeSilver's Philadelphia City Directory, 1823.* Philadelphia: Robert DeSilver, 1823; p. 191.

[18] *DeSilver's Philadelphia City Directory, 1824.* Philadelphia: Robert DeSilver, 1824; P. 210.

[19] *DeSilver's Philadelphia City Directory, 1825.* Philadelphia: Robert DeSilver, 1825; p. 68.

[20] Kite-Tunis-Sellars-Hobson Family Bible. Original in possession of Kerry Gans Douglas.

[21] *DeSilver's Philadelphia City Directory, 1829.* Philadelphia: Robert DeSilver, 1829; p. 88.

[22] *1830 United States Census*, Philadelphia, PA. *1830 United States Census*; Census Place: Philadelphia High Street Ward, Philadelphia, Pennsylvania; Page: 41; NARA Series: M19; Roll Number: 159; Family History Film: 0020633.

[23] *DeSilver's Philadelphia City Directory, 1831.* Philadelphia: Robert DeSilver, 1831; p. 96.

[24] *DeSilver's Philadelphia City Directory, 1833.* Philadelphia: Robert DeSilver, 1833; p. 96.

[25] *1840 United States Census*, Philadelphia, PA. Year: 1840; Census Place: Spring Garden Ward 1, Philadelphia, Pennsylvania; Roll: 487; Page: 368; Image: 1226; Family History Library Film: 0020555.

[26] *McElroy's Philadelphia City Directory 1841.* Philadelphia: A. McElroy & Co., 1841; p. 122.

[27] *1850 United States Census*, Philadelphia, PA. Year: 1850; Census Place: Spring Garden Ward 3 Precinct 2, Philadelphia, Pennsylvania; Roll: M432_818; Page: 1A; Image: 495.

[28] *1860 United States Census*, Philadelphia, PA. 1860 U.S. Census: Pennsylvania, Philadelphia (Ward 15): Series M653, Roll 1165, Sheet 102, Line 26

[29] Warren-Leinau Family Bible. Original in possession of Kerry Gans Douglas.

[30] Family Search.org: Pennsylvania,_ Philadelphia_City_Death_Certificates,_1803-1915_4010019_234

Hobson Family Bible Entries

JOHN HOBSON, SR.
DEPARTED THIS LIFE
14TH OCTOBER 1812
AGED 87 YEARS

JOHN HOBSON, JUNIOR
SON OF
JOHN AND ELIZABETH HOBSON
WAS BORN 31ST OF NOVEMBER 1763
ON THE SECOND DAY OF THE WEEK

JOHN HOBSON, JR., SON OF
JOHN AND ELIZABETH HOBSON
DEPARTED THIS LIFE
7TH NOVEMBER 1793
AGED 29 YEARS
11 MONTHS AND 7 DAYS

MARY SELLARS HOBSON
DAUGHTER OF
BENJAMIN AND HANNAH HOBSON
WAS BORN MAY 7TH, 1821 ON THE
2ND DAY OF THE WEEK AT
8 O'CLOCK IN THE MORNING

HOBSON FAMILY BIBLE ENTRIES, CON'T.

**BENJAMIN HOBSON
DEPARTED THIS LIFE
FEBRUARY 22ND, 1827
IN HIS 43RD YEAR**

**HANNAH HOBSON DIED
ON THE 7TH DAY OF FEBRUARY 1865
AGED 79 YEARS & 6 MONTHS
AT 8 1/2 O'CLOCK PM
IN PHILADELPHIA, PENN.,
IN PEACE WITH GOD**

The Kite Lineage

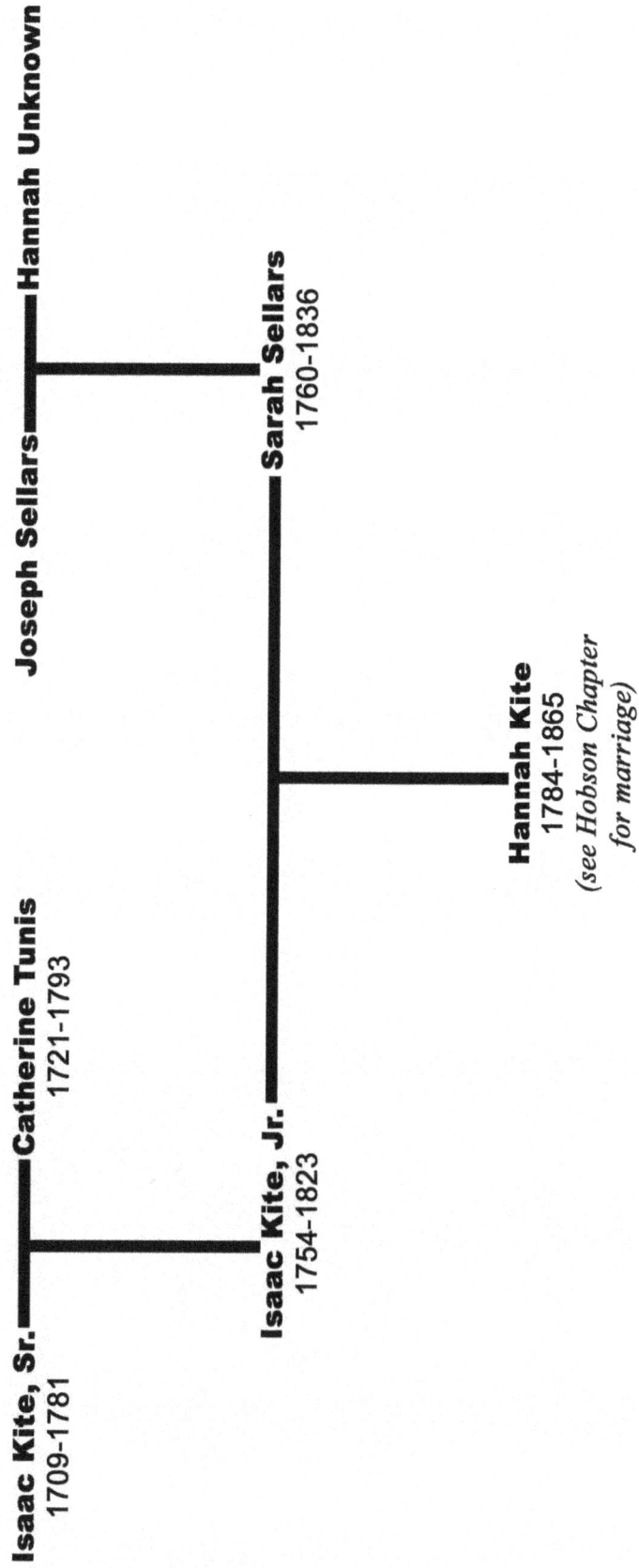

Isaac Kite, Sr.
1709-1781

Catherine Tunis
1721-1793

Joseph Sellars

Hannah Unknown

Isaac Kite, Jr.
1754-1823

Sarah Sellars
1760-1836

Hannah Kite
1784-1865
(see Hobson Chapter
for marriage)

The Kite Lineage

Isaac Kite, Sr., (1709–1781) and Catherine Tunis (1721–1793)[1]

Isaac Kite, Sr., was born in Philadelphia, PA, 11 May 1709.[2] He married Catherine Tunis (born 10 December 1721) in Lower Merion, PA, on 2 April 1749.[3] Isaac was 39; Catherine was 27.

Issac and Catherine had 7 known children:[4]

Elizabeth (b. 1751)
Isaac, Jr. (1754–1823) – *married Sarah Sellars.*
Mary (1757–1788)
Anthony (1760–1829)
Deborah (1762–1842)
Hannah (1763–1793)
Catherine (1765–1793)

Isaac Kite, Sr., died 7 March 1781 in Blockley Township, Philadelphia, PA, at age 71.[5] Please note, however, an entry in the family Bible seems to indicate Isaac, Sr., died 1 September 1823 at age 70. This would be impossible, however, given his children's birth dates, unless he was much older than 70.[6]

In the 1790 Census, Catherine Tunis Kite lived in Blockley Township. There were 3 females in her household—herself (69) and likely her 2 youngest girls, Hannah (27) and Catherine (25).[7]

Catherine Tunis Kite died 13 January 1793 in Blockley Township, Philadelphia, PA, at the age of 71.[8] An odd occurrence is that both of her youngest daughters, Hannah and Catherine, are also recorded as dying in 1793, although I have no exact date. It does make me wonder if they all died together in a house fire or other accident, or perhaps all contracted the same illness.[9]

Isaac Kite, Jr., (1754–1823) and Sarah Sellars (1760–1836)

Isaac Kite, Jr., was born 24 December 1754 in Blockley Township, Philadelphia, PA. [10] On 30 June 1785, Isaac married Sarah Sellars in Darby, Chester County, PA.[11] Isaac was 30; Sarah was 25. Sarah was born on 28 February 1760 and was the daughter of Joseph and Hannah Sellars.[12]

Isaac, Jr., and Sarah had 8 known children:[13] [14]

Hannah (1784–1865) – *married Benjamin Hobson.*
Mary Pearce (1787–1844)
Isaac, III (1790–1825)
Joseph Sellars (1792–1830)
William (1) (1794–1795)
William (2) (1795–1830)
Benjamin (1799–1824)
Paschal (1803–1869)

Kite

In 1790, Isaac, Jr., and his family lived on Water Street East Side in Philadelphia, PA. Isaac's household consisted of 3 males over 16 (one was himself, 36, the other 2 unknown), 1 male under 16 (probably Isaac, III), and 4 females (wife Sarah, 30, children Hannah and Mary and 1 unknown). Isaac was a carpenter.[15]

In 1791,[16] 1793,[17] and 1794[18] carpenter Isaac lived on 8th Street between Chestnut and Walnut. In 1795[19] his residence is South 8th Street, and in 1796[20] his residence is 8th Street between Cherry and Walnut. These are all likely the same residence.

In 1800, Isaac's family lived in the North Mulberry Ward of Philadelphia, PA. Isaac's household consisted of 4 males under 10 (Isaac III, 10; Joseph Sellars, 8; William [2], 5, and Benjamin, 1), 1 male over 45 (himself, 46), 2 females 10–15 (Hannah, 15, and Mary Pearce, 13) , and 1 female 26–44 (wife Sarah, 40).[21]

In 1803–1805,[22] the family lived on Juniper above Race (also called Sassafrass). From 1807–1811[23] they lived at 91 North 9th Street. Isaac still made his living as a carpenter.

The 1810 Census found the Kite family in South Mulberry Ward of Philadelphia, PA. Isaac's household consisted of 1 male under 10 (Paschal, 7), 2 males 10–15 (Benjamin, 11, and William [2], 15), 2 males 16–25 (Joseph Sellars, 18, and Isaac, III, 20), 1 male 45+ (himself, 56), 1 female 16–25 (Mary Pearce, 23), and 1 female 45+ (wife Sarah, 50).[24]

In 1814, Isaac's family lived at 11 Hause's Court.[25] In 1816, they moved to Nicholson's Court.[26] In 1818, the Kites lived at 12th above Race.[27]

In 1820, the Kites lived in Blockley Township, Philadelphia, PA. Isaac's household consisted of 1 male 16–18 (Paschal, 17), 1 male 16–26 (Benjamin, 21, or William [2], 25), 1 male 45+ (himself, 66), 1 female 45+ (wife Sarah, 60), with 1 person engaged in manufacturing.[28]

Isaac Kite, Jr., died on 21 September 1823 in Blockley Township at the age of 68.[29]

In 1830, widow Sarah Sellars Kite lived with her youngest child, Paschal, in the High Street Ward of Philadelphia, PA. This Census has Paschal as head of household (1 male 20–29), with one female 70–79 (Sarah, 70).[30] By 1830, 5 of Sarah's 8 children have died—only her two daughters and son Paschal were still alive.

Sarah Sellars Kite died 7 September 1836 at age 76 in Philadelphia, PA.[31]

Isaac, Jr., and Sarah's daughter *Hannah Kite* married Benjamin Hobson in 1807. She was 22; Benjamin was 23. (*See The Hobson Lineage chapter.*)

[1] Kite-Tunis-Sellars-Hobson Family Bible. Original in possession of Kerry Gans Douglas.
[2] George Jenkins Research. http://trees.ancestry.com/tree/8903857/family?cfpid=-877720051
[3] George Jenkins Research. http://trees.ancestry.com/tree/8903857/family?cfpid=-877720051
[4] George Jenkins Research. http://trees.ancestry.com/tree/8903857/family?cfpid=-877720051
[5] George Jenkins Research. http://trees.ancestry.com/tree/8903857/family?cfpid=-877720051
[6] Kite-Tunis-Sellars-Hobson Family Bible. Original in possession of Kerry Gans Douglas.
[7] *1790 United States Census*, Philadelphia, PA. Year: 1790; Census Place: Blockley, Philadelphia, Pennsylvania; Series: M637; Roll: 9; Page: 271; Image: 554; Family History Library Film: 0568149.
[8] George Jenkins Research. http://trees.ancestry.com/tree/8903857/family?cfpid=-877720051
[9] George Jenkins Research. http://trees.ancestry.com/tree/8903857/family?cfpid=-877720051

[10] Kite-Tunis-Sellars-Hobson Family Bible. Original in possession of Kerry Gans Douglas.

[11] Fulton Research. http://familytreemaker.genealogy.com/users/f/u/l/C-Fulton/FILE/0012text.txt

[12] Kite-Tunis-Sellars-Hobson Family Bible. Original in possession of Kerry Gans Douglas.

[13] Kite-Tunis-Sellars-Hobson Family Bible. Original in possession of Kerry Gans Douglas.

[14] George Jenkins Research. http://trees.ancestry.com/tree/8903857/family?cfpid=-877720051

[15] *1790 United States Census.* Year: 1790; Census Place: Water Street East Side, Philadelphia, Pennsylvania; Series: M637; Roll: 9; Page: 61; Image: 392; Family History Library Film: 0568149.

[16] *Biddle's Philadelphia City Directory, 1791.* Clement Biddle, ed., Philadelphia: James & Johnson, 1791; p. 70.

[17] *Hardie's Philadelphia City Directory, 1793.* James Hardie, ed., Philadelphia: T. Dobson, 1793; p. 79.

[18] *Hardie's Philadelphia City Directory, 1794.* James Hardie, ed., Philadelphia: Jacob Johnson & Co., 1794; p.84.

[19] *Hogan's Philadelphia City Directory, 1795.* Edmund Hogan, ed., Philadelphia: Francis & Robert Bailey, 1795; p. 136.

[20] *Stephens's Philadelphia City Directory, 1796.* Thomas Stephens, ed., Philadelphia: W. Woodward, 1796; p. 104.

[21] *1800 United States Census.* Year: 1800; Census Place: Philadelphia North Mulberry Ward, Philadelphia, Pennsylvania; Roll: 43; Page: 164,165; Image: 59; Family History Library Film: 363346.

[22] *Robinson's Philadelphia City Directory,* James Robinson, ed., Philadelphia: W. Woodhouse, 1803, p. 143; Year: 1804, p. 129; Year: 1805, p. 134.

[23] *Philadelphia City Directory, Robinson's;* Year: 1807, p. 173; Year: 1808, p. 185; Year: 1809, p. 161; Year: 1810, p. 160; *Aitken's,* Year: 1811, p. 179.

[24] *1810 United States Census.* Year: 1810; Census Place: Philadelphia South Mulberry Ward, Philadelphia, Pennsylvania; Roll: 55; Page: 342; Image: 0193681; Family History Library Film: 00122.

[25] *Kite's Philadelphia City Directory, 1814.* Philadelphia: B & T Kite, 1814; p. 274.

[26] *Robinson's Philadelphia City Directory, 1816.* Philadelphia: James Robinson, 1816; p. 238.

[27] *Paxton's Philadelphia City Directory, 1818.* John Adems Paxton, ed. Philadelphia: E & R Parker,1818; p. 203.

[28] *1820 United States Census.* 1820 U S Census; Census Place: Blockley, Philadelphia, Pennsylvania; Page: 8A; NARA Roll: M33_109; Image: 19.

[29] Kite-Tunis-Sellars-Hobson Family Bible. Original in possession of Kerry Gans Douglas.

[30] *1830 United States Census*; Census Place: Philadelphia High Street Ward, Philadelphia, Pennsylvania; Page: 40; NARA Series: M19; Roll Number: 159; Family History Film: 0020633.

[31] Kite-Tunis-Sellars-Hobson Family Bible. Original in possession of Kerry Gans Douglas.

KITE FAMILY BIBLE ENTRIES

Isaac Kite Sr.
Departed this life
Sept 1st 1823 in his 70th year

ISAAC KITE, SR. DEPARTED THIS LIFE
SEPTEMBER 1, 1823 IN HIS 70TH YEAR

Isaac Kite = Son of
Isaac and Catherine
Kite was Born the 24th
Day of the 12th Month, on
the third day of the week,
in the year of our Lord 1754
in County of Philadelphia
P.A. in Blockley Township

Sarah Sellers = Daughter
of Joseph and Hannah
Sellers was Born on the 28th
Day of February 1760

Isaac Kite Jun.
Departe this life
July 21st 1825. Aged 35 years

ISAAC KITE, JR. DEPARTED THIS LIFE
JULY 21ST, 1825
AGE 35 YEARS

Sarah Kite
Departed this life
on the 7th day of
September 1836.
Aged 79 years

SARAH KITE DEPARTED THIS LIFE
ON THE 7TH DAY OF
SEPTEMBER 1836
AGED 79 YEARS

ISAAC KITE, SON OF ISAAC AND CATHERINE
KITE WAS BORN THE 24TH DAY
OF THE 12TH MONTH,
ON THE THIRD DAY OF THE WEEK, IN THE
YEAR OF OUR LORD 1754 IN COUNTY OF
PHILADELPHIA PA IN BLOCKLEY TOWNSHIP.

SARAH SELLERS= DAUGHTER OF
JOSEPH AND HANNAH SELLERS
WAS BORN ON THE
28TH DAY OF FEBRUARY 1760

Benjamin Hobson
And
Hannah Kite
Were Married August 8th
1807.

BENJAMIN HOBSON AND HANNAH KITE
WERE MARRIED AUGUST 8TH, 1807

The Lathrop-Tyler Lineage

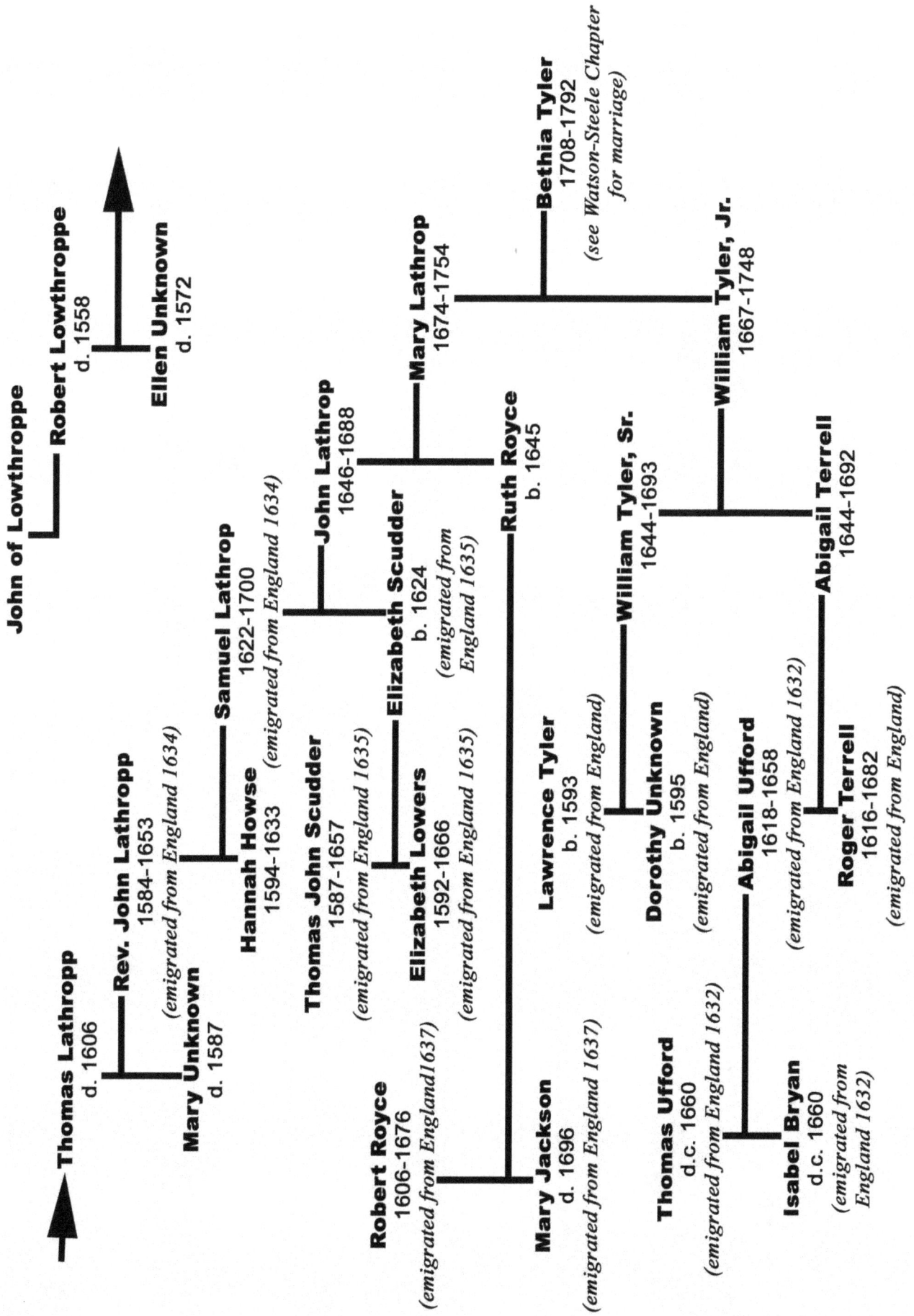

John of Lowthroppe

Robert Lowthroppe
d. 1558

Ellen Unknown
d. 1572

Thomas Lathropp
d. 1606

Rev. John Lathropp
1584-1653
(emigrated from England 1634)

Mary Unknown
d. 1587

Samuel Lathrop
1622-1700
(emigrated from England 1634)

Hannah Howse
1594-1633

Thomas John Scudder
1587-1657
(emigrated from England 1635)

John Lathrop
1646-1688

Elizabeth Scudder
b. 1624
(emigrated from England 1635)

Elizabeth Lowers
1592-1666
(emigrated from England 1635)

Mary Lathrop
1674-1754

Ruth Royce
b. 1645

Bethia Tyler
1708-1792

(see Watson-Steele Chapter
for marriage)

Robert Royce
1606-1676
(emigrated from England 1637)

Mary Jackson
d. 1696
(emigrated from England 1637)

Lawrence Tyler
b. 1593
(emigrated from England)

William Tyler, Sr.
1644-1693

William Tyler, Jr.
1667-1748

Dorothy Unknown
b. 1595
(emigrated from England)

Thomas Ufford
d.c. 1660
(emigrated from England 1632)

Abigail Ufford
1618-1658

Abigail Terrell
1644-1692

Isabel Bryan
d.c. 1660
(emigrated from England 1632)

Roger Terrell
1616-1682
(emigrated from England)

(emigrated from England 1632)

The Lathrop–Tyler Lineage

John of Lowthroppe and Unknown[1]

John of Lowthroppe[2] is the earliest known relation – we have no record of his parents or siblings. He lived in Lowthorpe, Wapentake of Dickering, East Riding of Yorkshire. Early in the 16th century, he lived in Cherry Burton, and owned extensive landed estates.[3]

He appeared on the 1545 Yorkshire subsidy roll.[4]

He had 4 children, but only 1 of their names is known:[5]

Robert (d. 1558) – *married Ellen Unknown.*

Robert Lowthroppe (d. 1558) and Ellen Unknown (d. 1572)

Robert Lowthroppe[6] married Ellen[7], maiden name unknown. They had 4 known children:[8]

John
Thomas (d. 1606) – *married Elizabeth Unknown, then Mary Unknown, then Jane*
       Unknown.
Margaret
Lawrence

Robert Lowthroppe died in 1558 in North Burton (Sheriburton), Yorkshire, England. His will was dated 16 July 1558, and was proven on 20 October 1558. His wife, Ellen, died in 1572, also in North Burton, Yorkshire.[9]

Thomas Lathropp (d. 1606) and Mary Unknown (d. 1587)

Thomas Lathropp[10] was born in Cherry Burton, Yorkshire, England. He was a very busy man, having 3 wives and 22 known children!

About 1561, Thomas married his first wife, Elizabeth, maiden name unknown, although she was a widow of a man surnamed Clark.[11] Thomas and Elizabeth had 8 known children:[12]

Robert – *married Ann Pattison.*
Catherine – *married William Akett/Akeit.*
Awdrey – *married Unknown Wickham/Wykham.*
Elizabeth – *married Thomas Rowood.*
Anne (b. 1569)
Isabell (b. 1570)
Martin (1572–1572)
Andrew (b. 1574)

At some time around 1574, but definitely by 1576, Thomas had moved his family from Cherry Burton to Etton in the Harthill Wapentake of East Riding, Yorkshire, England.[13]

Thomas' first wife died in July 1574. Elizabeth was buried on 29 July 1574 in Etton.[14]

Thomas then married Mary,[15] maiden name unknown, sometime after Elizabeth's death and before the 1576 birth of their first child. They had 5 known children:[16]

Anne (b. 1576)
Mary – *married John Gallaut/Garwood.*
Thomas, Jr. (1582–1628) – *married Elizabeth Unknown.*
John (1584–1653) – *married Hannah Howse/House, then Anna Hammond.*
William (b. 1587)

Thomas' second wife, Mary, died in January 1587/88, and was buried 6 January 1587/88 in Etton.[17]

Thomas then married Jane,[18] maiden name unknown, after Mary's death and before the 1591 birth of their first child. They had 9 known children:[19]

Margaret (b. 1591)
Isabell (b. 1592)
Lucy (b. 1593) – *married Richard Cawnsby.*
Richard (1595–1641) – *married Dorothy Lowdon.*
Mark (1597–1660)
Lawrence (b. 1599)
Jane (b. 1601)
Joseph (b. 1602)
Bartholomew (b. 1605)

It is unknown when Jane died, but Thomas Lathropp died in 1606, just a year after his youngest child was born. Thomas died in Etton.[20]

Thomas' son **John** by his second wife, Mary, is our line—he is the immigrant to America.

The Rev. John Lathropp (1584–1653) and Hannah Howse (1594–1633)

The Rev. John Lathropp was born in England in December 1584,[21] the 12th child of his father, Thomas, the fourth child by Thomas' second wife, Mary. He was christened 20 December 1584 in Etton in the Harthill Wapentake of East Riding, Yorkshire, England.[22] John enrolled at Queen's College, Cambridge. In 1605 he attained his B.A.; in 1609 he earned his M.A.[23]

John married his first wife, Hannah Howse, born 1590, around 1610.[24] He was 26; Hannah was 20. They had 8 known children:[25] [26]

Jane (b. 1614)
Ann (1616–1619)
John (b. 1618)
Barbara (b. 1619)
Thomas (b. 1621)
Samuel (1622–1700) – *married Elizabeth Scudder.*
Joseph (1624–1702)
Benjamin

From 1611 to 1619 John was the parish minister in Egerton, Lower Half Hundred of Calehill, Lathe of Scray, Kent County, England.[27]

In 1623, John left the Church of England and became an Independent preacher, preaching to the Independents or Congregationalists (ana baptists or Baptists) who met in hiding.[28]

In 1624 John moved to London, where he took over the First Independent Church of London, Southwark, from the Rev. Henry Jacob, who left for Virginia.[29] As a result of his illegal preaching, John and members of his congregation were arrested 22 April 1632 by the Church of England and charged with heresy. His parishioners were released, but John was denied bail because he was their leader.[30]

However, his wife, Hannah Howse, died in 1633,[31] [32] and the authorities took pity on the Lathropp children by releasing their father—although they ordered him to leave England. As a result, John and some of his children sailed to Boston, Massachusetts, on the ship *Griffin*, arriving 18 September 1634. Also on board were some members of John's London congregation.[33]

John did not stay long in Boston. On 27 September 1634 he moved to the small, new town of Scituate, MA, where many of his old London congregants had settled. He was quickly made their pastor.[34]

John married his second wife, Anna Hammond, in Scituate, MA, on 17 February 1636/37. John and Anna had 6 children:[35]

Barnabas (1636–1715)
Unknown Daughter (1638–1638)
Abigail (b. 1639)
Bathshua (1641–1723)
John (1644–1727)
Unknown Son (1649–1649)

The Rev. John had a falling out with his Scituate parish, apparently over baptisms, and moved his family to Barnstable, MA, on Cape Cod, on 11 October 1639.[36] He was one of the founders of that town.

The Reverend John Lathropp died in Barnstable, MA, on 8 November 1653 at age 68. [37] [38]

Samuel Lathrop (1622–1700) and Elizabeth Scudder (b. 1624)

Samuel Lathrop was born in 1622 in England.[39] [40] He arrived in Boston with his father, the Rev. John Lathropp, on 18 September 1634 at the age of 12. He moved with his father to Scituate and then to Barnstable at age 17.

On 28 November 1644, Samuel married Elizabeth Scudder at his father's house in Barnstable.[41] [42] [43] Samuel was 22; Elizabeth was 20. Elizabeth was born in Grofton, Suffolk, England, on 12 May 1624.[44] [45] She was the daughter of Thomas John Scudder and Elizabeth Lowers.

- Thomas Scudder was born in Suffolk, England, in 1587,[46] and died in Salem, MA, in 1657.[47] Elizabeth Lowers was born in Suffolk, England, in 1592, and died in Salem, MA, in 1666.[48] The family, including son John,[49] apparently came over in 1635.[50] [51]

Samuel Lathrop and Elizabeth Scudder had at least 9 children:[52] [53]

John (1646–1688) – *married Ruth Royce.*
Elizabeth (1648–1690) – *married Isaac Royce.*
Samuel (b. 1652)
Sarah (1655–1706) – *married Nathaniel Royce.*
Martha (b. 1657) – *married John Moss.*
Israel (b. 1659)
Joseph (b. 1661)
Ann (d. 1745) – *married William Heugh.*
Unknown Daughter

Samuel began as a house builder in Boston and continued at that trade his entire life, although he did combine that with several farming ventures.[54]

In 1648, he moved from Barnstable to Pequot (present day New London), Connecticut. [55]

In May 1649, Samuel, along with John Winthrop, Esq., and Thomas Minor, was appointed by the General Court of the State as a judge on the newly established local court.[56]

In 1657, the Narragansett Indians besieged the fort at the head of the Nahantick. Samuel, Lt. James Avery, Mr. Brewster, and others came to the defense of the besieged fort after the commander was routed by the Indians.[57]

In 1668, Samuel and his family moved into Norwich, CT. He built his house in town there by 1670.[58]

From 1673 to 1682, Samuel was a constable of Norwich.[59]

In 1679, Samuel was contracted to build the Second Church of New London.[60]

In 1685, Samuel was appointed "Townsman" in Norwich. This was some type of dignified office—it did not simply mean that he lived there.[61]

Samuel married Abigail Doane/Donne, daughter of Deacon John Doane/Donne of Plymouth, MA, in 1690, so Samuel's first wife, Elizabeth Scudder Lathrop, had died prior to that date. Abigail was born 29 January 1631/1632 and died in 1734 in Norwich, CT.[62]

Samuel Lathrop died 29 February 1699/1700 in Norwich, New London, CT, at the age of 78.[63] His will was proven in 1701.[64]

John Lathrop (1646–1688) and Ruth Royce (b. 1645)

John Lathrop was born in 1646 in Barnstable, MA, and baptized 7 December 1646.[65] [66] When John was 2 years old, his father, Samuel, moved the family to Pequot (now New London), CT.

John married Ruth Royce on 15 December 1669 in New London, CT.[67] [68] Ruth was born 7 December 1645 in New Haven, CT.[69] [70] John was 23; Ruth was 24.

- Ruth was the daughter of Robert Royce (sometimes spelled Royse) (1606–1676) and Mary Jackson (d. 1696), both born in England.[71]

- Robert Royce and Mary Jackson were married 8 April 1627 at St. Michael, Stamford, Lincolnshire, England.[72] They emigrated in 1637,[73] possibly as part of the Puritan migration, and lived in Stratford, New Haven, and New London. They had 10 children—John (1), John (2), Mary, Jonathan (3), Sarah, Nehemiah, Samuel, **Ruth**, Nathaniel, and Isaac—although 3 (John 1, John 2, and Mary) died young in England. The children from Samuel on were born in Connecticut.[74]

Ruth married John Lathrop, and it seems the families were quite close: Ruth's brothers Nathaniel and Isaac married John's sisters Sarah and Elizabeth.[75]

John Lathrop and Ruth Royce had 8 children:[76] [77]

Samuel (d.c. 1745) – *married Ruth Peck, then Lydia Elcock.*
Ruth (d. 1750) – *married Samuel Post.*
Mary (1674–1754) – *married William Tyler, Jr.*
Elizabeth (b. 1678) – *married Bowley Arnold.*
John (b. 1680) – *married Hannah Hough.*
Bethia (b. 1682)
Barnabas (b. 1686)
Hannah (b. 1686) – *married Samuel Thompson.*

In 1677, John moved from Pequot to Wallingford, CT, where he was given the commission to build a mill.[78]

In 1681, John was given full control of the mill, which his family sold in 1704.[79]

John Lathrop died at age 41 on 26 August 1688 in Wallingford, CT.[80] Ruth Royce Lathrop died sometime after 1689 in New Haven, CT.[81]

Their daughter *Mary Lathrop* married William Tyler, Jr., in 1692.

Mary Lathrop (1674–1754) and William Tyler, Jr. (c. 1667–1748)

Mary Lathrop was born in 1674 in Wallingford, New Haven, CT.[82] She married William Tyler, Jr., on 3 June 1692 in Derby, CT.[83] [84] Mary was 18; William was 27.

William Tyler, Jr., was born about 1667 in Wallingford, CT, the son of William Tyler, Sr., and Abigail Terrell.[85]

- William Tyler, Sr., was born in 1644 in Milford, CT. He was the son of Lawrence Tyler (b. 1593) and Dorothy (b. 1595). In 1662, William, Sr., married Abigail Terrell.[86] Abigail was born in New Haven in 1644 and died in Milford in 1692. William, Sr., died in Wallingford on 3 June 1693. William and Abigail had 12 children: Mary, Elizabeth, Abigail, **William, Jr.**, John, twins who died in infancy, Sarah, Hannah, Thomas, Ephraim, and Ruth.[87]

- Abigail Terrell was the daughter of Roger Terrell (1616–1682)[88] and Abigail Ufford (1618–1658).[89] [90] Roger Terrell was born in Stepney, Middlesex, England,[91] and died in Milford, CT.[92]

- Abigail Ufford was born in England and died in Milford, CT.[93] She was the daughter of Thomas Ufford (1590–1660) and Isabel Bryan (1594–1660), both of whom were born in England.[94]

- Thomas Ufford and Isabel Bryan left Nazeing, Essex, England, on the ship *Lyon* in 1632 and settled in Roxbury, CT. They moved from Roxbury to Springfield, CT, in 1636, then from Springfield to Wethersfield, CT, by 1640. By 1644 they had moved again, from Wethersfield to Milford, CT, where they both died in or before 1660. They had 3 children: *Abigail*, Thomas, Jr., and John.[95]

Mary Lathrop and William Tyler, Jr. had 9 known children:[96]

Ruth (c. 1693–1727) – *married Samuel Culver.*
Mary (1695–1774) – *married Francis Guitteau.*
Sarah (1697–1716) – *married John Beach.*
Phebe (1700–1731) – *married Samuel Beach.*
Samuel (b. 1702) – *married Mary Unknown.*
Martha (b. 1706) – *married Abram Clarke.*
Bethia (1708–1792) – *married John Watson, IV.*
Ephraim (b. 1713) – *married Elizabeth DeWolf.*
Mehitabel (b. 1717)

William Tyler, Jr., died on 21 July 1748 at age 81 in Wallingford, CT. Mary Lathrop Tyler died on 14 March 1754 at age 80 in Wallingford.[97]

Their daughter ***Bethia Tyler*** married John Watson, IV, in 1730. She was 21; he was 20. (*See The Watson–Steele Lineage chapter.*)

---

[1] Otis, Amos. *Genealogical Notes of Barnstable Families.* Genealogical Notes of Barnstable Families, being a reprint of the Amos Otis Papers originally published in the Barnstable Patriot. Revised and completed by C.F. Swift largely from notes made by the author. Volume II. Barnstable, Mass: F.B. & F.P. Goss, Publishers and Printers, 1890; p. 162.

[2] Huntington, Rev. E.B., A.M. *Genealogical Memoir of the Lo-Lathrop Family.* A Genealogical Memoir of the Lo-Lathrop Family in this country, embracing the descendants, as far as known, of the Rev. John Lopthropp of Scituate and Barnstable, Mass., and Mark Lothrop of Salem and Bridgewater, Mass. and the first generation of descendants of other names. Copyright Mrs. Julia M. Huntington, Ridgefield, CT, 1884. Hartford, CT: Case, Lockwood, & Brainard Company, 1884; p. 15.

[3] Otis, Amos. *Genealogical Notes of Barnstable Families.* Genealogical Notes of Barnstable Families, being a reprint of the Amos Otis Papers originally published in the Barnstable Patriot. Revised and completed by C.F. Swift largely from notes made by the author. Volume II. Barnstable, Mass: F.B. & F.P. Goss, Publishers and Printers, 1890; p. 162.

[4] Huntington, Rev. E.B., A.M. *Genealogical Memoir of the Lo-Lathrop Family.* A Genealogical Memoir of the Lo-Lathrop Family in this country, embracing the descendants, as far as known, of the Rev. John Lopthropp of Scituate and Barnstable, Mass., and Mark Lothrop of Salem and Bridgewater, Mass. and the first generation of descendants of other names. Copyright Mrs. Julia M. Huntington, Ridgefield, CT, 1884. Hartford, CT: Case, Lockwood, & Brainard Company, 1884; p. 15.

[5] Otis, Amos. *Genealogical Notes of Barnstable Families.* Genealogical Notes of Barnstable Families, being a reprint of the Amos Otis Papers originally published in the Barnstable Patriot. Revised and completed by C.F. Swift largely from notes made by the author. Volume II. Barnstable, Mass: F.B. & F.P. Goss, Publishers and Printers, 1890; p.162.

[6] Huntington, Rev. E.B., A.M. *Genealogical Memoir of the Lo-Lathrop Family.* A Genealogical Memoir of the Lo-Lathrop Family in this country, embracing the descendants, as far as known, of the Rev. John Lopthropp of Scituate and Barnstable, Mass., and Mark Lothrop of Salem and Bridgewater, Mass. and the first generation of descendants of other names. Copyright Mrs. Julia M. Huntington, Ridgefield, CT, 1884. Hartford, CT: Case, Lockwood, & Brainard Company, 1884; p. 15.

[7] Huntington, Rev. E.B., A.M. *Genealogical Memoir of the Lo-Lathrop Family.* A Genealogical Memoir of the Lo-Lathrop Family in this country, embracing the descendants, as far as known, of the Rev. John Lopthropp of Scituate and Barnstable, Mass., and Mark Lothrop of Salem and Bridgewater, Mass. and the first generation of descendants of other names. Copyright Mrs. Julia M. Huntington, Ridgefield, CT, 1884. Hartford, CT: Case, Lockwood, & Brainard Company, 1884; p. 15.

[8] Huntington, Rev. E.B., A.M. *Genealogical Memoir of the Lo-Lathrop Family*. A Genealogical Memoir of the Lo-Lathrop Family in this country, embracing the descendants, as far as known, of the Rev. John Lopthropp of Scituate and Barnstable, Mass., and Mark Lothrop of Salem and Bridgewater, Mass. and the first generation of descendants of other names. Copyright Mrs. Julia M. Huntington, Ridgefield, CT, 1884. Hartford, CT: Case, Lockwood, & Brainard Company, 1884; p. 16.

[9] Huntington, Rev. E.B., A.M. *Genealogical Memoir of the Lo-Lathrop Family*. A Genealogical Memoir of the Lo-Lathrop Family in this country, embracing the descendants, as far as known, of the Rev. John Lopthropp of Scituate and Barnstable, Mass., and Mark Lothrop of Salem and Bridgewater, Mass. and the first generation of descendants of other names. Copyright Mrs. Julia M. Huntington, Ridgefield, CT, 1884. Hartford, CT: Case, Lockwood, & Brainard Company, 1884; p. 15.

[10] Huntington, Rev. E.B., A.M. *Genealogical Memoir of the Lo-Lathrop Family*. A Genealogical Memoir of the Lo-Lathrop Family in this country, embracing the descendants, as far as known, of the Rev. John Lopthropp of Scituate and Barnstable, Mass., and Mark Lothrop of Salem and Bridgewater, Mass. and the first generation of descendants of other names. Copyright Mrs. Julia M. Huntington, Ridgefield, CT, 1884. Hartford, CT: Case, Lockwood, & Brainard Company, 1884; p. 16.

[11] Huntington, Rev. E.B., A.M. *Genealogical Memoir of the Lo-Lathrop Family*. A Genealogical Memoir of the Lo-Lathrop Family in this country, embracing the descendants, as far as known, of the Rev. John Lopthropp of Scituate and Barnstable, Mass., and Mark Lothrop of Salem and Bridgewater, Mass. and the first generation of descendants of other names. Copyright Mrs. Julia M. Huntington, Ridgefield, CT, 1884. Hartford, CT: Case, Lockwood, & Brainard Company, 1884; p. 17.

[12] Huntington, Rev. E.B., A.M. *Genealogical Memoir of the Lo-Lathrop Family*. A Genealogical Memoir of the Lo-Lathrop Family in this country, embracing the descendants, as far as known, of the Rev. John Lopthropp of Scituate and Barnstable, Mass., and Mark Lothrop of Salem and Bridgewater, Mass. and the first generation of descendants of other names. Copyright Mrs. Julia M. Huntington, Ridgefield, CT, 1884. Hartford, CT: Case, Lockwood, & Brainard Company, 1884; p. 18.

[13] Huntington, Rev. E.B., A.M. *Genealogical Memoir of the Lo-Lathrop Family*. A Genealogical Memoir of the Lo-Lathrop Family in this country, embracing the descendants, as far as known, of the Rev. John Lopthropp of Scituate and Barnstable, Mass., and Mark Lothrop of Salem and Bridgewater, Mass. and the first generation of descendants of other names. Copyright Mrs. Julia M. Huntington, Ridgefield, CT, 1884. Hartford, CT: Case, Lockwood, & Brainard Company, 1884; p. 17.

[14] Huntington, Rev. E.B., A.M. *Genealogical Memoir of the Lo-Lathrop Family*. A Genealogical Memoir of the Lo-Lathrop Family in this country, embracing the descendants, as far as known, of the Rev. John Lopthropp of Scituate and Barnstable, Mass., and Mark Lothrop of Salem and Bridgewater, Mass. and the first generation of descendants of other names. Copyright Mrs. Julia M. Huntington, Ridgefield, CT, 1884. Hartford, CT: Case, Lockwood, & Brainard Company, 1884; p. 17.

[15] Huntington, Rev. E.B., A.M. *Genealogical Memoir of the Lo-Lathrop Family*. A Genealogical Memoir of the Lo-Lathrop Family in this country, embracing the descendants, as far as known, of the Rev. John Lopthropp of Scituate and Barnstable, Mass., and Mark Lothrop of Salem and Bridgewater, Mass. and the first generation of descendants of other names. Copyright Mrs. Julia M. Huntington, Ridgefield, CT, 1884. Hartford, CT: Case, Lockwood, & Brainard Company, 1884; p. 17.

[16] Huntington, Rev. E.B., A.M. *Genealogical Memoir of the Lo-Lathrop Family*. A Genealogical Memoir of the Lo-Lathrop Family in this country, embracing the descendants, as far as known, of the Rev. John Lopthropp of Scituate and Barnstable, Mass., and Mark Lothrop of Salem and Bridgewater, Mass. and the first generation of descendants of other names. Copyright Mrs. Julia M. Huntington, Ridgefield, CT, 1884. Hartford, CT: Case, Lockwood, & Brainard Company, 1884; p. 18-19.

[17] Huntington, Rev. E.B., A.M. *Genealogical Memoir of the Lo-Lathrop Family*. A Genealogical Memoir of the Lo-Lathrop Family in this country, embracing the descendants, as far as known, of the Rev. John Lopthropp of Scituate and Barnstable, Mass., and Mark Lothrop of Salem and Bridgewater, Mass. and the first generation of descendants of other names. Copyright Mrs. Julia M. Huntington, Ridgefield, CT, 1884. Hartford, CT: Case, Lockwood, & Brainard Company, 1884; p. 17.

[18] Huntington, Rev. E.B., A.M. *Genealogical Memoir of the Lo-Lathrop Family*. A Genealogical Memoir of the Lo-Lathrop Family in this country, embracing the descendants, as far as known, of the Rev. John Lopthropp of Scituate and Barnstable, Mass., and Mark Lothrop of Salem and Bridgewater, Mass. and the first generation of descendants of other names. Copyright Mrs. Julia M. Huntington, Ridgefield, CT, 1884. Hartford, CT: Case, Lockwood, & Brainard Company, 1884; p. 17.

[19] Huntington, Rev. E.B., A.M. *Genealogical Memoir of the Lo-Lathrop Family*. A Genealogical Memoir of the Lo-Lathrop Family in this country, embracing the descendants, as far as known, of the Rev. John Lopthropp of Scituate and Barnstable, Mass., and Mark Lothrop of Salem and Bridgewater, Mass. and the first generation of descendants of other names. Copyright Mrs. Julia M. Huntington, Ridgefield, CT, 1884. Hartford, CT: Case, Lockwood, & Brainard Company, 1884; p. 19-20.

[20] Otis, Amos. *Genealogical Notes of Barnstable Families*. Genealogical Notes of Barnstable Families, being a reprint of the Amos Otis Papers originally published in the Barnstable Patriot. Revised and completed by C.F. Swift largely from notes made by the author. Volume II. Barnstable, Mass: F.B. & F.P. Goss, Publishers and Printers, 1890; p.162.

[21] Huntington, Rev. E.B., A.M. *Genealogical Memoir of the Lo-Lathrop Family*. A Genealogical Memoir of the Lo-Lathrop Family in this country, embracing the descendants, as far as known, of the Rev. John Lopthropp of Scituate and Barnstable, Mass., and Mark Lothrop of Salem and Bridgewater, Mass. and the first generation of descendants of other names. Copyright Mrs. Julia M. Huntington, Ridgefield, CT, 1884. Hartford, CT: Case, Lockwood, & Brainard Company, 1884; p. 19.

[22] Huntington, Rev. E.B., A.M. *Genealogical Memoir of the Lo-Lathrop Family*. A Genealogical Memoir of the Lo-Lathrop Family in this country, embracing the descendants, as far as known, of the Rev. John Lopthropp of Scituate and Barnstable, Mass., and

Mark Lothrop of Salem and Bridgewater, Mass. and the first generation of descendants of other names. Copyright Mrs. Julia M. Huntington, Ridgefield, CT, 1884. Hartford, CT: Case, Lockwood, & Brainard Company, 1884; p. 23.

[23] Huntington, Rev. E.B., A.M. *Genealogical Memoir of the Lo-Lathrop Family*. A Genealogical Memoir of the Lo-Lathrop Family in this country, embracing the descendants, as far as known, of the Rev. John Lopthropp of Scituate and Barnstable, Mass., and Mark Lothrop of Salem and Bridgewater, Mass. and the first generation of descendants of other names. Copyright Mrs. Julia M. Huntington, Ridgefield, CT, 1884. Hartford, CT: Case, Lockwood, & Brainard Company, 1884; p. 23.

[24] *US and International Marriage Records, 1560-1900*, [database online] Yates Publishing, The Generations Network, Provo, UT. Found on Ancestry.com.

[25] Huntington, Rev. E.B., A.M. *Genealogical Memoir of the Lo-Lathrop Family*. A Genealogical Memoir of the Lo-Lathrop Family in this country, embracing the descendants, as far as known, of the Rev. John Lopthropp of Scituate and Barnstable, Mass., and Mark Lothrop of Salem and Bridgewater, Mass. and the first generation of descendants of other names. Copyright Mrs. Julia M. Huntington, Ridgefield, CT, 1884. Hartford, CT: Case, Lockwood, & Brainard Company, 1884; p. 27, 33, 34, 38.

[26] Otis, Amos. *Genealogical Notes of Barnstable Families*. Genealogical Notes of Barnstable Families, being a reprint of the Amos Otis Papers originally published in the Barnstable Patriot. Revised and completed by C.F. Swift largely from notes made by the author. Volume II. Barnstable, Mass: F.B. & F.P. Goss, Publishers and Printers, 1890; p.162.

[27] Huntington, Rev. E.B., A.M. *Genealogical Memoir of the Lo-Lathrop Family*. A Genealogical Memoir of the Lo-Lathrop Family in this country, embracing the descendants, as far as known, of the Rev. John Lopthropp of Scituate and Barnstable, Mass., and Mark Lothrop of Salem and Bridgewater, Mass. and the first generation of descendants of other names. Copyright Mrs. Julia M. Huntington, Ridgefield, CT, 1884. Hartford, CT: Case, Lockwood, & Brainard Company, 1884; p. 23.

[28] Huntington, Rev. E.B., A.M. *Genealogical Memoir of the Lo-Lathrop Family*. A Genealogical Memoir of the Lo-Lathrop Family in this country, embracing the descendants, as far as known, of the Rev. John Lopthropp of Scituate and Barnstable, Mass., and Mark Lothrop of Salem and Bridgewater, Mass. and the first generation of descendants of other names. Copyright Mrs. Julia M. Huntington, Ridgefield, CT, 1884. Hartford, CT: Case, Lockwood, & Brainard Company, 1884; p. 23.

[29] Huntington, Rev. E.B., A.M. *Genealogical Memoir of the Lo-Lathrop Family*. A Genealogical Memoir of the Lo-Lathrop Family in this country, embracing the descendants, as far as known, of the Rev. John Lopthropp of Scituate and Barnstable, Mass., and Mark Lothrop of Salem and Bridgewater, Mass. and the first generation of descendants of other names. Copyright Mrs. Julia M. Huntington, Ridgefield, CT, 1884. Hartford, CT: Case, Lockwood, & Brainard Company, 1884; p. 24.

[30] Huntington, Rev. E.B., A.M. *Genealogical Memoir of the Lo-Lathrop Family*. A Genealogical Memoir of the Lo-Lathrop Family in this country, embracing the descendants, as far as known, of the Rev. John Lopthropp of Scituate and Barnstable, Mass., and Mark Lothrop of Salem and Bridgewater, Mass. and the first generation of descendants of other names. Copyright Mrs. Julia M. Huntington, Ridgefield, CT, 1884. Hartford, CT: Case, Lockwood, & Brainard Company, 1884; p. 24.

[31] Huntington, Rev. E.B., A.M. *Genealogical Memoir of the Lo-Lathrop Family*. A Genealogical Memoir of the Lo-Lathrop Family in this country, embracing the descendants, as far as known, of the Rev. John Lopthropp of Scituate and Barnstable, Mass., and Mark Lothrop of Salem and Bridgewater, Mass. and the first generation of descendants of other names. Copyright Mrs. Julia M. Huntington, Ridgefield, CT, 1884. Hartford, CT: Case, Lockwood, & Brainard Company, 1884; p. 24-25.

[32] Otis, Amos. *Genealogical Notes of Barnstable Families*. Genealogical Notes of Barnstable Families, being a reprint of the Amos Otis Papers originally published in the Barnstable Patriot. Revised and completed by C.F. Swift largely from notes made by the author. Volume II. Barnstable, Mass: F.B. & F.P. Goss, Publishers and Printers, 1890; p.162.

[33] Huntington, Rev. E.B., A.M. *Genealogical Memoir of the Lo-Lathrop Family*. A Genealogical Memoir of the Lo-Lathrop Family in this country, embracing the descendants, as far as known, of the Rev. John Lopthropp of Scituate and Barnstable, Mass., and Mark Lothrop of Salem and Bridgewater, Mass. and the first generation of descendants of other names. Copyright Mrs. Julia M. Huntington, Ridgefield, CT, 1884. Hartford, CT: Case, Lockwood, & Brainard Company, 1884; p. 25.

[34] Huntington, Rev. E.B., A.M. *Genealogical Memoir of the Lo-Lathrop Family*. A Genealogical Memoir of the Lo-Lathrop Family in this country, embracing the descendants, as far as known, of the Rev. John Lopthropp of Scituate and Barnstable, Mass., and Mark Lothrop of Salem and Bridgewater, Mass. and the first generation of descendants of other names. Copyright Mrs. Julia M. Huntington, Ridgefield, CT, 1884. Hartford, CT: Case, Lockwood, & Brainard Company, 1884; p. 25-26.

[35] Otis, Amos. *Genealogical Notes of Barnstable Families*. Genealogical Notes of Barnstable Families, being a reprint of the Amos Otis Papers originally published in the Barnstable Patriot. Revised and completed by C.F. Swift largely from notes made by the author. Volume II. Barnstable, Mass: F.B. & F.P. Goss, Publishers and Printers, 1890; p.162.

[36] Huntington, Rev. E.B., A.M. *Genealogical Memoir of the Lo-Lathrop Family*. A Genealogical Memoir of the Lo-Lathrop Family in this country, embracing the descendants, as far as known, of the Rev. John Lopthropp of Scituate and Barnstable, Mass., and Mark Lothrop of Salem and Bridgewater, Mass. and the first generation of descendants of other names. Copyright Mrs. Julia M. Huntington, Ridgefield, CT, 1884. Hartford, CT: Case, Lockwood, & Brainard Company, 1884; p. 31.

[37] Otis, Amos. *Genealogical Notes of Barnstable Families*. Genealogical Notes of Barnstable Families, being a reprint of the Amos Otis Papers originally published in the Barnstable Patriot. Revised and completed by C.F. Swift largely from notes made by the author. Volume II. Barnstable, Mass: F.B. & F.P. Goss, Publishers and Printers, 1890; p.175.

[38] Huntington, Rev. E.B., A.M. *Genealogical Memoir of the Lo-Lathrop Family*. A Genealogical Memoir of the Lo-Lathrop Family in this country, embracing the descendants, as far as known, of the Rev. John Lopthropp of Scituate and Barnstable, Mass., and Mark Lothrop of Salem and Bridgewater, Mass. and the first generation of descendants of other names. Copyright Mrs. Julia M. Huntington, Ridgefield, CT, 1884. Hartford, CT: Case, Lockwood, & Brainard Company, 1884; p. 33.

[39] Huntington, Rev. E.B., A.M. *Genealogical Memoir of the Lo-Lathrop Family*. A Genealogical Memoir of the Lo-Lathrop Family in this country, embracing the descendants, as far as known, of the Rev. John Lopthropp of Scituate and Barnstable, Mass., and Mark Lothrop of Salem and Bridgewater, Mass. and the first generation of descendants of other names. Copyright Mrs. Julia M. Huntington, Ridgefield, CT, 1884. Hartford, CT: Case, Lockwood, & Brainard Company, 1884; p. 38.

[40] *Ancestry Family Data Collection*. Edmund West, comp.. Family Data Collection - Births [database on-line]. Provo, UT, USA: The Generations Network, Inc., 2001. Available on Ancestry.com.

[41] Huntington, Rev. E.B., A.M. *Genealogical Memoir of the Lo-Lathrop Family*. A Genealogical Memoir of the Lo-Lathrop Family in this country, embracing the descendants, as far as known, of the Rev. John Lopthropp of Scituate and Barnstable, Mass., and Mark Lothrop of Salem and Bridgewater, Mass. and the first generation of descendants of other names. Copyright Mrs. Julia M. Huntington, Ridgefield, CT, 1884. Hartford, CT: Case, Lockwood, & Brainard Company, 1884; p. 38.

[42] *US and International Marriage Records, 1560-1900*, [database online] Yates Publishing, The Generations Network, Provo, UT. Found on Ancestry.com.

[43] Jacobus, Donald Lines. *Families of Ancient New Haven*. Baltimore: Genealogical Publishing Company, Inc., 1997. Originally published as *New Haven Genealogical Magazine, Vol. I-VIII*, Rome, NY, 1922-32.; p. 1081.

[44] *US and International Marriage Records, 1560-1900*, [database online] Yates Publishing, The Generations Network, Provo, UT. Found on Ancestry.com.

[45] *Ancestry Family Data Collection*. Edmund West, comp.. Family Data Collection - Births [database on-line]. Provo, UT, USA: The Generations Network, Inc., 2001. Available on Ancestry.com.

[46] *US and International Marriage Records, 1560-1900*, [database online] Yates Publishing, The Generations Network, Provo, UT. Found on Ancestry.com. Source number: 825.000; Source type: Electronic Database; Number of Pages: 1; Submitter Code: HDG.

[47] *Ancestry Family Data Collection*. Edmund West, comp.. Family Data Collection - Births [database on-line]. Provo, UT, USA: The Generations Network, Inc., 2001. Available on Ancestry.com.

[48] *Ancestry Family Data Collection*. Edmund West, comp.. Family Data Collection - Births [database on-line]. Provo, UT, USA: The Generations Network, Inc., 2001. Available on Ancestry.com.

[49] Huntington, Rev. E.B., A.M. *Genealogical Memoir of the Lo-Lathrop Family*. A Genealogical Memoir of the Lo-Lathrop Family in this country, embracing the descendants, as far as known, of the Rev. John Lopthropp of Scituate and Barnstable, Mass., and Mark Lothrop of Salem and Bridgewater, Mass. and the first generation of descendants of other names. Copyright Mrs. Julia M. Huntington, Ridgefield, CT, 1884. Hartford, CT: Case, Lockwood, & Brainard Company, 1884; p. 38.

[50] *Passenger and Immigration Lists Index, 1500s-1900s* [database on-line]. Provo, UT, USA: The Generations Network, Inc., 2006. Original data: Filby, P. William, ed.. *Passenger and Immigration Lists Index, 1500s-1900s*. Farmington Hills, MI, USA: Gale Research, 2006. VIRKUS, FREDERICK A., editor. Immigrant Ancestors: A List of 2,500 Immigrants to America before 1750. Baltimore: Genealogical Publishing Co., 1964. 75p. Repr. 1986. p. 60.

[51] Otis, Amos. *Genealogical Notes of Barnstable Families*. Genealogical Notes of Barnstable Families, being a reprint of the Amos Otis Papers originally published in the Barnstable Patriot. Revised and completed by C.F. Swift largely from notes made by the author. Volume II. Barnstable, Mass: F.B. & F.P. Goss, Publishers and Printers, 1890; p.223.

[52] Otis, Amos. *Genealogical Notes of Barnstable Families*. Genealogical Notes of Barnstable Families, being a reprint of the Amos Otis Papers originally published in the Barnstable Patriot. Revised and completed by C.F. Swift largely from notes made by the author. Volume II. Barnstable, Mass: F.B. & F.P. Goss, Publishers and Printers, 1890; p.163.

[53] Jacobus, Donald Lines. *Families of Ancient New Haven*. Baltimore: Genealogical Publishing Company, Inc., 1997. Originally published as *New Haven Genealogical Magazine, Vol. I-VIII*, Rome, NY, 1922-32.; p. 1081.

[54] Huntington, Rev. E.B., A.M. *Genealogical Memoir of the Lo-Lathrop Family*. A Genealogical Memoir of the Lo-Lathrop Family in this country, embracing the descendants, as far as known, of the Rev. John Lopthropp of Scituate and Barnstable, Mass., and Mark Lothrop of Salem and Bridgewater, Mass. and the first generation of descendants of other names. Copyright Mrs. Julia M. Huntington, Ridgefield, CT, 1884. Hartford, CT: Case, Lockwood, & Brainard Company, 1884; p. 38.

[55] Huntington, Rev. E.B., A.M. *Genealogical Memoir of the Lo-Lathrop Family*. A Genealogical Memoir of the Lo-Lathrop Family in this country, embracing the descendants, as far as known, of the Rev. John Lopthropp of Scituate and Barnstable, Mass., and Mark Lothrop of Salem and Bridgewater, Mass. and the first generation of descendants of other names. Copyright Mrs. Julia M. Huntington, Ridgefield, CT, 1884. Hartford, CT: Case, Lockwood, & Brainard Company, 1884; p. 39.

[56] Huntington, Rev. E.B., A.M. *Genealogical Memoir of the Lo-Lathrop Family*. A Genealogical Memoir of the Lo-Lathrop Family in this country, embracing the descendants, as far as known, of the Rev. John Lopthropp of Scituate and Barnstable, Mass., and Mark Lothrop of Salem and Bridgewater, Mass. and the first generation of descendants of other names. Copyright Mrs. Julia M. Huntington, Ridgefield, CT, 1884. Hartford, CT: Case, Lockwood, & Brainard Company, 1884; p. 39.

[57] Huntington, Rev. E.B., A.M. *Genealogical Memoir of the Lo-Lathrop Family*. A Genealogical Memoir of the Lo-Lathrop Family in this country, embracing the descendants, as far as known, of the Rev. John Lopthropp of Scituate and Barnstable, Mass., and Mark Lothrop of Salem and Bridgewater, Mass. and the first generation of descendants of other names. Copyright Mrs. Julia M. Huntington, Ridgefield, CT, 1884. Hartford, CT: Case, Lockwood, & Brainard Company, 1884; p. 39.

[58] Huntington, Rev. E.B., A.M. *Genealogical Memoir of the Lo-Lathrop Family*. A Genealogical Memoir of the Lo-Lathrop Family in this country, embracing the descendants, as far as known, of the Rev. John Lopthropp of Scituate and Barnstable, Mass., and Mark Lothrop of Salem and Bridgewater, Mass. and the first generation of descendants of other names. Copyright Mrs. Julia M. Huntington, Ridgefield, CT, 1884. Hartford, CT: Case, Lockwood, & Brainard Company, 1884; p. 39.

[59] Huntington, Rev. E.B., A.M. *Genealogical Memoir of the Lo-Lathrop Family*. A Genealogical Memoir of the Lo-Lathrop Family in this country, embracing the descendants, as far as known, of the Rev. John Lopthropp of Scituate and Barnstable, Mass., and Mark Lothrop of Salem and Bridgewater, Mass. and the first generation of descendants of other names. Copyright Mrs. Julia M. Huntington, Ridgefield, CT, 1884. Hartford, CT: Case, Lockwood, & Brainard Company, 1884; p. 40.

[60] Huntington, Rev. E.B., A.M. *Genealogical Memoir of the Lo-Lathrop Family*. A Genealogical Memoir of the Lo-Lathrop Family in this country, embracing the descendants, as far as known, of the Rev. John Lopthropp of Scituate and Barnstable, Mass., and Mark Lothrop of Salem and Bridgewater, Mass. and the first generation of descendants of other names. Copyright Mrs. Julia M. Huntington, Ridgefield, CT, 1884. Hartford, CT: Case, Lockwood, & Brainard Company, 1884; p. 39.

[61] Huntington, Rev. E.B., A.M. *Genealogical Memoir of the Lo-Lathrop Family*. A Genealogical Memoir of the Lo-Lathrop Family in this country, embracing the descendants, as far as known, of the Rev. John Lopthropp of Scituate and Barnstable, Mass., and Mark Lothrop of Salem and Bridgewater, Mass. and the first generation of descendants of other names. Copyright Mrs. Julia M. Huntington, Ridgefield, CT, 1884. Hartford, CT: Case, Lockwood, & Brainard Company, 1884; p. 40.

[62] Huntington, Rev. E.B., A.M. *Genealogical Memoir of the Lo-Lathrop Family*. A Genealogical Memoir of the Lo-Lathrop Family in this country, embracing the descendants, as far as known, of the Rev. John Lopthropp of Scituate and Barnstable, Mass., and Mark Lothrop of Salem and Bridgewater, Mass. and the first generation of descendants of other names. Copyright Mrs. Julia M. Huntington, Ridgefield, CT, 1884. Hartford, CT: Case, Lockwood, & Brainard Company, 1884; p. 40.

[63] Jacobus, Donald Lines. *Families of Ancient New Haven*. Baltimore: Genealogical Publishing Company, Inc., 1997. Originally published as *New Haven Genealogical Magazine, Vol. I-VIII*, Rome, NY, 1922-32.; p. 1081.

[64] Huntington, Rev. E.B., A.M. *Genealogical Memoir of the Lo-Lathrop Family*. A Genealogical Memoir of the Lo-Lathrop Family in this country, embracing the descendants, as far as known, of the Rev. John Lopthropp of Scituate and Barnstable, Mass., and Mark Lothrop of Salem and Bridgewater, Mass. and the first generation of descendants of other names. Copyright Mrs. Julia M. Huntington, Ridgefield, CT, 1884. Hartford, CT: Case, Lockwood, & Brainard Company, 1884; p. 40.

[65] Jacobus, Donald Lines. *Families of Ancient New Haven*. Baltimore: Genealogical Publishing Company, Inc., 1997. Originally published as *New Haven Genealogical Magazine, Vol. I-VIII*, Rome, NY, 1922-32.; p. 1081.

[66] Otis, Amos. *Genealogical Notes of Barnstable Families*. Genealogical Notes of Barnstable Families, being a reprint of the Amos Otis Papers originally published in the Barnstable Patriot. Revised and completed by C.F. Swift largely from notes made by the author. Volume II. Barnstable, Mass: F.B. & F.P. Goss, Publishers and Printers, 1890; p.163.

[67] Jacobus, Donald Lines. *Families of Ancient New Haven*. Baltimore: Genealogical Publishing Company, Inc., 1997. Originally published as *New Haven Genealogical Magazine, Vol. I-VIII*, Rome, NY, 1922-32.; p. 1552.

[68] Huntington, Rev. E.B., A.M. *Genealogical Memoir of the Lo-Lathrop Family*. A Genealogical Memoir of the Lo-Lathrop Family in this country, embracing the descendants, as far as known, of the Rev. John Lopthropp of Scituate and Barnstable, Mass., and Mark Lothrop of Salem and Bridgewater, Mass. and the first generation of descendants of other names. Copyright Mrs. Julia M. Huntington, Ridgefield, CT, 1884. Hartford, CT: Case, Lockwood, & Brainard Company, 1884; p. 46.

[69] *Ancestry Family Data Collection*. Edmund West, comp.. Family Data Collection - Births [database on-line]. Provo, UT, USA: The Generations Network, Inc., 2001. Available on Ancestry.com.

[70] *US and International Marriage Records, 1560-1900*, [database online] Yates Publishing, The Generations Network, Provo, UT. Found on Ancestry.com.

[71] Jacobus, Donald Lines. *Families of Ancient New Haven*. Baltimore: Genealogical Publishing Company, Inc., 1997. Originally published as *New Haven Genealogical Magazine, Vol. I-VIII*, Rome, NY, 1922-32.; p. 1549.

[72] Charles Julian research, found on Genealogy.com. http://genforum.genealogy.com/cgi-bin/pageload.cgi?charles,julian::royce::893.html – Data taken from parish records.

[73] *Passenger and Immigration Lists Index, 1500s-1900s* [database on-line]. Provo, UT, USA: The Generations Network, Inc., 2006. Original data: Filby, P. William, ed.. *Passenger and Immigration Lists Index, 1500s-1900s*. Farmington Hills, MI, USA: Gale Research, 2006. Available on Ancestry.com.

[74] Jacobus, Donald Lines. *Families of Ancient New Haven*. Baltimore: Genealogical Publishing Company, Inc., 1997. Originally published as *New Haven Genealogical Magazine, Vol. I-VIII*, Rome, NY, 1922-32.; p. 1549.

[75] Jacobus, Donald Lines. *Families of Ancient New Haven*. Baltimore: Genealogical Publishing Company, Inc., 1997. Originally published as *New Haven Genealogical Magazine, Vol. I-VIII*, Rome, NY, 1922-32.; p. 1549.

[76] Huntington, Rev. E.B., A.M. *Genealogical Memoir of the Lo-Lathrop Family*. A Genealogical Memoir of the Lo-Lathrop Family in this country, embracing the descendants, as far as known, of the Rev. John Lopthropp of Scituate and Barnstable, Mass., and Mark Lothrop of Salem and Bridgewater, Mass. and the first generation of descendants of other names. Copyright Mrs. Julia M. Huntington, Ridgefield, CT, 1884. Hartford, CT: Case, Lockwood, & Brainard Company, 1884; p. 56-57

[77] Jacobus, Donald Lines. *Families of Ancient New Haven*. Baltimore: Genealogical Publishing Company, Inc., 1997. Originally published as *New Haven Genealogical Magazine, Vol. I-VIII*, Rome, NY, 1922-32.; p. 1922.

[78] Huntington, Rev. E.B., A.M. *Genealogical Memoir of the Lo-Lathrop Family*. A Genealogical Memoir of the Lo-Lathrop Family in this country, embracing the descendants, as far as known, of the Rev. John Lopthropp of Scituate and Barnstable, Mass., and Mark Lothrop of Salem and Bridgewater, Mass. and the first generation of descendants of other names. Copyright Mrs. Julia M. Huntington, Ridgefield, CT, 1884. Hartford, CT: Case, Lockwood, & Brainard Company, 1884; p. 46.

[79] Huntington, Rev. E.B., A.M. *Genealogical Memoir of the Lo-Lathrop Family*. A Genealogical Memoir of the Lo-Lathrop Family in this country, embracing the descendants, as far as known, of the Rev. John Lopthropp of Scituate and Barnstable, Mass., and Mark Lothrop of Salem and Bridgewater, Mass. and the first generation of descendants of other names. Copyright Mrs. Julia M. Huntington, Ridgefield, CT, 1884. Hartford, CT: Case, Lockwood, & Brainard Company, 1884; p. 46.

[80] Jacobus, Donald Lines. *Families of Ancient New Haven*. Baltimore: Genealogical Publishing Company, Inc., 1997. Originally published as *New Haven Genealogical Magazine, Vol. I-VIII*, Rome, NY, 1922-32.; p. 1081.

[81] Huntington, Rev. E.B., A.M. *Genealogical Memoir of the Lo-Lathrop Family*. A Genealogical Memoir of the Lo-Lathrop Family in this country, embracing the descendants, as far as known, of the Rev. John Lopthropp of Scituate and Barnstable, Mass., and Mark Lothrop of Salem and Bridgewater, Mass. and the first generation of descendants of other names. Copyright Mrs. Julia M. Huntington, Ridgefield, CT, 1884. Hartford, CT: Case, Lockwood, & Brainard Company, 1884; p. 46.

[82] *Ancestry Family Data Collection*. Edmund West, comp.. Family Data Collection - Births [database on-line]. Provo, UT, USA: The Generations Network, Inc., 2001. Available on Ancestry.com.

[83] Jacobus, Donald Lines. *Families of Ancient New Haven*. Baltimore: Genealogical Publishing Company, Inc., 1997. Originally published as *New Haven Genealogical Magazine, Vol. I-VIII*, Rome, NY, 1922-32.; p. 1922.

[84] *US and International Marriage Records, 1560-1900*, Yates Publishing, The Generations Network, Provo, UT. Found on Ancestry.com. Source number: 206.000; Source type: Electronic Database; Number of Pages: 1; Submitter Code: ASB.

[85] Jacobus, Donald Lines. *Families of Ancient New Haven*. Baltimore: Genealogical Publishing Company, Inc., 1997. Originally published as *New Haven Genealogical Magazine, Vol. I-VIII*, Rome, NY, 1922-32.; p. 1922.

[86] *US and International Marriage Records, 1560-1900*, [database online] Yates Publishing, The Generations Network, Provo, UT. Found on Ancestry.com. Source number: 484.000; Source type: Electronic Database; Number of Pages: 1; Submitter Code: CGF.

[87] Jacobus, Donald Lines. *Families of Ancient New Haven*. Baltimore: Genealogical Publishing Company, Inc., 1997. Originally published as *New Haven Genealogical Magazine, Vol. I-VIII*, Rome, NY, 1922-32.; p. 1922

[88] *Ancestry Family Data Collection*. Edmund West, comp.. Family Data Collection - Births [database on-line]. Provo, UT, USA: The Generations Network, Inc., 2001. Available on Ancestry.com.

[89] *US and International Marriage Records, 1560-1900*, Yates Publishing, The Generations Network, Provo, UT. Found on Ancestry.com. Source number: 490.000; Source type: Electronic Database; Number of Pages: 1; Submitter Code: CGF.

[90] *Ancestry Family Data Collection*. Edmund West, comp.. Family Data Collection - Births [database on-line]. Provo, UT, USA: The Generations Network, Inc., 2001. Available on Ancestry.com.

[91] *US and International Marriage Records, 1560-1900*, [database online] Yates Publishing, The Generations Network, Provo, UT. Found on Ancestry.com. Source number: 490.000; Source type: Electronic Database; Number of Pages: 1; Submitter Code: CGF.

[92] Jacobus, Donald Lines. *Families of Ancient New Haven*. Baltimore: Genealogical Publishing Company, Inc., 1997. Originally published as *New Haven Genealogical Magazine, Vol. I-VIII*, Rome, NY, 1922-32.; p. 1549.

[93] Anderson, Robert Charles. *Great Migration Begins: Immigrants to New England, 1620-33* [database on-line]. Provo, UT, USA: The Generations Network, Inc., 2000. Original data: Anderson, Robert Charles. *The Great Migration Begins: Immigrants to New England, 1620-1633. Vol. 1-3*. Boston, MA, USA: New England Historic Genealogical Society, 1995.

[94] Anderson, Robert Charles. *Great Migration Begins: Immigrants to New England, 1620-33* [database on-line]. Provo, UT, USA: The Generations Network, Inc., 2000. Original data: Anderson, Robert Charles. *The Great Migration Begins: Immigrants to New England, 1620-1633. Vol. 1-3*. Boston, MA, USA: New England Historic Genealogical Society, 1995.

[95] Anderson, Robert Charles. *Great Migration Begins: Immigrants to New England, 1620-33* [database on-line]. Provo, UT, USA: The Generations Network, Inc., 2000. Original data: Anderson, Robert Charles. *The Great Migration Begins: Immigrants to New England, 1620-1633. Vol. 1-3*. Boston, MA, USA: New England Historic Genealogical Society, 1995.

[96] Jacobus, Donald Lines. *Families of Ancient New Haven*. Baltimore: Genealogical Publishing Company, Inc., 1997. Originally published as *New Haven Genealogical Magazine, Vol. I-VIII*, Rome, NY, 1922-32.; p. 1922.

[97] Jacobus, Donald Lines. *Families of Ancient New Haven*. Baltimore: Genealogical Publishing Company, Inc., 1997. Originally published as *New Haven Genealogical Magazine, Vol. I-VIII*, Rome, NY, 1922-32.; p. 1922.

The McCall Lineage

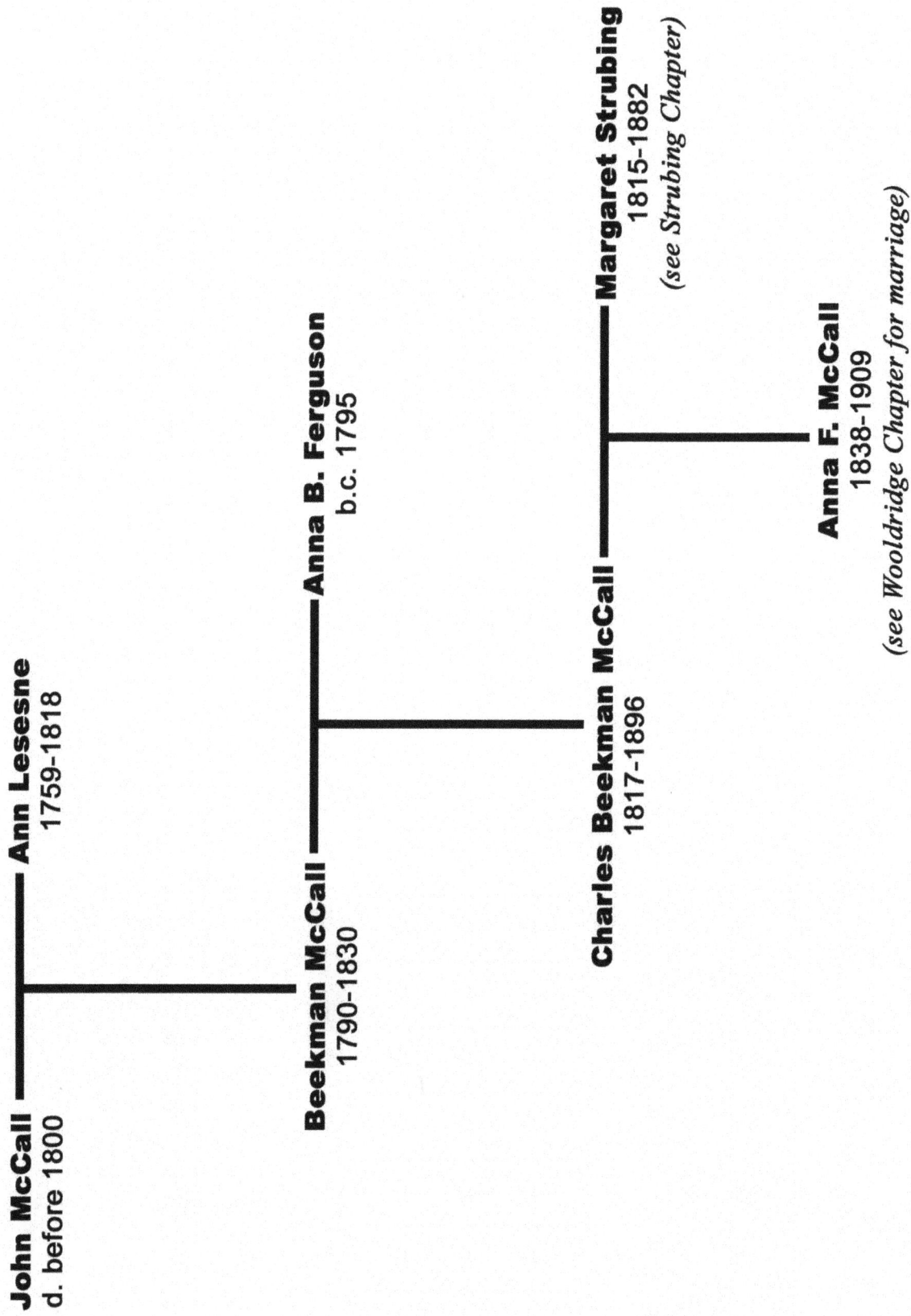

John McCall
d. before 1800

Ann Lesesne
1759-1818

Beekman McCall
1790-1830

Anna B. Ferguson
b.c. 1795

Charles Beekman McCall
1817-1896

Margaret Strubing
1815-1882
(see Strubing Chapter)

Anna F. McCall
1838-1909
(see Wooldridge Chapter for marriage)

The McCall Lineage

John McCall (d. before 1800) and Ann Lesesne (c. 1759–c. 1818)

I found John McCall's name because one of the Charleston, South Carolina, City Directories listed his widow as "Widow of John McCall."[1] The first documentation of the family I have is from the 1800 United States Census, at which point his wife, Ann, is already a widow. So he had died prior to 1800.[2] According to the 1800 Census, Ann was born between 1756 and 1774. Given their marriage date, I would guess at a birth date c. 1759.

There are 2 John McCalls listed in the 1790 Census. Both lived at St. Philips and St. Michaels, Charleston, SC.

One John's family is: 4 males under 16, 5 males 16 and over, 3 females, and 7 slaves.[3]

The other John's family is: 2 males under 16, 1 male over 16, 4 females, and 14 slaves.[4]

I am leaning toward John #2 as our family, since he and Ann would have been a young couple, and in 1800 the family had 15 slaves. However, more research is needed.

John McCall and Ann Lesesne married on 3 April 1777 in Charleston, SC.[5] Ann would have been about 20. While I am not 100% sure that this is the correct couple's marriage, it was the only John McCall and Ann anyone who appeared in the South Carolina Marriages, 1641–1965 database on Ancestry. There were numerous Lesesne families in the area in 1790, including an Isaac Lesesne on the St. Philips and St. Michaels plantation where both John McCalls lived.

John and Ann had at least 4 children, but I only know 1 by name:

Beekman (1790–1830)[6] – *married Anna B. Ferguson.*

In the 1800 Census, widow Ann had 4 children in her household: 2 boys under 10 (Beekman was 9), 1 male 10–15, and 1 female under 10. The family also had 15 slaves.[7]

From 1803 to 1809, Ann's family lived at 105 Church Street, Charleston, SC.[8 9 10 11] In 1803, there was also a grocers, Gordon & McCall, at 27 Wentworth.[12] It did not appear in the search results in any of the later directories, so I wonder if perhaps the McCall was her husband and the grocers closed or changed names after he died? In the directories, the name is always spelled M'Call.

In the 1810 Census, Ann's household consisted of 2 males 16–25 (Beekman, 20), 2 females 16–25, and 1 female 45+ (Ann).[13] Since Ann is over 45 years old here, her birth date could not be later than 1765. But that would have made her 12 at her wedding, so a birth date of about 1759 still seems the most likely.

In 1813, Ann lived at 130 Church St.—at the same address as Beekman McCall.[14]

In 1816, Ann lived at 132 Church St.[15]

Since she is not listed in the 1819 City Directory, Ann Lesesne McCall probably died sometime between 1816 and 1819.

Beekman McCall (1790–1830) and Anna B. Ferguson (b. c. 1795)

I have no absolute proof that this man is related to our Charles Beekman McCall. But with an odd name like Beekman popping up twice, and the ages and places being correct, I believe this is our Charles' father. Plus, according to the records, Beekman married a woman named Anna Ferguson. Our Charles' firstborn daughter was named Anna F.

Please note: On Anna Wooldridge McFarlin's handwritten DAR application, Charles' middle name is clearly Beekman. However, when Marge Warren Gondolf typed up her DAR application based on Anna's, she mis-transcribed the double E in Beekman as Bukman.

Beekman McCall was born in 1790 in Charleston, SC.[16] In 1813, he is in the City Directory, living with his widowed mother, Ann, at 130 Church St. He was an accountant.[17]

On 20 October 1813, Beekman married Anna B. Ferguson in Charleston, SC.[18] They had at least 4 children, but I have the name of only one:

Charles Beekman (1817–1896) – *married Margaret Strubing.*

In 1816, Beekman and Anna lived at 1 Hasell St., Charleston, SC.[19] Please note that although the address notations in the City Directories keep changing, they seem to reside in the same house at least through 1829. Beekman was a clerk at the State Bank.

In 1819, Beekman was still a bank clerk, and lived at the corner of East Bay and Hasell Streets.[20]

In the 1820 Census, his name was misspelled Bakman. His household consisted of 2 males under 10 (1 would have been our Charles, age 3), 1 male 26–45 (himself, age 30), 2 females under 10, 1 female 26–45 (wife Anna). He is listed as "Engaged in Commerce." He did own slaves. He had 1 male under 14, and 1 male 26–45, 1 female under 14, and 1 female 14–26.[21]

1822 found Beekman still a clerk at the State Bank. The family resided at 259 East Bay St.[22] In 1825 they are listed as at 159 East Bay St., with Beekman now a bookkeeper at the State Bank.[23]

The 1828[24] and 1829[25] Directories have the family residence as the south corner of East Bay and Hasell Streets. There is no occupation given in Beekman's 1829 entry. Given that he died early the next year, perhaps he was too ill to work.

Beekman McCall died 10 March 1830 at age 40, and is buried in St. Philip's Episcopal Church in Charleston, SC.[26]

Although her husband died prior to the 1830 Census, the only Anna McCall I could locate in Charleston had a household that could not possibly be the family we want. Our Anna's household should have contained at least 4 children between 10–20 (2 boys and 2 girls) and perhaps more younger children. There were no children at all in the Anna McCall household I found.

I have no further information or death information for Anna Ferguson McCall. If she moved in with a married daughter (her daughters could both have been over 18 in 1830) then she will be pretty much impossible to trace.

Charles Beekman McCall (1817–1896) and Margaret Strubing (1815–1882)
(see the Strubing Lineage chapter)

Charles Beekman McCall was born in Charleston, SC, on 5 February 1817.[27][28][29] He lived in Charleston with his parents until his father's death in 1830. Charles was 13 at that time. The remaining family disappeared from the records at this point.

Charles surfaced 6 years later in Philadelphia, PA. Charles married Margaret Strubing on 5 September 1836 in a ceremony by the Rev. Charles Pitman.[30] The Rev. Pitman appears to be a Presbyterian minister, but I could not find which specific church, if any, he was affiliated with. Margaret Strubing was born 4 October 1815 in Bloomsburg, Columbia County, PA.[31] At the time they married, Margaret was 21; Charles was 19.

The 1839 City Directory[32] had Charles Beekman McCall and family living at 33 Wood. He was a tailor.

Charles did NOT appear in the 1840 Philadelphia City Directory. In the 1840 Census, however, a family matching his exactly does appear in Weakley, Tennessee. Charles' household consisted of 1 male 20–30 (himself, 23), 1 female under 5 (Anna, 2), and 1 female 20–30 (wife Margaret, 25).[33]

I do not know for certain that this is our Charles (the name on the census was "C McCall"), as I have no idea what he'd be doing in Tennessee. But this is the only family that came up in the 1840 Census that matched (and it does match his exactly), so I am putting this here to be confirmed or denied as further information flows.

1841 found the family back in Philadelphia, living at 322 North 3rd Street.[34]

By 1845 they had moved to Holmes' Alley in Philadelphia, PA, with Charles still supporting the family as a tailor.[35]

In 1850, Charles and Margaret lived in Wilmington, DE. Charles was 34; Margaret was 33. I found that Margaret's ages on the censuses were consistently placing her as born in 1817, not 1815, but such discrepancies are not unusual.

This is definitely our Charles. He is 34, a tailor born in South Carolina. His household consists of wife Margaret (33) and children Anna F. (12), Catherine (9), Emma (8), Margaretta (2), and Charles (3 months).[36]

Anna and Emma were born in Pennsylvania, with the rest born in Delaware. They must have traveled quite a lot for them to have had Anna in Pennsylvania, then 3 years later Catherine in Delaware, then a year later Emma in Pennsylvania, then 6 years later have the last 2 in DE. I have also wondered if there were children who died in the large gaps between Anna and Kate, and Emma and Margaret.

Charles and Margaret had 7 known children:[37][38]

Anna F. (1838–1909) – *married Captain William M. Wooldridge, then George Nitzky.*
Catherine (Kate) (b. 1841) – *married Henry (Harry) Ebsen.*
Emma (b. 1845)
Margaretta (Margaret) (b. 1848) – *married Henry Kain.*
Charles, Jr. (b. May 1850)
Ida (b. 1851)
Laura (b. 1854) – *married Unknown Wink.*

By 1854, the family was back in Philadelphia, PA. From 1854–1857 they lived at Prime (present day Washington Ave.) above 9th St.[39][40][41] In 1858 through 1867, they lived at 625 Federal St.[42][43][44][45][46][47][48][49][50]

In 1860, Charles (42) was still making his living as a tailor, and had a personal estate of $400. Wife Margaret (42) watched over the 5 remaining children: Kate (19), Emma (15), Margaret (12), Ida (9), and Laura (7). Margaret, Ida, and Laura were all still at school.[51] Since Charles, Jr., who should have been 10 on this Census, is not listed, it is likely that he died.

In yet another inexplicable move, 1870 finds the family living in Pleasantville, Vernango County, PA. Charles (50) was a tailor, living with wife Margaret (50) and daughter Laura (14).[52]

In 1880, Charles (63) and Margaret (64) were empty–nesters, living at 1154 Linnan St., Philadelphia, PA. Charles was still working as a tailor, and this Census tells us that not only was he born in South Carolina, but both his parents were, too. A 10-year-old boy named Charles Cain lived with them, occupation listed as School. This was Charles and Margaret's grandson, son of young Margaret and her husband, Henry Kain.[53]

Margaret Strubing McCall died just 2 years later, on 1 August 1882, at age 65 of chronic Bright's disease (a kidney ailment). She was buried at Machpelah Cemetery Vault, Philadelphia, PA.[54][55] Machpelah was closed in 1895, and the bodies moved to North Mount Moriah Cemetery.[56]

Charles Beekman McCall died 1 December 1896, at age 80, of apoplexy. According to his death certificate, he lived at 2222 Manton St., Philadelphia, PA. He was buried on 4 December in Odd Fellows Cemetery.[57][58] Odd Fellows was closed in 1951, and bodies removed to Lawnview and Mount Peace cemeteries. A housing development was built on the land. During renovations in 1999, caskets of those not moved were found on the site.[59]

Anna McCall married William M. Wooldridge in 1857. She was 19; he was 21. (*See The Wooldridge Lineage chapter.*)

---

[1] Hagy, James W. *Charleston, South Carolina City Directories for the Years 1816, 1819, 1822, 1825, and 1829*. Baltimore, MD, USA: Genealogical Publishing Co., 2002.; Year 1816, p. 17.

[2] *1800 United States Census*, Charleston, SC. Year: 1800; Census Place: Charleston, South Carolina; Roll: 48; Page: 129; Image: 196; Family History Library Film: 181423.

[3] *1790 United States Census*, Charleston, SC. Year: *1790*; Census Place: *St Phillips and St Michaels, Charleston, South Carolina*; Series: *M637*; Roll: *11*; Page: *277*; Image: *175*; Family History Library Film: *0568151*.

[4] *1790 United States Census*, Charleston, SC. Year: *1790*; Census Place: *St Phillips and St Michaels, Charleston, South Carolina*; Series: *M637*; Roll: *11*; Page: *291*; Image: *182*; Family History Library Film: *0568151*.

[5]*South Carolina Magazine of Ancestral Research*, Vol 5, # 3

[6] *1820 United States Census*, Charleston, SC. 1820 U S Census; Census Place: Charleston, Charleston, South Carolina; Page: 29; NARA Roll: M33_119; Image: 65.

[7] *1800 United States Census*, Charleston, SC. Year: 1800; Census Place: , Charleston, South Carolina; Roll: 48; Page: 129; Image: 196; Family History Library Film: 181423.

[8] Hagy, James W. *City Directories for Charleston, South Carolina for the Years 1803, 1806, 1807, 1809, and 1813*. Baltimore, MD, USA: Genealogical Publishing Co., 2000; Year 1803, p. 13.

[9] Hagy, James W. *City Directories for Charleston, South Carolina for the Years 1803, 1806, 1807, 1809, and 1813*. Baltimore, MD, USA: Genealogical Publishing Co., 2000; Year 1806, p. 42.

[10] Hagy, James W. *City Directories for Charleston, South Carolina for the Years 1803, 1806, 1807, 1809, and 1813*. Baltimore, MD, USA: Genealogical Publishing Co., 2000; Year 1807, p. 75.

[11] Hagy, James W. *City Directories for Charleston, South Carolina for the Years 1803, 1806, 1807, 1809, and 1813*. Baltimore, MD, USA: Genealogical Publishing Co., 2000; Year 1809, p. 116.

[12] Hagy, James W. *City Directories for Charleston, South Carolina for the Years 1803, 1806, 1807, 1809, and 1813.* Baltimore, MD, USA: Genealogical Publishing Co., 2000; Year 1809, p. 13.

[13] *1810 United States Census*, Charleston, SC. Year: 1810; Census Place: Charleston, Charleston, South Carolina; Roll: 60; Page: 319; Image: 0181419; Family History Library Film: 00174.

[14] Hagy, James W. *City Directories for Charleston, South Carolina for the Years 1803, 1806, 1807, 1809, and 1813.* Baltimore, MD, USA: Genealogical Publishing Co., 2000; Year 1813, p. 152.

[15] Hagy, James W. *Charleston, South Carolina City Directories for the Years 1816, 1819, 1822, 1825, and 1829.* Baltimore, MD, USA: Genealogical Publishing Co., 2002.; Year 1816, p. 17.

[16] Death Return for the City of Charleston, SC. Week of 7th to 14th of March, 1830

[17] Hagy, James W. *City Directories for Charleston, South Carolina for the Years 1803, 1806, 1807, 1809, and 1813.* Baltimore, MD, USA: Genealogical Publishing Co., 2000; Year 1813, p. 152.

[18] South Carolina Marriages 1641-1965 [database online]. Available on Ancestry.com

[19] Hagy, James W. *Charleston, South Carolina City Directories for the Years 1816, 1819, 1822, 1825, and 1829.* Baltimore, MD, USA: Genealogical Publishing Co., 2002.; Year 1816, p. 17.

[20] Hagy, James W. *Charleston, South Carolina City Directories for the Years 1816, 1819, 1822, 1825, and 1829.* Baltimore, MD, USA: Genealogical Publishing Co., 2002.; Year 1819, p. 52.

[21] *1820 United States Census*, Charleston, SC. 1820 U S Census; Census Place: Charleston, Charleston, South Carolina; Page: 29; NARA Roll: M33_119; Image: 65.

[22] Hagy, James W. *Charleston, South Carolina City Directories for the Years 1816, 1819, 1822, 1825, and 1829.* Baltimore, MD, USA: Genealogical Publishing Co., 2002.; Year 1822, p. 89.

[23] Hagy, James W. *Charleston, South Carolina City Directories for the Years 1816, 1819, 1822, 1825, and 1829.* Baltimore, MD, USA: Genealogical Publishing Co., 2002.; Year 1825, p. 123.

[24] *Directory of the City of Charleston, 1828,* CROMWELL, O., ed., Charleston: James S. Burges, No. 44 Queen street, 1829. Found in UK and US Directories 1680-1830 [database online] on Ancestry.com.

[25] Hagy, James W. *Charleston, South Carolina City Directories for the Years 1816, 1819, 1822, 1825, and 1829.* Baltimore, MD, USA: Genealogical Publishing Co., 2002.; Year 1829, p. 152.

[26] Death Return for the City of Charleston, SC. Week of 7th to 14th of March, 1830. Ancestry.com. *South Carolina, Death Records, 1821-1960* [database on-line]. Provo, UT, USA: Ancestry.com Operations Inc, 2008. Original data: South Carolina. *South Carolina death records.* Columbia, SC, USA: South Carolina Department of Archives and History.

[27] *1860 United States Census*, Philadelphia, PA. Year: 1860; Census Place: Philadelphia Ward 2, Philadelphia, Pennsylvania; Roll: M653_1152; Page: 568; Image: 574; Family History Library Film: 805152.

[28] *Philadelphia Public Ledger* marriage notice. October 8, 1836

[29] Daughters of the American Revolution Lineage – Marjory Warren Gondolf #533004. Original in possession of Kerry Gans Douglas.

[30] *Philadelphia Public Ledger* marriage notice. October 8, 1836

[31] Strubing Family Bible. Originals housed at Historical Society of Pennsylvania, 1300 Locust Street Philadelphia, PA 19107.

[32] *McElroy's Philadelphia City Directory 1839.* Philadelphia: A. McElroy & Co., 1839; p. 154.

[33] *1840 United States Census*, Weakley, TN. Year: 1840; Census Place: , Weakley, Tennessee; Roll: 530; Page: 279; Image: 1140; Family History Library Film: 0024547.

[34] *McElroy's Philadelphia City Directory 1841.* Philadelphia: A. McElroy & Co., 1841; p. 163.

[35] *McElroy's Philadelphia City Directory 1845.* Philadelphia: A. McElroy & Co., 1845; p. 218.

[36] *1850 United States Census*, Wilmington, DE. Year: 1850; Census Place: Wilmington, New Castle, Delaware; Roll: M432_53; Page: 62A; Image: 390.

[37] *1850 United States Census*, Wilmington, DE. Year: 1850; Census Place: Wilmington, New Castle, Delaware; Roll: M432_53; Page: 62A; Image: 390.

[38] *1860 United States Census*. Year: 1860; Census Place: Philadelphia Ward 2, Philadelphia, Pennsylvania; Roll: M653_1152; Page: 568; Image: 574; Family History Library Film: 805152.

[39] *McElroy's Philadelphia City Directory 1854.* Philadelphia: A. McElroy & Co., 1854; p. 319.

[40] *McElroy's Philadelphia City Directory 1855.* Philadelphia: A. McElroy & Co., 1855; p. 333.

[41] *McElroy's Philadelphia City Directory 1857.* Philadelphia: A. McElroy & Co., 1857; p. 408.

[42] *McElroy's Philadelphia City Directory 1858.* Philadelphia: A. McElroy & Co., 1858; p. 412.

[43] *McElroy's Philadelphia City Directory 1859.* Philadelphia: A. McElroy & Co., 1859; p. 433.

[44] *McElroy's Philadelphia City Directory 1860.* Philadelphia: A. McElroy & Co., 1860; p. 597.

[45] *McElroy's Philadelphia City Directory 1861.* Philadelphia: A. McElroy & Co., 1861; p. 597.

[46] *McElroy's Philadelphia City Directory 1863.* Philadelphia: A. McElroy & Co., 1863; p. 467.

[47] *McElroy's Philadelphia City Directory 1864.* Philadelphia: A. McElroy & Co., 1864; p. 452.

[48] *McElroy's Philadelphia City Directory 1865.* Philadelphia: A. McElroy & Co., 1865; p. 420.

[49] *McElroy's Philadelphia City Directory 1866.* Philadelphia: A. McElroy & Co., 1866; p. 445.

[50] *McElroy's Philadelphia City Directory 1867.* Philadelphia: A. McElroy & Co., 1867; p. 633.

[51] *1860 United States Census*, Philadelphia, PA. Year: 1860; Census Place: Philadelphia Ward 2, Philadelphia, Pennsylvania; Roll: M653_1152; Page: 568; Image: 574; Family History Library Film: 805152.

[52] *1870 United States Census*, Pleasantville, PA. Year: 1870; Census Place: Pleasantville, Venango, Pennsylvania; Roll: M593_1459; Page: 32B; Image: 69; Family History Library Film: 552958.

[53] *1880 United States Census*, Philadelphia, PA. Year: 1880; Census Place: Philadelphia, Philadelphia, Pennsylvania; Roll: 1185; Family History Film: 1255185; Page: 551B; Enumeration District: 553; Image: 0367.

[54] Death Notice of Margaret Strubing McCall. *Philadelphia Inquirer,* August 3, 1882.

[55] Philadelphia Cemetery Returns. 1882, Roll 1099, Frames 1244 and 1247. Original housed at Philadelphia City Archives, 3101 Market Street, Philadelphia, PA 19104.

[56] Find A Grave.com, http://www.findagrave.com/cgi-bin/fg.cgi?page=cr&CRid=2153890

[57] Death Notice of Charles Beekman McCall. *Philadelphia Inquirer,* December 4, 1896.

[58] Philadelphia Death Certificate, year 1896, #11304, Roll 121, Frame 1441. Original housed at Philadelphia City Archives, 3101 Market Street, Philadelphia, PA 19104.

[59] Christine Bahls, Daily News staff writer, with staff writer Gloria Campisi contributing, *PHA Finds Forgotten Casket* (posted on Philly.com December 13, 1999.) http://articles.philly.com/1999-12-13/news/25479676_1_casket-housing-project-pha

**BORN FEB 5, 1817
IN CHARLESTON, SC
PHOTO TAKEN FEB 1, 1873
AGE 56 YEARS
IN PLEASANTVILLE, PA**

CHARLES BUKMAN MCCALL
(1817-1896)

The Sheppard-Abbott-Elton-Long Lineage

Thomas Sheppard
b. 1590

David Sheppard
1624-1685
(emigrated to Ireland from England)

John Sheppard
1655-1710
(emigrated from Ireland by 1683)

Rachel Wausborough
(emigrated to Ireland from England)

Magritt Unknown
1659-1706
(emigrated from Ireland by 1683)

Dickason Sheppard, Sr.
1685-1749

Dickason Sheppard, Jr.
1710-1769

Samuel Abbott
b.c. 1642
(emigrated from England 1690)

Eve Abbott
1682-1749
(emigrated from England 1690)

Anthony Elton
b.c. 1632
(emigrated from England)

Jane Elton
b.c. 1649
(emigrated from England 1690)

Susanna Unknown
(emigrated from England)

Prudence Sheppard
1746-1800
(see Stites Chapter for marriage)

Eleanor Long
b. 1724

Grace Unknown
1703-1775

William Long
1675-1743

Peter Long
1700-1754

The Sheppard–Abbott–Elton–Long Lineage

Unless otherwise noted, all information in this section originated from a PDF file given to me by Dave Bates, the current head of The New Jersey Dare Family Association. Original documents supporting this PDF, "1746 – Ancestor Genealogy of Prudence Sheppard," are housed in the Gloucester County Historical Society in Woodbury, NJ.[1]

Thomas Sheppard (b. 1590)

Thomas Sheppard was born about 1590 in England. He and his unknown wife had 1 known son:

David (1624–1685) – *married Rachel Wausborough.*

David Sheppard (1624–1685) and Rachel Wausborough

David Sheppard immigrated to Cleagh Keating in County Tipperary, Ireland, where they lived at least until 1683. Some accounts say David immigrated to Cumberland County, NJ, in 1683 with his family, others say he died in England around 1685. David was born around 1624 in England. He married Rachel Wausborough around 1647, when he was about 23.

They had 7 known children:

David, Jr. (1648–1695) – *married Eve Walen.*
Giles (1650–1690) – *married Elizabeth Wausborough.*
Jonathan (1653–1692)
John (1655–1710) – *married Margritt Unknown.*
Thomas (1657 – 1721) – *married Anne Wausborough.*
Jonadab (1660–1692)
James (1665–1691) – *married Hester Walen.*

John Sheppard (1655–1710) and Margritt Unknown (c. 1659–c. 1706)

John Sheppard was born in 1655 in Cleagh Keating, Tipperary, Ireland. He and Margritt married about 1678. John was 23; Margritt was 19. His wife Margritt was born about 1659 in Ireland. By 1683, the couple had settled in Back Neck, Cumberland County, NJ.

They had 7 children:

Hannah (b.c. 1675) – *married Obediah Holmes, Jr., then Timothy Brooks, IV.*
Job (b.c. 1680)
Enoch (1684–1718) – *married Elizabeth Sheppard.*
Dickason (1685–1749) – *married Eve Abbott.*
Margaret (b.c. 1690) – *married Thomas Abbott.*
John, Jr. (b.c. 1698)
David (1690–1771) – *married Sarah Unknown.*

John was a member of the Baptist Church of Cleagh Keating in Tipperary, Ireland, and an original organizer of the first Cohansey Baptist Church at Shrewsbury Neck, NJ. The Sheppard, Westcott, and Reeves families were the principle owners of Back Neck and Shrewsbury Neck for almost a hundred years beginning in the later 1700s.

Margritt Sheppard died between 1704 and 1708 in New Jersey at age 45.

John Sheppard died in New Jersey in September 1710 at age 55. His estate was inventoried 9 September 1710, and the estate settled 6 October 1710. It was worth £257.[2]

Dickason Sheppard, Sr., (1685–1749) and Eve Abbott (1682–1749)

Dickason Sheppard, Sr., was born in 1685. He married Eve Abbott, daughter of Samuel Abbott and Jane Elton. Young Eve Abbott, born 1682, emigrated with her parents at age 8 from Ireland.

- Samuel (b.c. 1642) and Jane (b.c. 1649) married c. 1667, and immigrated to Connecticut in 1690 with 5 children, Thomas, John, George, Stephen, and *Eve*.

- Jane Elton's parents were Anthony Elton and Susanna. Anthony Elton was born c. 1631 in Yatesbury Parish, Wiltshire, England, and his will was dated 31 January 1685/86 in Rancocas Creek, NJ, at age 55. His estate was worth £938, and included land in England, Pennsylvania, and New Jersey, as well as 2 Negroes and a covenanted servant.[3] In addition to *Jane*, they had a daughter, Mary.

Dickason, Sr., and Eve had 8 children:

John (1703–1781) – *married Mary Unknown.*
Anna (b. 1705) – *married David Sheppard.*
Stephen (1708–1757) – *married Ruth Gibbon.*
Dickason, Jr. (1710–1769) – *married Eleanor Long.*
Hannah (b. 1712)
Jonadab (1713–1769) – *married Mary Unknown, then Phebe Reed.*
Patience (b. 1715) – *married William Paullin.*
Eve (1716–1761) – *married Lancelot Sockwell, III.*

Dickason Sheppard, Sr., made his will on 11 March 1742. His estate was inventoried on 5 November 1749, worth £142. The estate was settled on 28 November 1749.[4] He last lived in Newport, Cumberland County, NJ. Eve Abbott Sheppard's will was dated 3 February 1749/50. Her estate, worth £74, was inventoried 8 March 1749/50, and her estate was settled 12 March 1749/50.[5] Their wills show that Dickason could at least write his name, while Eve could only make her mark.

Dickason Sheppard, Jr., (1710–1769) and Eleanor Long (b. 1724)

Dickason Sheppard, Jr., was born in Salem, Cumberland County, NJ, around 1710. He married Eleanor Long around 1742. Eleanor was born around 1724. At their marriage he was about 32; Eleanor was about 18.

- Eleanor's parents were Peter Long (1700–1754) and Grace Unknown. Peter was born about 1700, and wrote a will 25 August 1754 in Cumberland County, NJ, at age 54. His estate was inventoried and settled 14 April 1755.[6] Grace was born about 1703 and died in 1775 at age 72. Peter and Grace married around 1722. They had 6 children: ***Eleanor***, John, Ansell, Pleasant, Andrew, and David. Peter left a will, which he signed, so he could at least write his name. His wife, Grace, could also at least sign her name, as seen on several of the probate papers.

- Peter's father was William Long (1675–1743). He died in Cohansey, Cumberland County, NJ, at age 68. He and his unknown wife had at least 4 children: Joseph, **Peter**, Elihu, and Elizabeth.

Dickason, Jr., and Eleanor had 10 children:

Hannah (b. 1744) – *married Jonadab Sheppard, Jr.*
Eleanor Long (b. 1745)
Prudence (1746–1800) – *married Jonathan Stites.*
Priscilla (b. 1747)
Sarah (b. 1748)
Alexander (b. 1750)
Dickason, III (1752–1776) – *married Phebe Sheppard.*
Peter Long (b. 1757)
Pleasant (1758–1822) – *married Matthias Taylor.*
Ansell Long (1759–1840) – *married Hannah Ward.*

Dickason Sheppard, Jr., wrote a will 6 October 1769. On his will, unlike his father, Dickason, Jr., could not even sign his name, making his mark instead. His estate was inventoried 13 November 1769, assessed at £110. His estate was settled 6 December 1769.[7] On some of the estate papers, his wife, Eleanor, signed her name.

His daughter **Prudence Sheppard** married Jonathan Stites around 1775. He was 43; she was 29. (*See The Stites Lineage chapter.*)

---

[1] New Jersey Dare Family Association. PDF entitled *1746 - Ancestor Genealogy of Prudence Sheppard.*
[2] Estate papers of John Sheppard, Burlington County, NJ
[3] Estate papers of Anthony Elton, Burlington County, NJ
[4] Estate papers of Dickason Sheppard, Sr., Cumberland County, NJ
[5] Estate papers of Eve Abbott Sheppard, Cumberland County, NJ
[6] Estate papers of Peter Long, Cumberland County, NJ
[7] Estate papers of Dickason Sheppard, Jr., Cumberland County, NJ

DICKASON SHEPPARD, SR.'S SIGNATURE
FROM HIS 1742 WILL

HIS WIFE EVA SHEPPARD'S MARK
FROM HER WILL, 1750

THEIR SON
DICKASON SHEPPARD, JR.'S MARK
FROM HIS WILL, 1769

SIGNATURE OF PETER LONG
FROM HIS WILL, 1754

SIGNATURE OF GRACE LONG
FROM PETER'S ESTATE PAPERS, 1755
UNUSUAL FOR A WOMAN TO BE LITERATE

The Steele-Barnard-Birchard Lineage

George Steele
1583-1664
(emigrated from England 1633)

James Steele, Sr.
b. 1622
(emigrated from England 1633)

Margery Sorrell
1587-1663
(emigrated from England 1663)

James Steele, Jr.
1658-1713

Bethia Bishop
1631-1674

John Bishop

Ann Stevens

Sarah Steele
1686-1732
(see Watson Chapter for marriage)

Sarah Barnard
b. 1648

Bartholomew Barnard, Jr.
1622-1698

Bartholomew Barnard, Sr.

Sarah Birchard
b. 1624
(emigrated from England 1635)

Thomas Birchard
1595-1658
(emigrated from England 1635)

Mary Robinson
b. 1596
(emigrated from England 1635)

The Steele–Barnard–Birchard Lineage

George Steele (1583–1664) and Margery Sorrell (1587–1663)

In 1633, two brothers came to the New World from England: George and John Steele. George, age 50, arrived with his wife and 6 surviving children. George and his family traveled from Fairstead, Essex, England, to Cambridge, Massachusetts.[1]

George Steele was born about 1583 in Fairstead, Essex, England. On 12 October 1608 he married Margery Sorrell. George was 25; Margery was 21. Margery was born in 1587.[2]

George and Margery had 8 known children:[3]

Richard (c. 1610–c. 1640)
Margery (b. 1612)
John (1) (1615–before 1618)
John (2) (b. 1618)
Mary (b. 1620)
James (b. 1622) – *married Bethia Bishop, then Bethia Hopkins.*
Elizabeth (b. 1628) – *married Thomas Watts.*
Sarah (d. 1629)

In 1633, the family immigrated to Cambridge, MA. In 1636, they moved to Hartford, Connecticut.[4]

Margery Sorrell Steele died before 24 May 1663 in Hartford, CT. That date was the date of George's will, and she is not mentioned in it, indicating that she passed away prior to the will's writing. George Steele died in 1664 in Hartford, CT, at the age of 81. His will was proven 2 March 1664/65.[5]

James Steele (b. 1622) and Bethia Bishop (1631–1674)

James Steele was born in 1622 in Fairstead, Essex, England.[6] He was christened 30 November 1622.[7] He was 11 at the time his family immigrated to New England. On 18 October 1651, he married Bethia Bishop in Guilford, New Haven, CT.[8] James was 29; Bethia was 20. Bethia was a Guilford native, born there in 1631. Her parents were John Bishop and Ann Stevens.[9]

James and Bethia had at least 2 children:[10] [11]

James, Jr. (1658–1713) – *married Sarah Barnard.*
Mary

Bethia Bishop Steele died in January 1674/75 in Guilford, at age 44.[12]

James remarried sometime before 1685, to Bethia Hopkins.[13]

James Steele, Jr., (1658–1713) and Sarah Barnard (b. 1648)

James Steele, Jr., was born in 1658 in Hartford, CT.[14] In 1685 he married Sarah Barnard.[15] James was 27; Sarah was 37. Sarah was born on 3 December 1648 in Hartford, CT. Her parents were Bartholomew Barnard, Jr., and Sarah Birchard.[16]

- Bartholomew Barnard, Jr., was born in 1622 in Hartford, CT.[17] He married Sarah Birchard in 1647 in Connecticut.[18] He died at age 76 in 1698 in Hartford, CT.[19] He was the son of Bartholomew Barnard, Sr.[20]

- Sarah Birchard was born 22 August 1624 in Fairstead, Essex, England.[21] She immigrated at age 9 with her family to Roxbury, MA.[22] She married Bartholomew Barnard, Jr.

- Sarah's parents were Thomas Birchard and Mary Robinson.[23] Thomas was born in 1595 in England.[24] His wife, Mary Robinson, was born about 1596 in England.[25] They married in 1620.[26] Thomas immigrated in 1635, and had with him wife Mary Robinson (38) and children Elizabeth (13), Mary (12), *Sarah* (9), Suzannah (8), John (7), and Hannah (18 months).[27] Thomas Birchard died at age 63 in 1658 in Norwich, New London, CT.[28]

James, Jr., and Sarah had 1 known child:[29]

Sarah (1686–1732) – *married John Watson, III.*

James Steele, Jr., died 15 May 1713 in Wethersfield, Hartford, CT at age 55.[30]

Sarah Steele married John Watson, III. (*See The Watson Lineage chapter.*)

---

[1] Anderson, Robert Charles. *Great Migration Begins: Immigrants to New England, 1620-33* [database on-line]. Provo, UT, USA: The Generations Network, Inc., 2000. Original data: Anderson, Robert Charles. *The Great Migration Begins: Immigrants to New England, 1620-1633. Vol. 1-3.* Boston, MA, USA: New England Historic Genealogical Society, 1995. p. 1754.

[2] Anderson, Robert Charles. *Great Migration Begins: Immigrants to New England, 1620-33* [database on-line]. Provo, UT, USA: The Generations Network, Inc., 2000. Original data: Anderson, Robert Charles. *The Great Migration Begins: Immigrants to New England, 1620-1633. Vol. 1-3.* Boston, MA, USA: New England Historic Genealogical Society, 1995.

[3] Anderson, Robert Charles. *Great Migration Begins: Immigrants to New England, 1620-33* [database on-line]. Provo, UT, USA: The Generations Network, Inc., 2000. Original data: Anderson, Robert Charles. *The Great Migration Begins: Immigrants to New England, 1620-1633. Vol. 1-3.* Boston, MA, USA: New England Historic Genealogical Society, 1995.

[4] Anderson, Robert Charles. *Great Migration Begins: Immigrants to New England, 1620-33* [database on-line]. Provo, UT, USA: The Generations Network, Inc., 2000. Original data: Anderson, Robert Charles. *The Great Migration Begins: Immigrants to New England, 1620-1633. Vol. 1-3.* Boston, MA, USA: New England Historic Genealogical Society, 1995.

[5] Anderson, Robert Charles. *Great Migration Begins: Immigrants to New England, 1620-33* [database on-line]. Provo, UT, USA: The Generations Network, Inc., 2000. Original data: Anderson, Robert Charles. *The Great Migration Begins: Immigrants to New England, 1620-1633. Vol. 1-3.* Boston, MA, USA: New England Historic Genealogical Society, 1995.

[6] *Ancestry Family Data Collection.* Edmund West, comp., The Generation Network Inc, 2001 Provo, UT, Edmund West, comp.. Family Data Collection - Births [database on-line]. Provo, UT, USA: The Generations Network, Inc., 2001.

[7] Anderson, Robert Charles. *Great Migration Begins: Immigrants to New England, 1620-33* [database on-line]. Provo, UT, USA: The Generations Network, Inc., 2000. Original data: Anderson, Robert Charles. *The Great Migration Begins: Immigrants to New England, 1620-1633. Vol. 1-3.* Boston, MA, USA: New England Historic Genealogical Society, 1995.

[8] Anderson, Robert Charles. *Great Migration Begins: Immigrants to New England, 1620-33* [database on-line]. Provo, UT, USA: The Generations Network, Inc., 2000. Original data: Anderson, Robert Charles. *The Great Migration Begins: Immigrants to New England, 1620-1633. Vol. 1-3.* Boston, MA, USA: New England Historic Genealogical Society, 1995.

[9] *Ancestry Family Data Collection.* Edmund West, comp., The Generation Network Inc, 2001 Provo, UT, Edmund West, comp.. Family Data Collection - Births [database on-line]. Provo, UT, USA: The Generations Network, Inc., 2001.

[10] *Ancestry Family Data Collection.* Edmund West, comp., The Generation Network Inc, 2001 Provo, UT, Edmund West, comp. Family Data Collection - Births [database on-line]. Provo, UT, USA: The Generations Network, Inc., 2001.

[11] Anderson, Robert Charles. *Great Migration Begins: Immigrants to New England, 1620-33* [database on-line]. Provo, UT, USA: The Generations Network, Inc., 2000. Original data: Anderson, Robert Charles. *The Great Migration Begins: Immigrants to New England, 1620-1633. Vol. 1-3.* Boston, MA, USA: New England Historic Genealogical Society, 1995.

[12] *Ancestry Family Data Collection,* Edmund West, comp.. Family Data Collection - Deaths [database on-line]. Provo, UT, USA: The Generations Network, Inc., 2001.

[13] Anderson, Robert Charles. *Great Migration Begins: Immigrants to New England, 1620-33* [database on-line]. Provo, UT, USA: The Generations Network, Inc., 2000. Original data: Anderson, Robert Charles. *The Great Migration Begins: Immigrants to New England, 1620-1633. Vol. 1-3.* Boston, MA, USA: New England Historic Genealogical Society, 1995.

[14] *Ancestry Family Data Collection.* Edmund West, comp., The Generation Network Inc, 2001 Provo, UT, Edmund West, comp. Family Data Collection - Births [database on-line]. Provo, UT, USA: The Generations Network, Inc., 2001.

[15] US and International Marriage Records, 1560-1900 [database on-line] - Ancestry.com. Yates Publishing, The Generations Network Inc., Provo, UT

[16] *Ancestry Family Data Collection,* Births - Edmund West, comp.. Family Data Collection - Births [database on-line]. Provo, UT, USA: The Generations Network, Inc., 2001.

[17] *Ancestry Family Data Collection,* Births - Edmund West, comp.. Family Data Collection - Births [database on-line]. Provo, UT, USA: The Generations Network, Inc., 2001.

[18] *US and International Marriage Records, 1560-1900* [database on-line]. Provo, UT, USA: The Generations Network, Inc., 2004. Original data: This unique collection of records was extracted from a variety of sources including family group sheets and electronic databases. Originally, the information was derived from an array of materials including pedigree charts, family history articles, querie. Source number: 23829.003; Source type: Pedigree chart; Number of Pages: 4.

[19] *Ancestry Family Data Collection,* Deaths - Edmund West, comp.. Family Data Collection - Deaths [database on-line]. Provo, UT, USA: The Generations Network, Inc., 2001.

[20] *Ancestry Family Data Collection,* Births - Edmund West, comp.. Family Data Collection - Births [database on-line]. Provo, UT, USA: The Generations Network, Inc., 2001.

[21] *Ancestry Family Data Collection,* Births - Edmund West, comp.. Family Data Collection - Births [database on-line]. Provo, UT, USA: The Generations Network, Inc., 2001.

[22] *Passenger and Immigration Lists Index, 1500s-1900s* [database on-line]. Provo, UT, USA: The Generations Network, Inc., 2006. Original data: Filby, P. William, ed. *Passenger and Immigration Lists Index, 1500s-1900s.* Farmington Hills, MI, USA: Gale Research, 2006. Place: Roxbury, Massachusetts; Year: 1635; Page Number: 293.

[23] *Passenger and Immigration Lists Index, 1500s-1900s* [database on-line]. Provo, UT, USA: The Generations Network, Inc., 2006. Original data: Filby, P. William, ed. *Passenger and Immigration Lists Index, 1500s-1900s.* Farmington Hills, MI, USA: Gale Research, 2006. Place: Roxbury, Massachusetts; Year: 1635; Page Number: 293.

[24] *US and International Marriage Records, 1560-1900* [database on-line]. Provo, UT, USA: The Generations Network, Inc., 2004. Original data: This unique collection of records was extracted from a variety of sources including family group sheets and electronic databases. Originally, the information was derived from an array of materials including pedigree charts, family history articles, querie. Source number: 4505.001; Source type: Family group sheet, FGSE, listed as parents; Number of Pages: 1.

[25] *US and International Marriage Records, 1560-1900* [database on-line]. Provo, UT, USA: The Generations Network, Inc., 2004. Original data: This unique collection of records was extracted from a variety of sources including family group sheets and electronic databases. Originally, the information was derived from an array of materials including pedigree charts, family history articles, querie. Source number: 4505.001; Source type: Family group sheet, FGSE, listed as parents; Number of Pages: 1.

[26] *US and International Marriage Records, 1560-1900* [database on-line]. Provo, UT, USA: The Generations Network, Inc., 2004. Original data: This unique collection of records was extracted from a variety of sources including family group sheets and electronic databases. Originally, the information was derived from an array of materials including pedigree charts, family history articles, querie. Source number: 4505.001; Source type: Family group sheet, FGSE, listed as parents; Number of Pages: 1.

[27] *Passenger and Immigration Lists Index, 1500s-1900s* [database on-line]. Provo, UT, USA: The Generations Network, Inc., 2006. Original data: Filby, P. William, ed. *Passenger and Immigration Lists Index, 1500s-1900s.* Farmington Hills, MI, USA: Gale Research, 2006. Place: Roxbury, Massachusetts; Year: 1635; Page Number: 293.

[28] *Ancestry Family Data Collection.* Edmund West, comp.. Family Data Collection - Deaths [database on-line]. Provo, UT, USA: The Generations Network, Inc., 2001.

[29] *Ancestry Family Data Collection.* Edmund West, comp., The Generation Network Inc, 2001 Provo, UT, Edmund West, comp.. Family Data Collection - Births [database on-line]. Provo, UT, USA: The Generations Network, Inc., 2001.

[30] *Ancestry Family Data Collection.* Edmund West, comp., The Generation Network Inc, 2001 Provo, UT, Edmund West, comp.. Family Data Collection - Deaths [database on-line]. Provo, UT, USA: The Generations Network, Inc., 2001.

The Stites Lineage

William Stites
b. c. 1550

Richard Stites
1570-1595

Dr. John Stites
1595-1717
(emigrated from England 1653)

Alice Stote
1600-1679

Richard Stites
1640-1702
(emigrated from England 1653)

Benjamin Stites
1674-1732

Mary Underhill
b. 1640
(emigrated from England before 1665;
see Underhill Chapter)

Jonathan Stites
1732-1792

Elizabeth Forman
b. 1685

Peter Stites
1777-1821

Prudence Sheppard
1746-1800
(see Sheppard Chapter)

Prudence Stites
1800-1882
(see Godshall Chapter
for marriage)

Hannah Wills
1777-1830

The Stites Lineage

Much of this chapter is based on other people's research. Although their research appears to be well documented, I have seen none of the original documents myself. Except where cited, all of this information comes from a Word document put together by Susan Schiller titled, "Combined Stites Family."[1] This document is an amalgamation of research from Nicolas Wingrove at www.genesreunited.com, Bill and Penny's genealogy page: www.swapware.org/resources/personal_home_pages_b4.html, www.ancestry.com, www.familysearch.org, and Gayle Falker and Linda Robinson's site. Unfortunately, Ms. Schiller did not note which information came from which source.

The Stites lineage takes us back to pre–Colonial England:

William Stites, born in England c. 1550, had a son –

Richard Stites, born in England in 1570, and died after 1595. He fathered *John Stites*.

Dr. John Stites (1595–1717) and Alice Stote (1600–1679)

Dr. John Stites was born 10 May 1595 in Derbyshire, England. John married Alice Stote, born c. 1600 in Boldre, Hampshire, England. Alice (aged 79) was buried 9 September 1679 in Boldre, Hampshire. John immigrated in 1653 at age 58 to Plymouth, Massachusetts, while his wife was still alive – which makes me wonder why she did not come with him. In 1657 he moved from Plymouth to Hempstead, Long Island, New York.[2] Dr. John Stites died 5 August 1717 in Hempstead, Nassau, Long Island, NY, at the ripe old age of 122!

Since this age seems somewhat unbelievable, I suggest an alternative theory. As seen below, John had 2 sons, Richard and John. It is my suggestion that the John Stites who came over to New York with Richard was his brother, not his father, and the 2 have become conflated over time. But I have no proof to support this theory.

John and Alice had 3 children:

John, Jr. (b.c. 1623) – *in Lyndhurst, Hampshire, England.*
Ann (b.c. 1625) – *in Lyndhurst, Hampshire, England.*
Richard (b. 1640) – *in Derbyshire, England.*

Richard Stites (1640–1702) and Mary Underhill (b. 1640)
(see the Underhill Lineage)

Richard Stites was born in 1640 in Derbyshire, England; died in 1702 at age 62 in Westbury, Hempstead, Long Island, NY, and is buried in Springfield, NJ. He presumably immigrated to New York in 1653 with his father. Richard was 13 when he immigrated.

Richard's second wife, Mary Underhill, was born c. 1640 in Whitechurch, England. Mary was baptized on 15 November 1640 in Clifford Chambers, England. She immigrated to the United States sometime prior to 1665/66. She was married to Thomas Naylor 14 February 1665/66 at the Dutch Reformed Church, New York, NY.[3] She had 1 child with him, Thomas Naylor, Jr. Mary was the daughter of Humphrey Underhill, Jr. and Unknown Hall.

Richard and Mary married 14 May 1668 in Hempstead, Long Island, NY. They were both 23.

Richard and Mary had 9 known children:

Henry (from Richard's first wife) – (1665–1749) – *married Hannah Garlick.*
Rebecca (b.c.1670) – *married Robert Denge.*
Benjamin (b c. 1674–1732) – *married Elizabeth Forman.*
Richard, Jr. (b.c. 1676–1740) – *married Abigail Garlick.*
William (b. 1676–1727) – *married Mary Hall.*
Mary (b.c. 1678) – *married Cornelius Schillinger.*
John (b.c. 1678–1714) – *married Unknown Beansher, then Priscilla Leaming.*
Margaret (b.c. 1679–1675) – *married Francis Hall.*
Elijah (b.c. 1680–bef. 1702)

Benjamin Stites (1674–1732) and Elizabeth Forman (b. 1685)

Benjamin Stites was born about 1674 in Hempstead, Long Island, NY.[4] [5] He married Elizabeth Forman, born about 1685 on Long Island, NY. Benjamin and Elizabeth had 5 children:[6] [7]

George (b.c. 1710–1754) – *married Esther Foster.*
Deborah (b.c. 1712–1767) – *married Joseph Page.*
Martha (b.c. 1714–1773) – *married Jeremiah Ludlum.*
Benjamin, Jr. (b.c. 1725–1792)
Jonathan (b. 1732–1792) – *married Prudence Sheppard.*

Benjamin died after 6 September 1732 (the date of his will) in Cape May, NJ, at age 58. The inventory of his estate took place on 18 September 1732, but the estate was not settled and distributed until 28 March 1733.[8] His will shows that he could not sign his name, and was therefore illiterate, which is something of a surprise to me, considering that his grandfather was a physician. Perhaps coming to the Colonies had a detrimental effect on the education of the younger generations.

Jonathan Stites (1732–1792) and Prudence Sheppard (1746–1800)
(see the Sheppard Lineage chapter)

Jonathan Stites was born in 1732 in Cape May, NJ.[9] [10] He married Prudence Sheppard around 1774, when he was about 42, and she about 28.[11] Prudence was born c. 1746 in Cape May, NJ.[12]

Jonathan is registered as a Patriot with the Daughters of the American Revolution. He did not serve in the military, but as a civil servant in Cumberland County, NJ. He was the Overseer of Highways in 1780, and in 1781 he was the constable of Downe Township.[13] Jonathan and Prudence had 6 children:[14] [15]

David (1775–1826) – *married Ann Long.*
Peter (c. 1777–1821) – *married Hannah Wills.*
Pleasant (b.c. 1780) – *married James Smith.*
Deborah (b.c. 1780) – *married Nathan Henderson.*
Uriah (b.c. 1785–1854) – *married Eunice D. Clark.*
Jonathan, Jr. (1791–1868) – *married Mary Hall.*

Jonathan Stites died 7 February 1792 at age 60 in Dividing Creek, NJ, and Prudence Sheppard Stites died 4 April 1800.[16] Her death in 1800 at age 54 may have been the inspiration for her son Peter to name his daughter Prudence.

Peter Stites (1777–1821) and Hannah Wills (1777–1830)

Peter Stites was born about 1777 in Downey, Cumberland County, NJ.[17] [18] He married Hannah Wills on 11 June 1799 at the Gloria Dei Church (now Old Swedes' Church) in Philadelphia, PA.[19] [20] Peter and Hannah would have been 22. Hannah was born about 1777 in Cumberland County, NJ.[21]

Peter and Hannah had 3 confirmed children, but only Prudence had any offspring:

Prudence (1800–1882) – *married Frederick Godshall, Jr.*
Deborah (b.c. 1804)
Henry (b.c. 1806)

According to the Philadelphia City Directories, Peter was a tailor. In 1801, the family lived at 30 N. Water St.[22] In 1813, they lived at 16 Little Water St.[23] From 1816 to 1819, they lived at 8 Little Water St.[24] [25]

In 1820, they lived in the Cedar Ward of Philadelphia, PA. Peter's household consisted of 1 male 10–15 (Henry, 14), 1 male 26–44 (himself, 46) , 2 females 10–15 (Deborah, 16, and Prudence, 20), 1 female 26–44 (wife Hannah, 43).

Peter Stites, aged 44, died in Philadelphia, PA, on 17 March 1821. He was buried at the 3rd Baptist Church Cemetery in Philadelphia, PA. He was buried with 4 young children, possibly his sons: male Stites, November 1811, 20 months old; Washington Stites, July 1818, 1 year old; George Stites April 1817, 10 weeks, 3 days old; and Humphrey Stites, 6 April 1822.[26] [27] [28] Hannah Wills Stites, aged 53, died in January 1830.[29]

Prudence Stites married Frederick Godshall in 1823. Both were 23 at the time of their marriage. (*See The Godshall Lineage chapter.*)

---

[1] Susan Schiller, *Combined Stites Family* Word document, an amalgamation of research from Nicolas Wingrove at www.genesreunited.com, Bill and Penny's genealogy pages www.swapware.org/resources/personal_home_pages_b4.html, www.familysearch.org, www.ancestry.com, and Gayle Falker and Linda Robinson's site.

[2] *Passenger and Immigration Lists Index, 1500s-1900s* [database on-line]. Provo, UT, USA: The Generations Network, Inc., 2006. Original data: Filby, P. William, ed. *Passenger and Immigration Lists Index, 1500s-1900s.* Farmington Hills, MI, USA: Gale Research, 2006. Found on Ancestry.com.

[3] Research from Lynette Jukes Wiltshire from GenesReunited.com, http://tree.genesreunited.co.uk/V3.4.0?tree_key=217649

[4] From Dave Bates of the New Jersey Dare Family Association. The original records are housed in the Gloucester County Historical Society in Woodbury, NJ.

[5] *Ancestry Family Data Collection.* Edmund West, comp.. Family Data Collection - Individual Records [database on-line]. Provo, UT, USA: The Generations Network, Inc., 2000. Found on Ancestry.com.

[6] From Dave Bates of the New Jersey Dare Family Association. The original records are housed in the Gloucester County Historical Society in Woodbury, NJ.

[7] Susan Schiller, *Combined Stites Family* Word document, an amalgamation of research from Nicolas Wingrove at www.genesreunited.com, Bill and Penny's genealogy pages www.swapware.org/resources/personal_home_pages_b4.html, www.familysearch.org, www.ancestry.com, and Gayle Falker and Linda Robinson's site.

[8] Estate papers of Benjamin Stites, Cape May, NJ, Registrar's Office

[9] *Ancestry Family Data Collection.* Edmund West, comp. Family Data Collection - Individual Records [database on-line]. Provo, UT, USA: The Generations Network, Inc., 2000.

[10] From Dave Bates of the New Jersey Dare Family Association. The original records are housed in the Gloucester County Historical Society in Woodbury, NJ.

[11] From Dave Bates of the New Jersey Dare Family Association. The original records are housed in the Gloucester County Historical Society in Woodbury, NJ.

[12] From Dave Bates of the New Jersey Dare Family Association. The original records are housed in the Gloucester County Historical Society in Woodbury, NJ.

[13] Daughters of the American Revolution, Application #532271. Originals housed with National Society Daughters of the American Revolution, 1776 D Street, NW, Washington, DC, 20006-5303.

[14] From Dave Bates of the New Jersey Dare Family Association. The original records are housed in the Gloucester County Historical Society in Woodbury, NJ.

[15] Emma Holbrook Buzby Family History 1925. Originals housed at Historical Society of Pennsylvania, 1300 Locust Street Philadelphia, PA 19107.

[16] From Dave Bates of the New Jersey Dare Family Association. The original records are housed in the Gloucester County Historical Society in Woodbury, NJ.

[17] Emma Holbrook Buzby Family History 1925. Originals housed at Historical Society of Pennsylvania, 1300 Locust Street Philadelphia, PA 19107.

[18] From Dave Bates of the New Jersey Dare Family Association. The original records are housed in the Gloucester County Historical Society in Woodbury, NJ.

[19] Emma Holbrook Buzby Family History 1925. Originals housed at Historical Society of Pennsylvania, 1300 Locust Street Philadelphia, PA 19107.

[20] *Marriages Gloria Dei 1791-1856*, film #0511808 at the Family History Library of the Latter-Day Saints in Salt Lake City, Utah.

[21] Emma Holbrook Buzby Family History 1925. Originals housed at Historical Society of Pennsylvania, 1300 Locust Street Philadelphia, PA 19107.

[22] *Stafford's Philadelphia City Directory, 1801*. Cornelius William Stafford, ed., Philadelphia: William W. Woodward, 1801; p. 19.

[23] *Paxton's Philadelphia City Directory, 1813*. John A. Paxton, ed., Philadelphia: B & T Kite, 1813; p. 402.

[24] *Robinson's Philadelphia City Directory, 1816*. Philadelphia: James Robinson, 1816, p. 405; Year: 1817, p. 417.

[25] *Paxton's Philadelphia City Directory, 1818*. John Adems Paxton, ed. Philadelphia: E & R Parker, 1818, p. 329; Year: 1819; p. 383.

[26] Emma Holbrook Buzby Family History 1925. Originals housed at Historical Society of Pennsylvania, 1300 Locust Street Philadelphia, PA 19107.

[27] From Dave Bates of the New Jersey Dare Family Association. The original records are housed in the Gloucester County Historical Society in Woodbury, NJ.

[28] 3rd Baptist Church, Philadelphia, PA, Cemetery Records. Originals housed at Historical Society of Pennsylvania, 1300 Locust Street Philadelphia, PA 19107.

[29] Emma Holbrook Buzby Family History 1925. Originals housed at Historical Society of Pennsylvania, 1300 Locust Street Philadelphia, PA 19107.

The Strubing Lineage

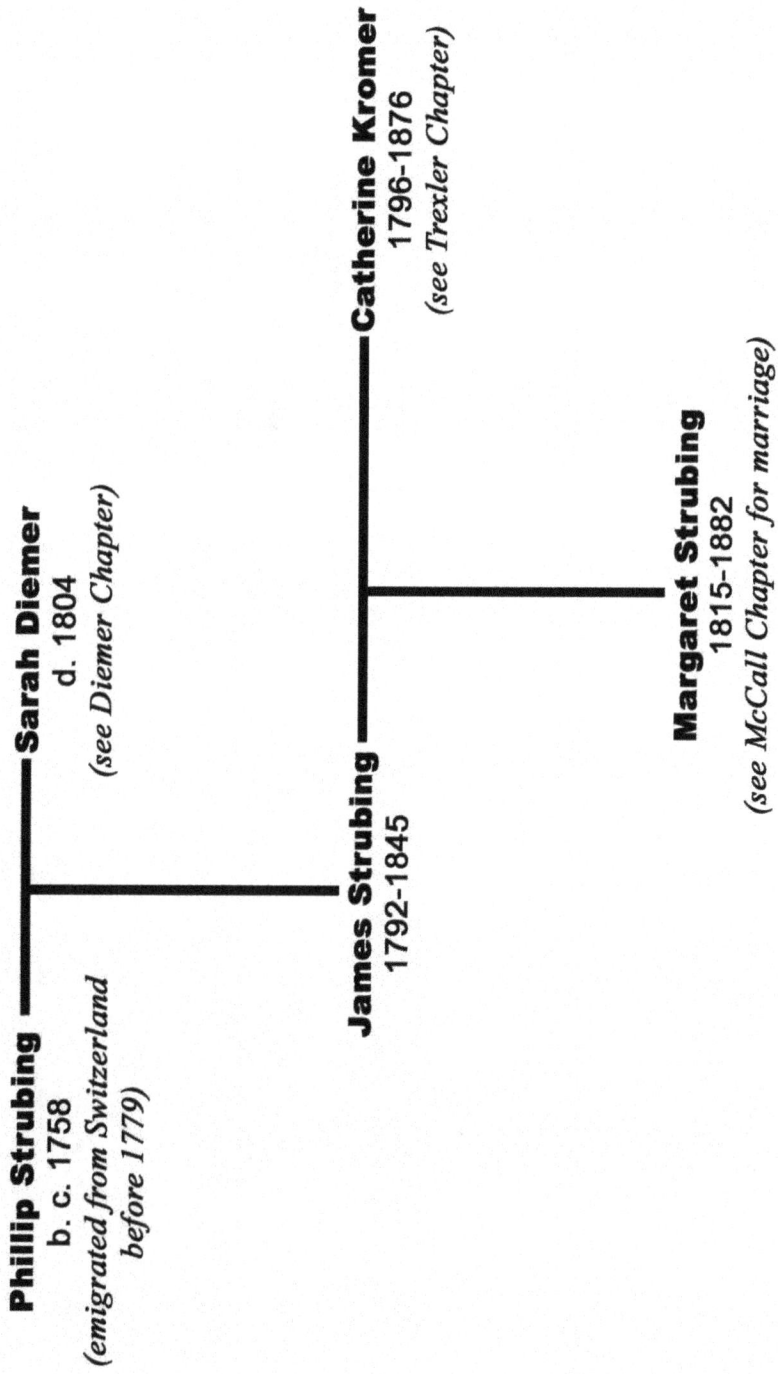

Phillip Strubing
b. c. 1758
(emigrated from Switzerland before 1779)

Sarah Diemer
d. 1804
(see Diemer Chapter)

James Strubing
1792-1845

Catherine Kromer
1796-1876
(see Trexler Chapter)

Margaret Strubing
1815-1882
(see McCall Chapter for marriage)

The Strubing Lineage

Philip Strubing (abt 1758–aft 1795) and Sarah Diemer (d. Oct 11, 1804)
(see the Diemer Lineage chapter)

Philip Strubing is a Patriot listed in the Daughters of the American Revolution. According to their records, Philip was born in Switzerland,[1] and came to America sometime before 1779. Philip served as a lieutenant in the Van Heers Independent Troop of Light Dragoons in the Revolutionary War. He was commissioned 1 September 1779 and his name was borne without remark on the company muster roll for December 1782.[2] Records further show that he was brevetted to captain on 15 April 1784. His commission was signed by Thomas Mifflin, then President of Congress.[3]

He was admitted to the Society of the Cincinnati of Pennsylvania, a veterans' association of sorts. He had letters of recommendation from George Washington and Friedrich Wilhelm Augustus von Steuben.[4]

He married Sarah Diemer, daughter of James Diemer. They lived in the Reading, PA, area, and had 4 known children:[5] [6]

Elizabeth (b. 1787)
Diemer (b. 1789) – *married Sarah Witz.*
James (1792–1845) – *married Catherine Kromer.*
Margarethe (b. 1794)

In James Diemer's 1819 will, grandchildren Elizabeth, James, and Diemer are mentioned. Elizabeth and Diemer were each given tracts of land in Columbia County, PA. James was given £1,000 and his young son, James, Jr., was given £100 to be awarded on his 21st birthday. The remainder of the estate was to be divided among the 3 grandchildren. I wonder if Margarethe had died prior to this date, as it is odd that her siblings would be recognized, but not her.[7]

The 1790 Census of the Robeson, PA, area shows a Philip Strubing with a household consisting of: 2 men aged 16 or older (Philip and someone unknown), 1 male under 16 (son Diemer, 1), and 3 females (daughter Elizabeth, 3; wife Sarah, and someone unknown).[8]

As of 11 April 1799, Philip still lived in Berks County, PA. Philip was a representative from Berks County on a Committee to elect Federalist James Ross for Governor of PA, according to a 1799 article in the *Philadelphia Gazette & Universal Daily Advertiser*.[9]

The 1800 Census near Hamburg, PA, had a Philip Strubing with a household of:
Free white males: 1 under age 10 (James, 2); 1 between 10–15 (Diemer, 11); 1 between 26–44 (Philip); Free white females: 2 under age 10 (Margarethe, 6, and unknown); 1 between 10–15 (Elizabeth, 13); 1 between 26–44 (Sarah); All other Free Persons: 1[10]

Children James and Margarethe were baptized into the Reformed Congregation Church in Reading, PA. James was baptized in 1793.[11] There was a Second Reformed Congregation Church built later in Hamburg, PA, where Philip Strubing lived in 1800.

There is also a story that indicates Philip had a falling out with another Reading area resident, and moved to the Bloomsburg, Columbia County, PA, area to avoid a libel suit. His wife's death in Fishing Creek seems to confirm this.

Also, there was an article in a German–language magazine, *Der Readinger Adler*, 16 April 1799, which concerns a falling out between Philip Strubing and Jonathan Machmer. Below is a rough translation:

"Herr Jonathan Machmer is writing this article in the paper (*Jungmann's Zeitung*[newspaper]) to set the record straight about lies that were told about him by Herr Philip. Herr Philip spread a rumor around the village that Jonathan cut the "Freedom Tree" down that stood next to Johann Weber's place. Several other men swore that they saw Jonathan do it. However, upon cross–examination, these other men later said that it wasn't true, that they did not see Jonathan cut it down. Jonathan is affirming in this letter that he swears he did not cut the tree down and that Herr Philip is a liar. So he is just clearing his name with the village."[12]

It is unknown when Philip Strubing died, or where he was buried. Sarah Diemer Strubing died 11 October 1804, in Fishing Creek, Northumberland County, PA, of a fever she contracted.[13]

James Strubing (1792–1845) and Catherine Kromer (1796–1876)
(see the Trexler Lineage chapter)

James Strubing, Sr., was born 9 March 1792, in Reading, PA. He was baptized at the First Reformed Congregation Church in Reading, PA, on 11 May 1793.[14] He married Catherine Kromer,[15] who was born 22 June 1796.[16] They had at least 2 children:[17]

Margaret (1815–1882) – *born in Bloomsburg, Columbia County, PA. Married Charles
    Beekman McCall.*
James, Jr. (b. 1817) – *born in Northern Liberties, Philadelphia, PA.*

James was a carpenter. From 1839–1841, the family lived at 10 Noble St., Philadelphia, PA.[18] From 1842 to 1845, they lived at 95 Callowhill,[19] and in 1845 James' workshop was at 116 Sassafrass (present day Race).[20]

James Strubing, Sr., died 20 September 1845 in Philadelphia, PA. He was 52, and died of pulmonary consumption.[21] He was buried in Mutual of Kensington Cemetery on 23 September 1845.[22] Mutual of Kensington closed in 1862, and the bodies were removed to Fernwood Cemetery.

In 1846, widowed Catherine Kromer Strubing lived at 116 Sassafrass (present day Race).[23] In 1850–1851, she lived at 17 Brown.[24]

Catherine Kromer Strubing, widow of James, makes an appearance in the *Journal of the Senate of the United States 1789–1873*. On Tuesday, 24 February 1852, she submitted a petition as a descendant of James Diemer "praying compensation" for lands granted to James Diemer and disposed of by the United States. This petition was referred to the Committee of Private Land Claims.[25] Dr. James Diemer had been granted 1,000 acres (see *The Diemer Lineage* chapter for details) by the British government in return for his services in the British Army. These tracts of land were in West Florida and were to be granted on condition of habitation and cultivation. Catherine's petition stated that the Revolutionary War made it impossible for James Diemer to fulfill the obligations of the grant, and that she, as his heir, should be compensated for the land. On 20 April 1852, the Senate Committee of Private Land Claims ruled against her, stating that James Diemer had lived for 40 years after the Revolution and never made claim or use of the lands in dispute, and that in any event the grants had been made 80 years ago and were therefore too stale to be eligible for compensation.[26]

This did not deter Catherine. She appeared in the House of Representatives on Wednesday, 14 December 1853, at which point her petition was referred to the Committee of Private Land Claims (again).[27] She then appears a third time on 23 February 1855, at which point a Mr. Nichols "made adverse reports thereon; which were laid upon the table and ordered to be printed." [28] On 23 February 1855, the House Committee ruled much the same as did the Senate, that the claim was too far out of date, and that James Diemer's siding with the British in the Revolutionary War (in spite of becoming a U.S. citizen in 1789), made it a matter between Catherine and the British government, not the U.S.[29]

In spite of this rejection, Catherine returns in 1860, appearing in front of the House on 1 March 1860, seeking confirmation of "a certain tract of land in the State of Florida." She was referred to the Committee on Private Land Claims (again).[30]

I couldn't find how it was resolved, but my guess is that she did not get what she wanted, for on 11 February 1874, Catherine was back in front of the House, asking for relief for services rendered by her husband and father during the Revolutionary War. This was referred to the Committee on Revolutionary Pensions and War of 1812.[31] Again, there is no note of how it was resolved, but seeing as she died 2 years later, her relief, if any, would have been short–lived.

In 1867[32] and 1871, [33] Catherine lived at 823 N. 9th Street.

In 1870, Catherine (74) lived with granddaughter Kate Wallace (30) and Kate's two children, Mary (15) and Roberta (10). Since there is no husband, I am assuming Kate is a widow. Kate has a personal estate of $1,000.[34]

In 1876, Catherine resided at 615 Dickenson St., Philadelphia, PA, the home of her granddaughter Kate Wallace.[35]

Catherine Kromer Strubing died of peritonitis at age 80 in Philadelphia, PA, 27 September 1876.[36] She was buried in the Wharton Street M.E. Church vault.[37]

Margaret Strubing (20) married Charles Beekman McCall (19) in 1836.[38] (*See The McCall Lineage chapter.*)

[1] Daughters of the American Revolution Lineage Application, Marge Warren Gondolf #533004. Original in possession of Kerry Gans Douglas.

[2] Copy of Muster Roll found in Daughters of the American Revolution Philip Strubing file documents. Originals housed with National Society Daughters of the American Revolution, 1776 D Street, NW, Washington, DC, 20006-5303.

[3] Copy of Commission found in Daughters of the American Revolution Philip Strubing file documents. Originals housed with National Society Daughters of the American Revolution, 1776 D Street, NW, Washington, DC, 20006-5303.

[4] Copies of recommendation letters found in Daughters of the American Revolution Philip Strubing file documents. Originals housed with National Society Daughters of the American Revolution, 1776 D Street, NW, Washington, DC, 20006-5303.

[5] Indiana Daughters of the American Revolution Records, p. 617-618. Originals housed with National Society Daughters of the American Revolution, 1776 D Street, NW, Washington, DC, 20006-5303.

[6] Strubing Family Bible found in Daughters of the American Revolution Philip Strubing file documents. Originals housed with National Society Daughters of the American Revolution, 1776 D Street, NW, Washington, DC, 20006-5303.

[7] Will of Dr. James Diemer, filed in Berks County, PA, Register of Wills office. 633 Court Street, 2nd Floor, Reading, PA 19601.

[8] *1790 United States Census*, Robeson, Berks County, PA. Year: 1790; Census Place: Robeson, Berks, Pennsylvania; Series: M637; Roll: 8; Page: 116; Image: 130; Family History Library Film: 0568148.

[9] *Philadelphia Gazette & Universal Daily Advertiser*, April 11, 1799, pg. 3.

[10] *1800 United States Census*, Hamburg, Berks, PA. Year: 1800; Census Place: Hamburg, Berks, Pennsylvania; Roll: 35; Page: 690; Image: 276; Family History Library Film: 363338.

[11] Pennsylvania Church Records - Adams, Berks, and Lancaster Counties, 1729-1881 Record - Ancestry, First United Church of Christ, Reformed Congregation in Reading, Record ID: 276059. First United Church of Christ, Washington & Reed Sts., Reading, Pennsylvania, by Jacqueline B. Nein, 1986., unpaginated. Computerized spreadsheet-based data of baptisms, marriages and deaths. These microfilmed records at HSP (XCH10) are not the original records but a typed transcript.

[12] *Der Readinger Adler*, April 16, 1799

[13] Strubing Family Bible found in Daughters of the American Revolution Philip Strubing file documents. Originals housed with National Society Daughters of the American Revolution, 1776 D Street, NW, Washington, DC, 20006-5303.

[14] Pennsylvania Church Records - Adams, Berks, and Lancaster Counties, 1729-1881 Record - Ancestry, First United Church of Christ, Reformed Congregation in Reading, Record ID: 276059. First United Church of Christ, Washington & Reed Sts., Reading, Pennsylvania, by Jacqueline B. Nein, 1986., unpaginated. Computerized spreadsheet-based data of baptisms, marriages and deaths. These microfilmed records at HSP (XCH10) are not the original records but a typed transcript. Microfilm housed at Historical Society of Pennsylvania, 1300 Locust Street Philadelphia, PA 19107.

[15] *History & Geneaology of the Trexler Family*, by John Trexler Warren. 1972, Allentown, PA by Schlechter's Publishers, p. 6.

[16] Daughters of the American Revolution Lineage Application, Marge Warren Gondolf #533004. Original in possession of Kerry Gans Douglas.

[17] Strubing Family Bible found in Daughters of the American Revolution Philip Strubing file documents. Originals housed with National Society Daughters of the American Revolution, 1776 D Street, NW, Washington, DC, 20006-5303.

[18] *McElroy's Philadelphia City Directory 1839*. Philadelphia: A. McElroy & Co., 1839, p. 246; Year: 1840, p. 245; Year: 1841, p. 262.

[19] *McElroy's Philadelphia City Directory 1842*. Philadelphia: A. McElroy & Co., 1842, p. 260; Year: 1843, p. 272; Year: 1844, p. 305; Year: 1845, p. 348.

[20] *McElroy's Philadelphia City Directory 1845*. Philadelphia: A. McElroy & Co., 1845; p. 348.

[21] Death Notice of James Strubing, Sr. *Philadelphia Public Ledger*, 22 Sept. 1845.

[22] Cemetery Returns, City of Philadelphia, 1845, Roll 560, Frames 1281 and 1283. Original housed at Philadelphia City Archives, 3101 Market Street, Philadelphia, PA 19104.

[23] *McElroy's Philadelphia City Directory 1846*. Philadelphia: A. McElroy & Co., 1846; p. 349.

[24] *McElroy's Philadelphia City Directory 1850*. Philadelphia: A. McElroy & Co., 1850, p. 404; Year: 1851, p. 414.

[25] *Journal of the Senate of the United States of America, Vol 43, the first session of the 32nd Congress*. Washington: A. Boyd Hamilton, 1851-52, p. 227

[26] Petition of Catharine Strubing, CIS#: 630 S.rp.193, Document #: S.rp.193, Committee on Private Land Claims, Senate, April 20, 1852, Volume: 630, p. 192. Found online at ProQuest: http://congressional.proquest.com

[27] *Journal of the House of Representatives of the United States, Vol. 49, the first session of the 33rd Congress*. Washington: Robert Armstrong, printer, 1853, p. 82.

[28] *Journal of the House of Representatives of the United States, Vol. 50, the second session of the 33rd Congress*. Washington: A.O.P. Nicholson, printer, 1854, p. 441.

[29] Reports on Private Bills; Strubing, Catharine, heir of James Dreiner; CIS#: 808 H.rp.130; Document #: H.rp.130; Committee on Private Land Claims, House; February 23, 1855; Volume 808, p. 1. Found online at ProQuest. Permalink: http://congressional.proquest.com/congressional/docview/t05.d06.808_h.rp.130_index?accountid=63787

[30] *Journal of the House of Representatives of the United States, Vol. 56, the first session of the 36th Congress*. Washington: Thomas H. Ford, 1859, p. 412.

[31] *Journal of the House of Representatives of the United States, Vol. 74, the first session of the 43rd Congress*. Washington: Government Printing Office, 1873. p. 419.

[32] *McElroy's Philadelphia City Directory 1867*. Philadelphia: A. McElroy & Co., 1867; p. 881.

[33] *Gopsill's Philadelphia City Directory 1871*. Philadelphia: Gopsill, 1871; p. 1364.

[34] *1870 United States Census*, Philadelphia, PA. Year: 1870; Census Place: Philadelphia Ward 13 District 39, Philadelphia, Pennsylvania; Roll: M593_1397; Page: 451B; Image: 420; Family History Library Film: 552896.

[35] Obituary of Catherine Kromer Strubing. *Philadelphia Inquirer*, September 30, 1876.

[36] Obituary of Catherine Kromer Strubing. *Philadelphia Inquirer*, September 30, 1876.

[37] Cemetery Returns of Philadelphia 1876, Roll 969, Frames 1185 and 1187. Original housed at Philadelphia City Archives, 3101 Market Street, Philadelphia, PA 19104.

[38] Marriage Notice of Margaret Strubing and Charles Beekman McCall. *Philadelphia Public Ledger*, October 8, 1836

ROLL OF CAPTAIN VON HEER'S DRAGOONS.

" State of a troop of light dragoons, having been raised in the Pennsylvania State, and commanded by Capt. Von Heer, September 16, 1780, (at Tappan, New York.)"

Captain.

Von Heer, Bartholomew,* Reading, from captain in Procter's artillery.

First Lieutenant.

Mytinger, Jacob.

Second Lieutenant.

Strubing, Philip.

Sergeants.

Harker, Franz, November 1, 1778.

Hess, George, Philadelphia, September 1, 1778.

Mutter, [Nutter,] John, July 1, 1778; promoted lieutenant.

Trumpeters.

Wolf, Lewis, Pottsgrove, July 1, 1778; died in Philadelphia, August 20, 1830, aged eighty-three.

Hiller, John George, Reading, January 1, 1778; resided in Jonestown, Lebanon county, in 1832.

Corporals.

Ekstine, David, Philadelphia, July 12, 1778.

Effinger, John Ignatius, Pottsgrove, August 1, 1778; discharged July, 1783; resided in Woodstock, Shenandoah county, Virginia, 1834.

Wachter, Anthony, Philadelphia, July 10, 1778.

Shafer, Jacob, Philadelphia, July 1, 1778.

Smith, Philip, Philadelphia, July 10, 1778; resided in Berks county, 1835, aged seventy-eight.

Privates.

Adam, John, Philadelphia, July 12, 1778.

Barth, [Bard,] Stephen, Lancaster, May 15, 1779; resided in Berks county, in 1835, aged eighty-one.

Baumann, John, Philadelphia, September 1, 1778.

Cunitz, Sebastian, Reading, April 1, 1780.

Dansler, Christian, Hessen, Philadelphia, September 1, 1778; died July 20, 1821, in Lebanon county, aged seventy-one.

Durie, John, Philadelphia, September 1, 1778.

---

* Capt. Von Heer removed with his family from Berks county in the spring of 1785, to near falls of Schuylkill, Philadelphia county.

1784 - Philip Strubing's Commission as Lieutenant Signed by Thomas Mifflin, President of Congress

Transcription of 1784 Commission as Lieutenant for Philip Strubing
From U.S. Congress, signed by Thomas Mifflin

The United States of America in Congress Assembled

To Philip Strubing, Gentleman. Greeting. We reposing official trust and confidence in your Patriotism, Valour, Conduct and Fidelity DO by these present constitute and appoint you to be a Lieutenant in Captain Von Heers Troop of Light Dragoons in the Army of the United States, to take rank as such from the 29th day of August 1779. You are therefore carefully and diligently to discharge the duty of a Lieutenant by doing and performing all manner of things thereunto belonging. AND we do strictly charge and require all Officers and Soldiers under your command to be obedient to your orders as Lieutenant. And you are to observe and follow such orders and directions from time to time as you shall receive from this or future Congress of the United States or Committee of Congress for the purpose appointed, a Committee of the States or Commander in Chief for the time being of the Army of the United States, or any other your superior Officer, according to the rules and discipline of War, in performance of the trust reposed in you. This Commission to continue in force until revoked by this, or a future Congress, the Committee of Congress before mentioned, or a Committee of the States.

Witness of His Excellency Thomas Mifflin, Esqr., President of the Congress of the United States of America at Annapolis, the 18th day of February AD 1784 and in the eighth year of our Independence.

Thomas Mifflin

Elisabeth Strubing Born
February the 24 1787

Diemer Strubing Born
July the 26 1789

James Strubing Born
March the 9 1792

Margaret Strubing Born
October the 29 1794

On the 11 of October Died on Fishing Creek Northum-
berland County Sarah Strubing Wife of Philip
Strubing from the City of Geneva Switzerland and
Daughter of James Diemer Esq one of the asosiate
Judges of Bucks County Practisioner of Physick
Her disease begun with a fever for which She took a
vomit which occasioned an inflamation in Her
Stomack and took Her of She was ~~such Woman that~~
beloved by all

Her Neighbours in Short Her equall might be
Found But Her better do not exist She left Four
Children two Daughters and two Boys and an
inusolable Husband

FROM STRUBING
FAMILY BIBLE:
PHILIP & SARAH STRUBING
JAMES STRUBING
MARGARET STRUBING

Margaret M Strubing
was born in October
24 1815 daughter
P Strubing
in Bloomsburg
Columbia County

Transcription of Strubing Family Bible

Elizabeth Strubing born February the 24, 1787
Diemer Strubing born July the 26, 1789
James Strubing born March the 9, 1792
Margaret Strubing born October the 29, 1794

On the 11 of October 1804, died on Fishing Creek Northumberland County Sarah Strubing, wife of Philip Strubing from the city of Geneva Switzerland and Daughter of James Diemer Esqr. One of the appointed judges of Berks County Practisioner of Physick. Her disease begun with a fever for which she took a vomit which occasioned an inflammation in her stomuck and took her of. She was beloved by all. Her neighbors in (illegible) her equall might be found but her better do not exist. She left four children, two daughters and two boys and an inconsolable husband.

Margaret Strubing was born in October 24, 1815, daughter of James Strubing, in Bloomsburg, Columbia County, PA

1783 - SOCIETY OF THE CINCINNATI
LETTER OF RECOMMENDATION FROM
GEORGE WASHINGTON FOR PHILIP STRUBING

By His Excellency George
Washington Esq.ʳ General and
Commander in Chief of the
Armies of the United States
of America.

This Certifies that the Bearer
M.ʳ Strubing has served as a Lieutenant
of Horse four years, in the Army of
the United States of America, in which
~~time he has conducted himself~~
as a faithful and deserving Officer.

Given at Princeton this 18ᵗʰ
day of September 1783

G Washington

His Excellency's
Command
David Cobb
Aid de Camp

Transcription of 1783 Letter of Recommendation from George Washington
For Philip Strubing's entrance into the Society of the Cincinnati

By His Excellency George Washington, Esqr. General and Commander in Chief of the Armies of the United States of America.

This certifies that the bearer Mr. Strubing has served as a Lieutenant of Horse four years in the Army of the United States of America, in which character he has conducted himself as a faithful and deserving officer.

Given at Princeton this 18th day of September 1783.

G. Washington

1784 - SOCIETY OF THE CINCINNATI
LETTER OF RECOMMENDATION FROM VON STEUBEN
FOR PHILIP STRUBING

Lieutenant Strubing late of Van Heer's Corps being requested of me a certificate of his conduct while in the Service of the United States, I with pleasure certify that his attention to duty always merited my approbation, the Corps in which he served being remarkable for its discipline & regularity which, next to its Commander is to be attributed to Lt Strubing's knowledge & attention.

Steuben
Maj: Gen

15 March 1784

**Transcription of 1784 Letter of Recommendation from von Steuben
For Philip Strubing's entrance into the Society of the Cincinnati**

Lieutenant Strubing late of Von Heers Corps, having requested of me a certificate of his conduct while in the service of the United States, I with pleasure certify that his attentions to duty always merited (paper torn). The Corps in which he served was remarkable for its discipline and regularity which, next to its Commander, is to be attributed to Lt. Strubing's knowledge and attentions.

Steuben, Maj. General

15th March 1784

1784 - SOCIETY OF THE CINCINNATI
PHILIP STRUBING ACCEPTANCE LETTER

This Certifies that Lieut. Strubing of Capt. Von Heer Troop of Light Dragoons, in virtue of His services in the American Army, intitled to become a Member of the Cincinaty, and having Signed the institution and complied with the Regulations therein, Specified is accordingly admitted a Member and is intitled to all the rights and privileges of the Said Society of the Cincinaty

Horatio Gates,
Vice President of
the Order of The
Cincinati:—

Given under my Hand and Seall at Philadelphie this 2
of Octobre 1784

A. St. Clair, President

Transcription of 1784 Letter of Acceptance into the Society of the Cincinnati For Philip Strubing

This certifies that Lieut. Strubing of Capt. Von Heer Troop of Light Dragoons in virtue of his services in the American Army is intitled to become a Member of the Cincinaty, and having signed the institution and complied with the Regulations therein specified is accordingly admitted a Member and is intitled to all the rights and priviledges of the said Society of the Cincinaty.

Given under the hand and seal at Philadelphia this 2(?) of October 1784

Signed by the president and vice president of the society

The Thomas Lineage

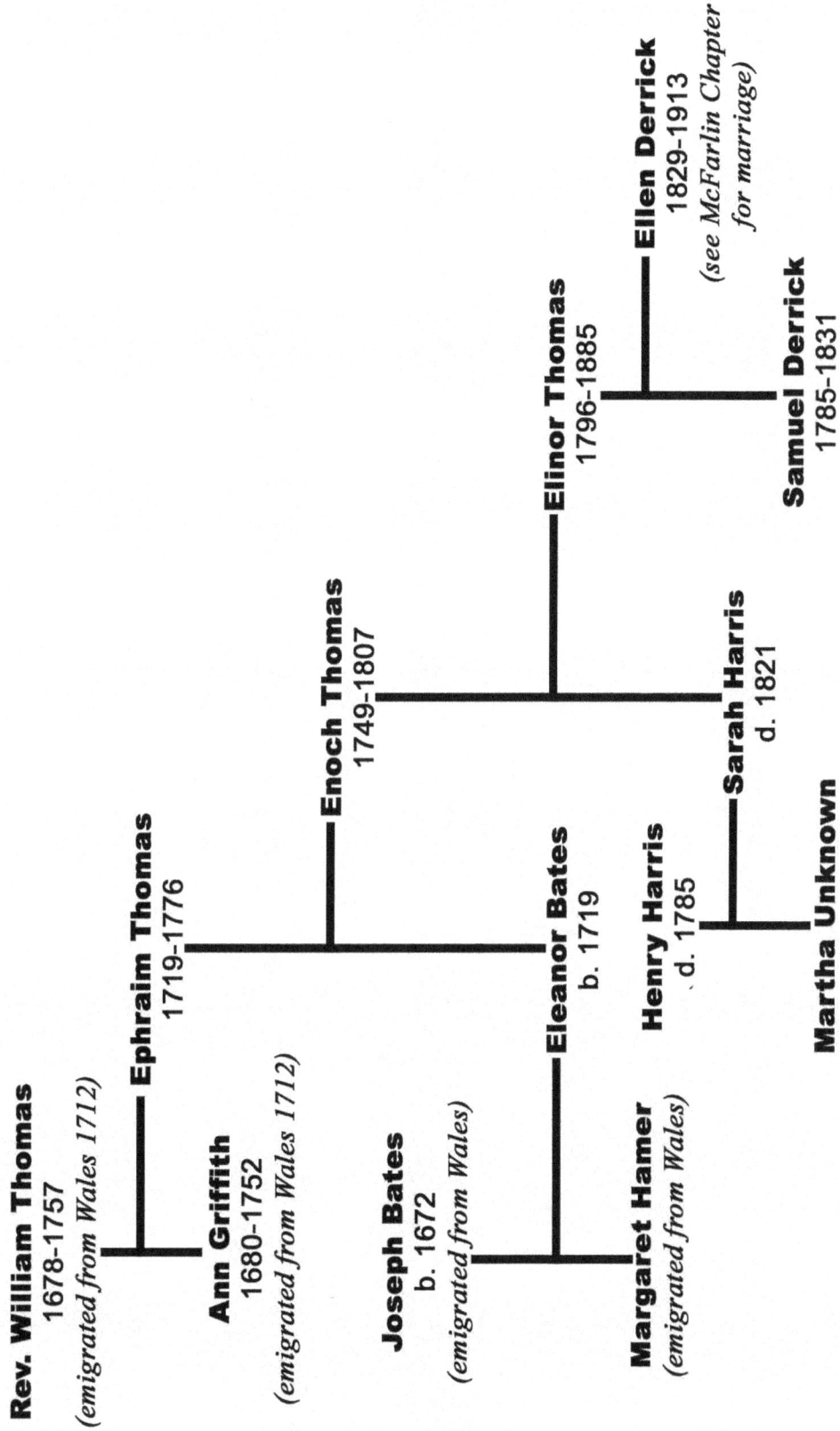

Rev. William Thomas
1678-1757
(emigrated from Wales 1712)

Ephraim Thomas
1719-1776

Ann Griffith
1680-1752
(emigrated from Wales 1712)

Enoch Thomas
1749-1807

Joseph Bates
b. 1672
(emigrated from Wales)

Eleanor Bates
b. 1719

Margaret Hamer
(emigrated from Wales)

Elinor Thomas
1796-1885

Henry Harris
d. 1785

Sarah Harris
d. 1821

Martha Unknown

Ellen Derrick
1829-1913
(see McFarlin Chapter for marriage)

Samuel Derrick
1785-1831

The Thomas Lineage

The following information is largely taken from a family history of the Thomas family written by Edward Mathews in 1884, later updated by Edward Arthur McFarlin, Jr., in 1930. Much of this history is unsupported by original documentation, so there may be errors. Unless otherwise cited, all information has been taken from this document.[1]

The Rev. William Thomas (1678–1757) and Ann Griffith (1680–1752)

William Thomas was born in Llanwenarth, in Monmouthshire, Wales, in 1678, during the reign of Charles II. Although he trained for the trade of a cooper, his superior education and ability in public speaking led him to the ministry. He married Ann Griffith (born in Wales in 1680) sometime after 1708 in Carmarthen, Wales.

In 1712, at age 34, William, his wife (32), and his eldest son, Thomas (1), came to Bristol, England, to embark to Pennsylvania. William had sold his late father's estate, and was quite wealthy at this time. He stowed all his goods and wealth onto a ship, but the ship was not ready to sail yet, so he took his family to the country until the appointed date of departure. He arrived back early, only to see the vessel, with all his worldly goods on board, leaving the harbor without him! He pursued in some other craft, but the vessel eluded them. The now destitute family booked passage on credit aboard another vessel headed for Philadelphia, PA.

When they arrived on 14 February 1712, they found the first vessel, but the master had run away with all of their wealth. This setback did not deter William from making a good life. In about 6 years, he had acquired enough money to move from Philadelphia, PA, to Hilltown, Bucks County, PA. Over the next 15 years, he bought and owned 1,258 acres of land in the area, erecting houses for each of his 7 children as they married.

William and Ann had 7 children:

Thomas (1711–1780) – *the only child born in Wales. Married Unknown Bates.*
John (1712–1790) – *the family arrived in February of 1712, so Ann would have been
        about 8 months pregnant during the turbulent voyage here.*
Gwently (1716–1785)
Anna (1719–1759)
Ephraim (1719–1776) – *married Eleanor Bates.*
Manasseh (1721–1802)
William, Jr. (1723–1764)

As William owned a great deal of land, he granted some of it to the community, and in 1737 erected a stone meetinghouse on the land, the first Hilltown Baptist Church. William (aged 59) did much of the work himself on this small and (by today's standards) crude building. The pulpit was made from a hollowed out gum tree. This little church stood for 44 years, until it was demolished in 1771, and a larger stone church erected on the site. William became a leading Elder of the church, and his sons followed in his spiritual footsteps, becoming prominent members of the Baptist community in Hilltown.

Ann Griffith Thomas died 5 November 1752 at age 72. William, perhaps spurred on by the death of his wife, made a will dated 11 December 1753.[2] As might be expected from a cleric, William was literate. William Thomas died 6 October 1757 at age 79. His estate was inventoried on 12 October 1757, and was settled on 13 October 1757.[3]

William and Ann are buried in the Hilltown Baptist Church cemetery in Hilltown, PA, which meant so much to them. On William's stone is the following inscription:

In yonder meeting house I spent my breath,
Now silent, mouldering here, I lie in death;
These silent lips shall wake, and yet declare
A dread amen to truths they publish here.

Ephraim Thomas (1719–1776) and Eleanor Bates (b. 1719)[4]

Ephraim Thomas was the third son of William, and was born about 1719. He married Eleanor Bates in 1740. Eleanor was also born around 1719. Both were about 21 when they married. Eleanor's father, Joseph Bates, had been born in Wales in 1672 and came to Pennsylvania with his wife, Margaret Hamer. Ephraim's brother Thomas had married Eleanor's sister.

Ephraim and Eleanor had 11 children:

Enoch (1) (b. 1741)
Margaret (b. 1742)
Elias (1743–1814)
Dinah (1747–1793)
Enoch (2) (1749–1807) – *married Sarah Harris.*
Rachel (b. 1750)
Sarah (b. 1754)
Elinor (b. 1756)
Joseph (b. 1758)
Ephraim, Jr. (b. 1759)
John (b. 1765)
There are 2 Enochs because 1 died as a child.

Ephraim Thomas, like his father, was an Elder in the Baptist Church and was also literate. He died at age 57 on 31 July 1776, during the summer of Independence. He is also buried in the Hilltown Baptist Church Cemetery, and his epitaph is as follows:

Entombed I here an elder lie
My work on Earth is done
The church I commit to God's care
The Spirit and the Son.

Enoch (2) Thomas (1749–1807) and Sarah Harris (d. 1821)[5]

Enoch Thomas was born 24 October 1749. He married Sarah Harris, daughter of Henry and Martha Harris. Sarah and her husband, Enoch Thomas, are mentioned in the 1785 will of Henry Harris, yeoman of New Britain, Bucks County, PA.[6] We know from Henry Harris' will that he was literate—at least enough to sign his name.

Enoch and Sarah were as prolific as his father, also having 11 children who grew to maturity, as well as others who died young. The 11 were:

John
William
Enoch, Jr.
Arthur
Martha
Elizabeth
Margaret
Mary
Isabella
Ann
Elinor (1796–1885) – *married Samuel P. Derrick.*

Enoch Thomas died on 19 April 1807 at age 58.
Sarah Harris Thomas died 27 November 1821.

Elinor (Ellen) Thomas (1796–1885) and Samuel Derrick (b.c. 1785–1831)

Elinor Thomas, youngest daughter of Enoch, was born 22 April 1796. She married Samuel Derrick (born between 1781–1790) in Pennsylvania, then moved to the vicinity of Wilmington, Delaware.[7] Although Samuel's parents are unknown, in 1800 there was a John Derrick living in Solebury, Bucks County, PA (not far from where the Thomas family lived), and he had a son who is the right age to be our Samuel.[8] More research is needed to prove a connection.

In 1820, Samuel and Elinor lived in the Christiana Hundred in Delaware (a Hundred is a land division much like a township or county). Samuel's household consisted of 2 males under 10 (John [1] and Samuel, Jr.), 1 male 26–45 (himself), 1 female under 10 (Mary Ann), and 1 female 16–26 (Elinor).[9]

In 1830, still in the Christiana Hundred, Samuel Derrick's household consisted of 1 male under 5 (John [2]), 1 male 5–under 10 (William), 1 male 10–under 15 (Samuel, Jr.), 1 male 15–under 20, 1 male 30–under 40, 1 male 40–under 50 (himself), 2 girls under 5 (Eliza and Ellen), 1 female 10–under 15 (Mary Ann), and 1 female 30–under 40 (his wife Elinor). I do not know who the other adult male and the 15–20-year-old male are. Perhaps Samuel's brothers or brothers–in–law or even farmworkers living at the house.[10]

Elinor and Samuel had 7 known children:[11]

John (1) (1817–1825)
Mary Ann (b.c. 1818)
Samuel, Jr. (b. between 1815–1820)
William (b. between 1820–1825)
Eliza (b. between 1825–1829)
John (2) (b. between 1825–1830)
Ellen (1829–1913) – *married Edward Arthur McFarlin, Sr.*

On 10 January 1832, Samuel Derrick's estate was probated in the New Castle, DE, probate records.[12] Samuel Derrick had a memorial service on 28 January 1832, presided over by Matthew Mead. Since the probate papers are dated 10 January 1832, we must assume this was a memorial of some sort, rather than the burial, even though the entry reads that Samuel Derrick "departed this life" on the January date.[13] Samuel apparently died without a will, as there is no will on record. However, there is an inventory and estate sale record on file in Delaware, dated 21 February 1833. Samuel's estate, when settled on 24 February 1834, amounted to $1,336.26—not a bad sum in those days.[14] As his wife, Elinor, could not even sign her name (she made her "mark"), it is apparent that she was not literate, even though the men in the Thomas family were.

In the 1840 Census of the Brandywine Hundred in Delaware, widowed Elleanor (Elinor) Derrick's household consisted of 1 male 5–10 (John [2]), 1 male 10–15 (William), 1 male 15–20 (Samuel, Jr.), 1 male 40–50, 1 female 10–15 (Ellen, 11), 1 female 15–20 (Eliza), 1 female 20–30 (Mary Ann, 22), and 1 female 40–50 (Elinor, 44). I have no idea who the older male is. I suspect it is someone working on the farm, perhaps even a brother–in–law to Elinor. [15]

After her daughter Ellen married Edward Arthur McFarlin, Sr., in 1851, Elinor lived with Ellen and her family throughout her later years. She moved with them around Delaware[16] [17] and eventually to the Ridley Park, PA,[18] area where she died on 4 February 1885[19] at age 89. Elinor Thomas Derrick is buried in the Mt. Lebanon Cemetery in Delaware, Plot 90S 44E, where at least 2 of her children are buried.[20]

A mystery surrounds the Samuel Derrick buried in the plot with Elinor, son John (1), and daughter Mary Ann. The cemetery assumed that it was Elinor and Samuel's son, Samuel, Jr. The gravestone is very degraded, but in a late attempt to catalog all the headstones (when the date was already well–worn), they deciphered the inscription as: "In Memory of Samuel Derrick, who departed this life December 28, 18__ in the 44th Year of his Age."[21] The question then becomes, is this Samuel, Elinor's husband, or Samuel, Jr., son of Samuel and Elinor?

The headstone clearly states that Mary Ann and John are children of Samuel and Elinor, but as you can see above, it says no such thing about Samuel.

I believe this to be Samuel the father, husband of Elinor, in spite of the fact that the church records record the date of death (which is illegible) as 1854. Here's why:

- Samuel, Sr., would have been in his 40s when he died. In 1830, he is listed as between 40–50 on the Census. A death age at 44 would make him born in 1787.
- If the 1854 date for the stone is correct, then Samuel, Jr., would have been born in 1810. Elinor, his mother, would have been 14 at the time—and that is very young, even for the times—especially since he is NOT the firstborn child.
- In addition, the 1820, 1830, and 1840 Censuses consistently put Samuel, Jr.'s birth date c. 1820, with the earliest date possible being 1815.
- Also, had Samuel, Jr., been born in 1810, he would have been 21 at the time of his father's death in 1831/2. In his father's estate settlement dated 1834, Samuel, Jr., was listed as a MINOR child – so he could not have been born prior to 1814 (consistent with Census data).
- Samuel, Sr.'s probate was dated 10 January 1832, so a death date of December 1831 is likely – which would match if the headstone actually reads 28 December 1831.
- Finally, I found a Samuel Derrick living in Delaware's Christiana Hundred in 1870 and 1880, born c. 1819. This date matches perfectly with where he fell in the list of minor children, AND it fits the earlier Census data, AND the Christiana Hundred is where his father and mother lived.

Ellen Derrick married Edward Arthur McFarlin, Sr., in 1851.[22] Ellen was 22; Edward was 27. (*See The McFarlin Lineage chapter.*)

[1] Mathews, Edward. *The Thomas Family of Hilltown, Bucks County, Pennsylvania*. Published by Arthur K. Thomas, Lansdale, PA 1884.

[2] Will of William Thomas, 1753. Hilltown, Bucks County, PA. Original housed in the Bucks County, PA, Register of Wills Office. Bucks County Courthouse, 55 East Court Street, 3rd Floor, Administration Building, Doylestown, PA 18901.

[3] Will of William Thomas, 1753. Hilltown, Bucks County, PA. Original housed in the Bucks County, PA, Register of Wills Office. Bucks County Courthouse, 55 East Court Street, 3rd Floor, Administration Building, Doylestown, PA 18901.

[4] Mathews, Edward. *The Thomas Family of Hilltown, Bucks County, Pennsylvania*. Published by Arthur K. Thomas, Lansdale, PA 1884.

[5] Mathews, Edward. *The Thomas Family of Hilltown, Bucks County, Pennsylvania*. Published by Arthur K. Thomas, Lansdale, PA 1884.

[6] Will of Henry Harris, 1785, New Britain Township, Bucks County, PA. Original housed in the Bucks County, PA, Register of Wills Office. Bucks County Courthouse, 55 East Court Street, 3rd Floor, Administration Building, Doylestown, PA 18901.

[7] Mathews, Edward. *The Thomas Family of Hilltown, Bucks County, Pennsylvania*. Published by Arthur K. Thomas, Lansdale, PA 1884.

[8] *1800 United States Census*. Year: *1800*; Census Place: *Solebury, Bucks, Pennsylvania*; Roll: *36*; Page: *278*; Image: *122*; Family History Library Film: *363339*.

[9] *1820 United States Census*, Christiana Hundred, Delaware. 1820 U S Census; Census Place: Christiana Hundred, New Castle, Delaware; Page: 116; NARA Roll: M33_4; Image: 124.

[10] *1830 United States Census*, Christiana Hundred, Delaware. *1830 United States Census*; Census Place: Christiana Hundred, New Castle, Delaware; Page: 37; NARA Series: M19; Roll Number: 12; Family History Film: 0006414.

[11] Samuel Derrick's estate probate papers, Jan 10, 1832. Original housed in the Historical Society of Delaware, 505 N. Market Street, Wilmington, DE 19801.

[12] Samuel Derrick's estate probate papers, Jan 10, 1832. Original housed in the Historical Society of Delaware, 505 N. Market Street, Wilmington, DE 19801.

[13] Bently-Sheild Book, 1736. Original housed in the Historical Society of Delaware, 505 N. Market Street, Wilmington, DE 19801.

[14] New Castle County Probate, Samuel Derrick, 1832-1834, RG 2545. Original housed in the Historical Society of Delaware, 505 N. Market Street, Wilmington, DE 19801.

[15] *1840 United States Census*, Brandywine Hundred, Delaware. Year: 1840; Census Place: Brandywine Hundred, New Castle, Delaware; Roll: 33; Page: 143; Image: 289; Family History Library Film: 0006434.

[16] *1860 United States Census*, New Castle, Delaware. Year: 1860; Census Place: Wilmington Ward 2, New Castle, Delaware; Roll: M653_98; Page: 747; Image: 114; Family History Library Film: 803098.

[17] *1870 United States Census*, New Castle, Delaware. Year: 1870; Census Place: New Castle Hundred, New Castle, Delaware; Roll: M593_120; Page: 634B; Image: 494; Family History Library Film: 545619.

[18] *1880 United States Census*, Ridley, Delaware County, Philadelphia, PA. Year: 1880; Census Place: Ridley, Delaware, Pennsylvania; Roll: 1125; Family History Film: 1255125; Page: 125B; Enumeration District: 007; Image: 0349.

[19] Cemetery Returns, City of Philadelphia. Original housed at Philadelphia City Archives, 3101 Market Street, Philadelphia, PA 19104.

[20] Mount Lebanon (Delaware) cemetery records. Originals housed at Mount Lebanon Church, 850 Mt Lebanon Rd Wilmington, DE 19803.

[21] Mount Lebanon (Delaware) cemetery headstone. Cemetery located at 850 Mt Lebanon Rd Wilmington, DE 19803.

[22] Marriage Register of New Castle, DE. Original housed in the Historical Society of Delaware, 505 N. Market Street, Wilmington, DE 19801.

(3)

And in Case My said Daughter Anna Shall happen to Die without any Lawfull Issue Living at the Time of her Decease, then and in Such Case, my Will is: And I Do give Devise and Bequeath unto my Son William and unto his Heirs & Assigns forever, the said Parcell of Land hereby Given unto My Daughter Anna As ye same is before Described, Ordering & Directing him my son William to pay at ye Expiration of one year after her Decease ye Sum of sixty Pounds lawfull Money of Pensilvania to be Equally Distributed Amongst his Surviving Brothers and Sister Provided Always that they Release and Quit all Claim & Demand of in & to ye said Tract of Now Devised to my said Daughter Anna, And in Case my Son William Should Decline to accept, or take to ye Same on ye Terms aforesd, I Desire my Son Thomas would Accept thereof on ye Lay & Terms aforesd, I Do not like it Should be Sold to Strangers

Item: I Give Devise and Bequeath unto my Son William Thomas And to his Heirs and Assigns for ever all the Remainder of the four hundred Acres I bought of Jeremiah Longhorn, being the Place I Now live on (My Mantion house) Together with all the Buildings Improvements and Appurtenances thereunto belonging to my said Son William Thomas Paying the Proportionable Part of the Quitrent Due for his part of the sd Tract of Land to the Proprietaries of this Province

And my Will is that if any Deficiency or Default be found in ye Title of any of my Lands hereby Devised as aforesd that then all My Sons shall Joyntly Contribute to Defray the Charge of Obtaining a Clear and Lawfull Title unto ye same

Item: I Give and Bequeath unto all & every of my said Children male & female the Sum of twenty Shillings each to be paid by My Exe___ at the Expiration of one year after My Decease And My Will further is that ___ Personall Estate Goods and Chattels whatsoever (after my Just Debts Charges & Legacies be Deducted) be Equally Divided Amongst my ____ Children share and share alike

And I Do nom___ Constitute and Appoint My afor___ ____ five Sons Thomas ____ ____ ____ ____ ____ William Thomas to be ___mes, ____ ____ Joynt Executors of this my last Will & Testament (And ____ ____ & ___point my Brother in Law Lewis Evans And my Trusty friends ____ ___ffith of hiltown aforsd and Evan Evans of Gwynedd And John Jones Carpenter of Mountgomery both of the County of Philadelphia to be Trustees or Overseers to see this My Will in all things fullfilled Performed And Accomplished And ffinally I Do hereby Disannull Revoke and Declare void all other & former Wills & Testaments by me at any Time before this Made Willed or Declared to be Made & Willed by word or writing; Ratifying and Confirming this and No other to be my last will & Testament (In Witness whereof I have hereunto Set my hand & Seal the Day and Year aforesd

N:B. that ye word (Issue) between ye 18th & 19th lines of the Second Page, And ye words (My Son) between ye fourth & fifth lines of third page were Interlined before the Signing & Sealing hereof

Signed Sealed And Declared by William Thomas Testator as his last will & Testament in ye Presence of us who in his Presence have Subscribed our Names

William Thomas (seal)

Abstract of Will of William Thomas, of Hilltown, Yeoman.

December 11, 1753. Proved October 13, 1757.

"Stricken in years" "To be buried on my own land in ye Grave Yard by ye Meeting House." Sons Thomas, Ephraim, John, Manassah, and William, exrs. Dau. Gwenllian, wife of Morris Morris, her son Cadwaller Morris. Dau. Anna Thomas. "To Inhabitants of Hilltown forever" the Meeting House erected by ye Grave Yard together 4 acres and some odd Perches for a Grave Yard to bury their dead in "and all other far and near" "Whites and Blacks" "Such as are guilty of self murder, only excepted." Preachers of all Denominations to hold services for funerals, "Paptists excepted" Baptists and Presbyterians to use the Meeting House jointly. My five sons, together with Lewis Evan, Junr., Nathaniel Griffith (eldest sons of Evan) and Jonathan Evans of Hilltown to serve as Trustees of said Meeting House and Grave Yard, they to name their successors in their wills. Son Ephraim, 150 acres part of 300 acres bought of James Logan; Son Manassah, 150 acres residue of 300 acres bought of James Logan; Son John, 200 acres adj. above bought of James Logan; Son Thomas, 300 acres bought of Rowland Ellis, Benj. Phillips and Jer. Langhorne. Dau. Anna, 100 acres adj. Henry Lewis and Evan Griffith; Dau. Gwenllian, 100 acres adj. Meeting House. Wit: Benj. Griffith, Benj. Griffith, Junr., and Joseph Griffith. Acknowledged before Simon Butler, Esq. by Testator as his Last Will and Testament. December 21, 1753. Codicil dated October 11, 1756. Letters granted to Thomas, John, Wm., and Mannasseh.

thinks the right

As My Trustees and Further my will is that all the s[ai]d personal
Estate or money that will be in the possession of my said wife
before her Decease She may will unto them She Likes best
Further I Do Nominate and apoint My Loving Son
John Harris and my Friend Amos Griffiths to be my
Whole and Sole Executors of this my Last Will and
Testament and I Do Revoke and utterly Disanull all
other and former wills and Testaments by me at anny time
made before this Ratifying and Confirming this and no other to be
My Last Will and Testament In Whereof Testimoney where of
I have here unto Set my hand and Seal the Day and year first
Above written

Sealed and Delivered

Pronounsd and Declar'd

In the presents of us

As his Last Will & Testament

Samuel Wier
David Reis
John Wier

Henry Harris

Transcription of Henry Harris' Will, 1786

In the name of God amen the twenty seventh day of March in the year of our Lord one thousand seventeen hundred and eighty six, I Henry Harris of the township of New Britain and County of Bucks and state of Pennsylvania, yeoman being weak and sick of body but of perfect mind and memory thanks to the almighty God for his mercies. Therefore, calling to mind the mortality of my body and knowing that it's appointed for all men once to die, do make and ordain this to be my last will and testament. That is principle and first of all I recommend my soul to God that gave it, and my body I recommend to the Earth to be buried in a Christian-like and decent manner at the discretion of my executors hereafter named. Nothing doubting but at the general resurrection I shall receive the same again. By the mighty power of God as touching such worldly estate wherewith it hath pleased God to bless me with in this life, I give, devise, and dispose in manner and form following: First of all my will is that all my just debts and funeral charges be discharged by my executors out of my personal estate.

Then I give and bequeath unto my well beloved wife Martha Harris the measure or tract of land which I now live on containing fifty-five and seventy six perches(?) agreeable to a late survey by Silas Watts which may appear with the draft of the said tract and likewise I give all my buildings and improvements and all the appurtenances therein to belonging during her natural life. I likewise give unto my wife all my horses and mares and all my horned cattle, sheep and swine and all my household furniture and all my grain of what kind so ever and all of my hay and other fodder that I do possess at the time of my decease, only such a part that should be sold to discharge my just debts and funeral charges.

Then I give and bequeath unto my son Samuel Harris the said tract of land that I give to my said wife during her natural life to him the said Samuel Harris, his heirs, and his assigns forever after the decease of his said mother, with all the appurtenances thereunto belonging in as full and ample a manner as I now possess it. Then I give and bequeath unto my daughter Sarah Thomas, the wife of Enoch Thomas, the sum of thirteen pounds and likewise a bond of seven pounds which they owed to me the said money to be paid in three years after my decease and the bond consigned to her and her heirs.

Then I give and bequeath unto my daughter Elizabeth Hines, the wife of William Hines, the sum of twenty pounds to be paid unto her or to her heirs in three years after my decease.

Then I give and bequeath unto my granddaughter Sarah Harris, daughter unto my son Thomas Harris twenty pounds to her or to her heirs in three years after my decease.

Then I give and bequeath unto my grandson Isaac Hines, son of William Hines, the sum of five pounds to be paid to him or to his heirs in three years after my decease.

Then I give and bequeath unto my son John Harris the house and plantation whereon he now lives with all the improvements and all the appurtenances thereunto belonging to hold to him, his heirs and assigns for ever. Containing all the remainder of my land about one hundred and forty five acres more or less. Further, my will is that my son John Harris shall pay each of my daughters the said legacies and each of my grandchildren their legacies at the time. Further I do nominate and entrust my friend David Davis and my friend Thomas Mathew, both of New Britain to be trustees to see this my last will in all things fulfilled and accomplished. Whereas I have given said tract to my said wife for her comfortable support, but if my said wife cannot have and enjoy such a maintenance in a sufficient manner to her contentment, my will is that then my estate hereafter named shall provide and allow all things necessary to her support at the expense of my said estate as my trustees think right, and further my will is that all the said personal estate or money that will be in the possession of my said wife before her decease she may will unto them she likes best. Further I do nominate and appoint my loving son John Harris and my friend Amos Griffith to be my whole and sole executors of this my last will and testament and I do revoke and utterly disannul all other and former wills and testaments by one at any time made before this ratifying and confirming this and no other to be my last will and testament. In testimony whereof I have here unto set my hand and seal the day and year first above written.

Henry Harris

1757 - Ephraim Thomas
Note Permitting Father's will
to be proved in his absence

I Ephraim Thomas of y Township of Hilltown Being Sick this many weeks Cannot attend with my Brethren at y Proving my fathers Last will & Testament: I Desire y Same may be Proved Givin from under my Hand this Twelvoth Day of october 1757

Ephraim Thomas

"I Ephraim Thomas of the township of Hilltown, being sick this many weeks cannot attend with my brethren at the proving of my father's last will and testament. I desire the same may be proved. Given from under my hand this 12th day of october, 1757."

MT. LEBANON METHODIST CHURCH
MT. LEBANON, DE

DERRICK
FAMILY
CHURCH

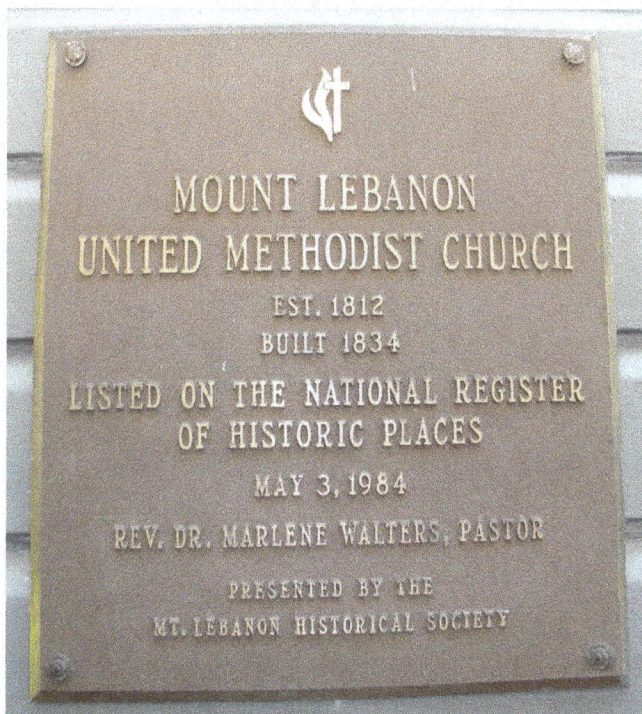

MOUNT LEBANON
UNITED METHODIST CHURCH

EST. 1812
BUILT 1834

LISTED ON THE NATIONAL REGISTER
OF HISTORIC PLACES

MAY 3, 1984

REV. DR. MARLENE WALTERS, PASTOR

PRESENTED BY THE
MT. LEBANON HISTORICAL SOCIETY

(PHOTOS TAKEN 29 AUGUST 2012)

MT. LEBANON METHODIST CHURCH
MT. LEBANON, DE

DERRICK
FAMILY
CHURCH

(PHOTOS TAKEN 29 AUG 2012)

FINAL SETTLEMENT OF SAMUEL DERRICK'S ESTATE, 1834

WIDOW:
ELLEN (ELINOR) DERRICK

MINOR CHILDREN:
MARYANN, SAMUEL, WILLIAM, ELIZA, JOHN & ELLEN

MT. LEBANON CEMETERY
MT. LEBANON, DE

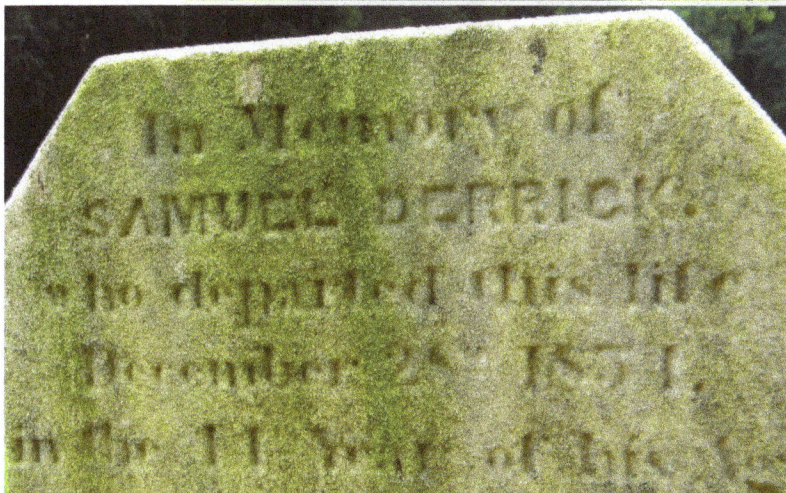

Derrick Family
Plot:
Ellen Thomas Derrick,
Samuel Derrick,
& children
John & Mary

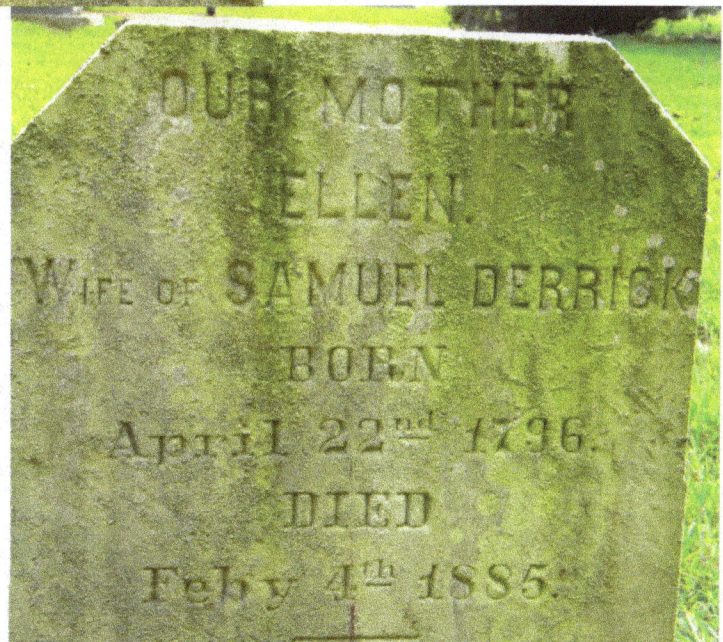

(Photos taken 1 Sept 2012)

The Trexler Lineage

Conrad Drechsler
1624-1694

Nicholaus Drechsler
1657-1690

Catherine Unknown

John Peter Trexler
1680-1758
(emigrated from Germany 1709)

Elizabeth Zimmerman
b. 1659

Catherine Breinig
d. 1760
(emigrated from Germany 1709)

Jeremiah Trexler
1708-1780
(emigrated from Germany 1709)

John Trexler
1729-1795

Mary Catherine Schumacher

Margaret Trexler
1771-1864

Mary Elizabeth Unknown

Catherine Kromer
1796-1876
(see Strubing Chapter for marriage)

John Kromer
1770-1850

The Trexler Lineage

There is a region known as the Palatinate, an area in southwest Germany that extends on both sides of the Rhine and its tributaries – the Main and the Neckar rivers. William Penn had traveled there several times to try to entice the Palatines to come to Pennsylvania, but to no avail.

The Palatinate was a war zone over and over, from the Thirty Years War (1618–1648) through the 18th century War of Spanish Succession. Again and again, the people rebounded and rebuilt their lives. They were also oppressed by feudal laws. The first was religious persecution – only 3 religions were recognized (Catholic, Lutheran, and Calvinist) and all people were forced to follow the religion of their ruler. They were also heavily taxed, as their princes learned of the opulence of Louis XIV's court, and tried to emulate him, leaving their people with very little food to eat.

The winter of 1708–1709 was the final straw. It was the coldest in over 100 years, and it was said that "birds froze in the air and beasts in the forest." After 4 long months, the thaw came, but all the fruit trees and vines had been destroyed. Many of the people decided to take up Queen Anne of England's offer to go settle in the Hudson Valley of New York. She promised them free passage to New York, a plot of land each, a monthly subsistence, and instruction in a new trade in production of naval stores for England's great navy.[1]

Our history begins a few generations prior to this massive German immigration to the New World.

Conrad Drechsler (1624–1694) and Catherine Unknown[2][3]

Conrad Drechsler was born in May 1624, and married Catherine, who was born in Hirelenbach, Germany. He and Catherine lived in the Palatinate region of Germany. They had 2 sons:

Valentine (b. 1656)
Nicholaus (1657–1690) – *married Elizabeth Zimmerman.*

Conrad Drechsler, aged 70, died 7 March 1694.[4]

Nicholaus Drechsler (1657–1690) and Elizabeth Zimmerman (b. 1659)

Nicholaus Drechsler was born 12 November 1657 in Germany. He married Elizabeth Zimmerman, who was born 5 May 1679 in Sternbach, Germany.[5] They had 4 children:[6]

George
Jacob
John Peter (1680–1758) – *married Catherine Breinig.*
A fourth – name unknown

Nicholaus Drechsler, aged 33, died 12 May 1690.[7][8]

John Peter Trexler (1680–1758) and Catherine Breinig (d. 1760)

John Peter Drechsler was born in Dettingen on the Mainz River in Hesse–Darmstadt, Germany,[9] on 26 February 1680[10]. He married Catherine Breinig.[11] In 1709, they and their year–old son, Jeremiah, left the Palatinate for London, England. This meant a 4- to 6-week journey down the Rhine to Holland, then a wait for transportation to London. They arrived at St. Catherine's (a dock near the Tower of London) in London on 3 May 1709.[12] In the British records from that time, John Peter is listed under "Husbandman and Vinedresser," and his religion is listed as Lutheran.[13]

After living in tents from May until December, the people were loaded into 5 ships, which left the Thames in December 1709 – but they did not sail for New York then. Instead, the immigrants were forced to spend the winter living in the cramped quarters of the ships as they lay at anchor off the Devon coast of England. Those who survived the winter set sail for New York on 7 April 1710. John Peter, aged 30, and family arrived sometime before 4 August 1710, when they were entered on the Governor's Lists.[14]

In 1710 and 1712, John Peter and his family were on the Sustenance Lists for the Mohawk Valley in New York State.[15] Their life in the New World was not all they had been promised. The land grant was smaller than agreed, and their training as apprentices in the ship building trade failed, largely because their teachers were also untrained. In 1714, George I became King of England, and he didn't care for the German people in New York (they had been Queen Anne's pet project), so he stopped the subsistence allowances they had been living on.[16]

A number of the Palatine families moved to Pennsylvania, settling in the Reading area. In 1720, John Peter (40) and his family were living in the Oley Valley, southeast of Reading, PA.[17]

On 18 November 1729, John Peter (49) bought 138.5 acres of land in Upper Macungie Township, PA, from Caspar Wistar. This was the first recorded deed in that area. The land was near Breinigsville, PA. Although that town contains his wife's last name, no relationship between the town and Catherine is known.[18]

It is to be noted that John Peter never learned to write. As a result, his last name took various forms over the years, as people heard it and wrote it differently. Eventually, the name evolved from Drechsler to Trexler.[19]

John Peter and Catherine had 5 children:[20] [21]

Jeremiah (1708–1780) – *born in Germany. Married Maria Catherine Schumacher.*
Anna (b. 1712) – *born in New York Colony .*
Maria Catherine (b. 1714) – *born in New York Colony. Married John*
    George Schumacher.
Margaretha (b. 1717) – *born in New York Colony. Married John Albright.*
Peter (b. 1721) – *born in Pennsylvania. Married Catherine Winck.*

On 9 January 1730, John Peter (50) fulfilled a 7–year residency requirement by owning land in Maxatawney Township, PA (Philadelphia County then, Berks County now), and was naturalized as a British citizen of the Colony of Pennsylvania.[22] He was a member of the Lutheran congregation of the Ziegel Church in Breinigsville, PA.[23]

On 1 November 1742, John Peter (62) secured more acreage adjoining his land. He and his family seemed to have a good relationship with the Indians of that area. Legend has it that "Mother" Trexler baked bread for them, and the Indians brought dried skins of wild animals in return.[24] On 16 June 1743, John Peter and his son Jeremiah were among the signers of a petition to erect a township in Macungie, PA, which at that time had about 650 residents.[25]

His will was dated 17 December 1744, and is on file in Philadelphia, PA.

John Peter Drechsler/Trexler, aged 78, died in 1758 – his will was probated on 21 October 1758.[26] Catherine Breinig Trexler died in 1760.[27] Both are buried in a private cemetery near Breinigsville, PA.[28]

Jeremiah Trexler (1708–1780) and Mary Catherine Schumacher

Jeremiah Trexler was born in the Palatinate, Germany, in 1708, and made the harrowing trip to the New World when he was only a year old.[29] After moving around with his father for many years, he settled in the Allentown, Lehigh Valley, PA, area. He was the first known white settler of Macungie Township, PA. He and his family came as early as 1719 and settled on land on Spring Creek known as Schwartz's Farm, near Trexlertown, PA.[30] It is likely that Trexlertown was named for our Trexler family.

Jeremiah married Maria Catherine Schumacher in 1726.[31] Jeremiah was 18.

Jeremiah and Maria Catherine had 3 children:[32]

John Peter (1727–1784) – *married Maria Catherine Albright.*
Margaret
John (1729–1795) – *married Mary Elizabeth Unknown, then Susanna Bauer Hesler.*

Jeremiah owned a tavern in Macungie, PA, in the current Lehigh County, as early as 1732, at about age 24.[33] [34] As noted above, on 16 June 1743, Jeremiah and his father were among the signers of a petition to erect a township in Macungie, which at that time had about 650 residents.[35]

Jeremiah was naturalized 5 September 1748.[36] He moved to Easton, PA, (at age 52) in 1760, where he was a tax collector at age 60 in 1768.[37]

He is a Patriot in the Daughters of the American Revolution. On 11 November 1776, at age 68, Jeremiah was appointed to the General Committee of Northampton County, PA, and served at numerous meetings between 1776 and 1777.[38] On 4 April 1778, Jeremiah took the Oath of Allegiance to the United States.[39]

At some time prior to 4 August 1779[40], Jeremiah Trexler moved back to Macungie, PA, where he died in 1780, at age 72.[41]

John Trexler (1729–1795) and Mary Elizabeth Unknown

John Trexler was born in 1729, most likely in Macungie, PA.[42] In 1760, John (31) received two tracts of land from his father when Jeremiah moved to Easton, including Jeremiah's tavern.[43] This tavern still exists today and is called the 1760 House.[44] John's will shows that he was literate, and since running a tavern likely required a lot of paperwork, this is not surprising.

He married a Mary Elizabeth, and they had 7 children:[45] [46]

Peter
Jeremiah
Emanuel – *married Catherine Cameron.*
Ferdinand – *married Catherine Swartz.*
Philippina – *married John Albright, then John Nyce.*
Margaret (1771 –1864) – *married John Kromer.*
Mary Elizabeth – *married Unknown Jarrett.*

After John's first wife died, he remarried a widow named Susanna Bauer Hesler.[47] Susanna and her first husband, John Hesler, were kidnapped by Indians around the time of the Revolutionary War. John Hesler escaped, and Susanna and most of the children were let go 3 years later. Two of the Hesler children were never released – Jacob and Elizabeth.[48] The other Hesler children – John, Jr., William, and Anna Maria – lived with John Trexler and Susanna.[49] Susanna and John Trexler had 1 son – Israel, who married Hannah Ott.[50]

John Trexler was a captain of the sixth company of the First Battalion of Northampton County Militia – commanded by Lt. Col. Stephen Balliet – from 1 November 1780 to 1 January 1782. His name also appears as captain of the same company in May 1780 and on 3 May 1783 as major of the Third Battalion of Northampton County Militia. He would have been in his 50s during his service.[51] There is some confusion if this John Trexler is our John or a younger Trexler. John and John Peter were very common first names in the Trexler family, and given that a man in his fifties was quite old for the times, it is likely to be another John. More research is needed.

John Trexler died at age 66 in 1795.[52] His will was written 6 January 1795. The inventory of his estate was on 7 March 1795, so John had passed away before that date. The estate, worth £1,153, was finally settled on 27 January 1802.[53]

Margaret Trexler (1771–1864) and John Kromer (b.c. 1770–1850)

Margaret Trexler was born 4 December 1771.[54] She was baptized at Lehigh Church, Macungie Township, PA, on 29 April 1772. The sponsors were Melchior Schmidt and his wife, Margaret.[55]

Margaret Trexler married John Kromer,[56] who was born between 1767 and 1774.[57] John Kromer's name is often found as Kroner. However, in John Trexler's will, it is clearly Kromer, and John's own signature as executor of the will is clearly Kromer, so I am continuing to use that spelling here.[58]

One of the signatories of John Trexler's will (of which John Kromer was executor) was William Kromer, Jr.[59] It is likely that this is our John Kromer's brother, which would make both of them sons of the William Kromer, Sr., who served the military in Northampton County, PA, on 18 June 1777.[60]

Margaret and John had 9 children:[61]

Emanuel G. (1809–1862) – *married Sarah Jones, then Margaret Unknown.*
Lavinia – *married William Smith.*
Jemima
Leah – *married Unknown Pettit.*
Elizabeth – *married James Soumelion, then Unknown Atkins.*
Catherine (1796–1876) – *married James Strubing.*
Anne – *married Jacob Souder.*
Levi
John, Jr.

In 1800, the family lived in Allen, Northampton, PA. John's household consisted of 1 male under 10, 1 male 16–25, 1 male 26–44, 2 females under 10, and 1 female 26–44. Although we have the names of his children, we have no birth dates for most of them. One of the younger girls is Catherine, who would have been 4. The eldest male and female are obviously John and Margaret (29). The 2 boys are likely Levi and John Jr., but I don't know which was older.[62]

In 1810, John's household consisted of 2 males under 10, 3 males 10–15, 1 male 26–44, 3 females under 10, 2 females 10–15, 1 female 16–25, and 1 female 26–44. Again, the eldest 2 are obviously John and Margaret (39). I have names for only 3 sons, so the remaining 2 are a mystery. One of the males under 10 is Emanuel G., who would have been 1 year old. Catherine would have been 1 of the females between 10–15, at age 14. We have names for 6 daughters, so it seems all of them are accounted for above.[63]

I could not locate the family on the 1820, 1830, or 1840 Censuses. On the 1820 Census, there are 2 Margaret Kromers found in Philadelphia, PA. The vagueness of the data makes it impossible to know if either is ours. The Margaret in the Northern Liberties Ward 4 is possible, which would place John's death earlier than we have noted below. That same Margaret Kromer is found in 1830 in Northern Liberties Ward 1, spelled Cromer. I found nothing in Philadelphia or in Northampton County that could be our family in 1840.

John Kromer died in 1850 in Philadelphia, PA.[64]

1850 found the widowed Margaret Trexler Kromer living in the Upper Delaware Ward of Philadelphia, PA, with her youngest son. Margaret (80) lived with her son Emanuel G. (41, tailor), wife Margaret (28), and his children: Elizabeth (18), Clamphe (15, probably Clara, misheard, given the 1860 Census), Edgar (13), John (11), Louisa (7), Margaret (5), Albert (3), and Thomas (4). Also living there was a servant, Catherine Fitzgerald (25).[65]

Wife Margaret seems to be a second wife, given her age and that we have information that Emanuel married a Sarah Jones. If her age is correct, Margaret could not be the mother of the older children, given that she would have been 10 at the time of Elizabeth's birth.

In 1860, Margaret (90) still lived with son Emanuel (50, real estate broker), and his family: wife Margaret (37), children Clara (23), John (21), Louisa (17), Margaret (15), Harry (7), Willie (6), and Emma (1). Also living there was servant Sarah Munick (20).[66]

Missing were Albert and Thomas, who should have been 13 and 14. They likely died in the interim. Also missing were Elizabeth and Edgar, but they would have been 28 and 23 and could easily have moved off into their own lives.

Margaret Trexler Kromer died at age 93 on 24 July 1864.[67]

Catherine Kromer married James Strubing.[68] (*See The Strubing Lineage chapter.*)

---

[1] Beitel, Jane C. *Proceedings of the Lehigh County Historical Society, vol. 42*, Mahlon H. Hellerich, ed., Allentown, PA: Lehigh County Historical Society, 2000. p. 195-196.

[2] Beitel, Jane C. *Proceedings of the Lehigh County Historical Society, vol. 42*, Mahlon H. Hellerich, ed., Allentown, PA: Lehigh County Historical Society, 2000. p. 197.

[3] Warren, John Trexler. *History & Geneaology of the Trexler Family.* Allentown, PA: Schlechter's Publishers, 1972. p. 1.

[4] Warren, John Trexler. *History & Geneaology of the Trexler Family.* Allentown, PA: Schlechter's Publishers, 1972. p. 1.

[5] Beitel, Jane C. *Proceedings of the Lehigh County Historical Society, vol. 42*, Mahlon H. Hellerich, ed., Allentown, PA: Lehigh County Historical Society, 2000. p. 197.

[6] Warren, John Trexler. *History & Geneaology of the Trexler Family.* Allentown, PA: Schlechter's Publishers, 1972. p. 1.

[7] Beitel, Jane C. *Proceedings of the Lehigh County Historical Society, vol. 42*, Mahlon H. Hellerich, ed., Allentown, PA: Lehigh County Historical Society, 2000. p. 197.

[8] Warren, John Trexler. *History & Geneaology of the Trexler Family.* Allentown, PA: Schlechter's Publishers, 1972. p. 1.

[9] Warren, John Trexler. *History & Geneaology of the Trexler Family.* Allentown, PA: Schlechter's Publishers, 1972. p. ix.

[10] Warren, John Trexler. *History & Geneaology of the Trexler Family.* Allentown, PA: Schlechter's Publishers, 1972. p. 1.

[11] Warren, John Trexler. *History & Geneaology of the Trexler Family.* Allentown, PA: Schlechter's Publishers, 1972. p. ix.

[12] Warren, John Trexler. *History & Geneaology of the Trexler Family.* Allentown, PA: Schlechter's Publishers, 1972. p. ix.

[13] Beitel, Jane C. *Proceedings of the Lehigh County Historical Society, vol. 42*, Mahlon H. Hellerich, ed., Allentown, PA: Lehigh County Historical Society, 2000. p. 197.

[14] Beitel, Jane C. *Proceedings of the Lehigh County Historical Society, vol. 42*, Mahlon H. Hellerich, ed., Allentown, PA: Lehigh County Historical Society, 2000. p. 198.

[15] Warren, John Trexler. *History & Geneaology of the Trexler Family.* Allentown, PA: Schlechter's Publishers, 1972. p. ix.

[16] Beitel, Jane C. *Proceedings of the Lehigh County Historical Society, vol. 42*, Mahlon H. Hellerich, ed., Allentown, PA: Lehigh County Historical Society, 2000. p. 196.

[17] Beitel, Jane C. *Proceedings of the Lehigh County Historical Society, vol. 42*, Mahlon H. Hellerich, ed., Allentown, PA: Lehigh County Historical Society, 2000. p. 198.

[18] Beitel, Jane C. *Proceedings of the Lehigh County Historical Society, vol. 42*, Mahlon H. Hellerich, ed., Allentown, PA: Lehigh County Historical Society, 2000. p. 199.

[19] Beitel, Jane C. *Proceedings of the Lehigh County Historical Society, vol. 42*, Mahlon H. Hellerich, ed., Allentown, PA: Lehigh County Historical Society, 2000. p. 198.

[20] Beitel, Jane C. *Proceedings of the Lehigh County Historical Society, vol. 42*, Mahlon H. Hellerich, ed., Allentown, PA: Lehigh County Historical Society, 2000. p. 197-200.

[21] Warren, John Trexler. *History & Geneaology of the Trexler Family.* Allentown, PA: Schlechter's Publishers, 1972. p. 1.

[22] Warren, John Trexler. *History & Geneaology of the Trexler Family.* Allentown, PA: Schlechter's Publishers, 1972. p. ix.

[23] Beitel, Jane C. *Proceedings of the Lehigh County Historical Society, vol. 42*, Mahlon H. Hellerich, ed., Allentown, PA: Lehigh County Historical Society, 2000. p. 199.

[24] Warren, John Trexler. *History & Geneaology of the Trexler Family.* Allentown, PA: Schlechter's Publishers, 1972. p. xi.

[25] Warren, John Trexler. *History & Geneaology of the Trexler Family.* Allentown, PA: Schlechter's Publishers, 1972. p. xiii.

[26] Beitel, Jane C. *Proceedings of the Lehigh County Historical Society, vol. 42*, Mahlon H. Hellerich, ed., Allentown, PA: Lehigh County Historical Society, 2000. p. 199.

[27] Beitel, Jane C. *Proceedings of the Lehigh County Historical Society, vol. 42*, Mahlon H. Hellerich, ed., Allentown, PA: Lehigh County Historical Society, 2000. p. 200.

[28] Warren, John Trexler. *History & Geneaology of the Trexler Family.* Allentown, PA: Schlechter's Publishers, 1972. p. xi.

[29] Beitel, Jane C. *Proceedings of the Lehigh County Historical Society, vol. 42*, Mahlon H. Hellerich, ed., Allentown, PA: Lehigh County Historical Society, 2000. p. 197.

[30] Warren, John Trexler. *History & Geneaology of the Trexler Family.* Allentown, PA: Schlechter's Publishers, 1972. p. xi.

[31] Warren, John Trexler. *History & Geneaology of the Trexler Family.* Allentown, PA: Schlechter's Publishers, 1972. p. 1.

[32] Warren, John Trexler. *History & Geneaology of the Trexler Family.* Allentown, PA: Schlechter's Publishers, 1972. p. 2.

[33] *Minutes and Proceedings of the First Reunion of the Trexler Family, Wednesday, August 28, 1907* (Kutztown Park, Kutztown, PA), pg. 7.

[34] Warren, John Trexler. *History & Geneaology of the Trexler Family.* Allentown, PA: Schlechter's Publishers, 1972. p. xi.

[35] Warren, John Trexler. *History & Geneaology of the Trexler Family.* Allentown, PA: Schlechter's Publishers, 1972. p. xiii.

[36] Beitel, Jane C. *Proceedings of the Lehigh County Historical Society, vol. 42*, Mahlon H. Hellerich, ed., Allentown, PA: Lehigh County Historical Society, 2000. p. 200.

[37] Warren, John Trexler. *History & Geneaology of the Trexler Family.* Allentown, PA: Schlechter's Publishers, 1972., p. xiii.

[38] Egle, M.D., William H., ed. *Pennsylvania in the War of the Revolution: Associated Battalions and Militia, 1775-1783.* Harrisburg: E.K. Meyes, State Printers, 1888. Pennsylvania Archive, Second Series, Vol XIV.

[39] Marx, Henry F., editor, *Oaths of Allegiance of Northampton County, Pennsylvania, 1777-1784, Also Oaths of Office 1700-1804: From Original Lists of John Arndt, Recorder of Deeds, 1777-1800* Easton: Easton Public Library, 1932. p. 55.

[40] *Minutes and Proceedings of the First Reunion of the Trexler Family, Wednesday, August 28, 1907* (Kutztown Park, Kutztown, PA), pg. 8.

[41] Warren, John Trexler. *History & Geneaology of the Trexler Family.* Allentown, PA: Schlechter's Publishers, 1972. p. 1.

[42] Warren, John Trexler. *History & Geneaology of the Trexler Family.* Allentown, PA: Schlechter's Publishers, 1972. p. 2.

[43] *Minutes and Proceedings of the First Reunion of the Trexler Family, Wednesday, August 28, 1907* (Kutztown Park, Kutztown, PA), pg. 7.

[44] Warren, John Trexler. *History & Geneaology of the Trexler Family.* Allentown, PA: Schlechter's Publishers, 1972. p. xi.

[45] Will of John Trexler, #1686 with Registrar of Wills in Northampton County, PA. Northampton County Courthouse, 669 Washington Street, Easton, PA 18042-7475.

[46] Warren, John Trexler. *History & Geneaology of the Trexler Family.* Allentown, PA: Schlechter's Publishers, 1972. p. 2.

[47] Warren, John Trexler. *History & Geneaology of the Trexler Family.* Allentown, PA: Schlechter's Publishers, 1972. p. 2.

[48] Warren, John Trexler. *History & Geneaology of the Trexler Family.* Allentown, PA: Schlechter's Publishers, 1972. p. xv.

[49] Will of John Trexler, #1686 with Registrar of Wills in Northampton County, PA. Northampton County Courthouse, 669 Washington Street, Easton, PA 18042-7475.

[50] Warren, John Trexler. *History & Geneaology of the Trexler Family.* Allentown, PA: Schlechter's Publishers, 1972. p. 2.

[51] Pennsylvania Archives, Fifth Series, Vol VIII: *Muster Rolls Relating to the Associators and Militia of the County of Northampton.* Thomas Lynch Montgomery, ed. Harrisburg: Harrisburg Publishing Company, State Printer, 1906. p. 56, 619.

[52] Warren, John Trexler. *History & Geneaology of the Trexler Family.* Allentown, PA: Schlechter's Publishers, 1972. p. 2.

[53] John Trexler Estate papers, found in the Northampton County, PA, Registrar's Office. Northampton County Courthouse, 669 Washington Street, Easton, PA 18042-7475.

[54] Warren, John Trexler. *History & Geneaology of the Trexler Family.* Allentown, PA: Schlechter's Publishers, 1972. p. 6.

[55] Church Records - Zion Lehigh Lutheran Church. Family History Center, call # 383, 520. Family History Library of the Latter-Day Saints in Salt Lake City, Utah.

[56] Warren, John Trexler. *History & Geneaology of the Trexler Family.* Allentown, PA: Schlechter's Publishers, 1972. p. 6.

[57] *1800 United States Census*, Allen, Northampton, PA. Year: 1800; Census Place: Allen, Northampton, Pennsylvania; Roll: 37; Page: 520; Image: 37; Family History Library Film: 363340.

[58] Will of John Trexler, #1686 with Registrar of Wills in Northampton County, PA. Northampton County Courthouse, 669 Washington Street, Easton, PA 18042-7475.

[59] Will of John Trexler, #1686 with Registrar of Wills in Northampton County, PA. Northampton County Courthouse, 669 Washington Street, Easton, PA 18042-7475.

[60] Daughters of the American Revolution Kromer file. Originals housed with National Society Daughters of the American Revolution, 1776 D Street, NW, Washington, DC, 20006-5303.

[61] Warren, John Trexler. *History & Geneaology of the Trexler Family.* Allentown, PA: Schlechter's Publishers, 1972. p. 6.

[62] *1800 United States Census*, Allen, Northampton, PA. Year: 1800; Census Place: Allen, Northampton, Pennsylvania; Roll: 37; Page: 520; Image: 37; Family History Library Film: 363340.

[63] *1810 United States Census*, Allen, Northampton, PA. Year: 1810; Census Place: Allen, Northampton, Pennsylvania; Roll: 51; Page: 90; Image: 0193677; Family History Library Film: 00144.

[64] Research of Jeanette Carroll, found on Genealogy.com http://genforum.genealogy.com/kromer/messages/115.html Original data: This information is found in the book titled *Trexler Family & Related Kin* by John Trexler Warren, Trexlertown, PA, copright 1972, Lib. of Cong. Catalog Card No. 72-75594.

[65] *1850 United States Census*, Philadelphia, PA. Year: 1850; Census Place: Philadelphia Upper Delaware Ward, Philadelphia, Pennsylvania; Roll: M432_816; Page: 121B; Image: 247.

[66] *1860 United States Census*, Phildelphia, PA. Year: 1860; Census Place: Philadelphia Ward 15, Philadelphia, Pennsylvania; Roll: M653_1165; Page: 325; Image: 331; Family History Library Film: 805165.

[67] Warren, John Trexler. *History & Geneaology of the Trexler Family.* Allentown, PA: Schlechter's Publishers, 1972. p. 6.

[68] Warren, John Trexler. *History & Geneaology of the Trexler Family.* Allentown, PA: Schlechter's Publishers, 1972. p. 6.

In the Name of God Amen The twenty Sixth day of January in the Year
of our Lord one thousand seven hundred and ninety five I John Trexler
of Maccungie Township Northampton County and State of Pennsylvania
Yeoman being very sick and weak in Body but of perfect mind and
Memory Thanks be given unto God therefore calling unto ———
Mortality of my Body and knowing that it is appointed for all
Men once to dye do make and ordain this my Last Will and testament
That is to say principally and first of all I give and recommend my
Soul into the Hands of God that gave it, and for my Body I recommend
✝ it to the Earth to be buried in a Christian - like and decent manner
at the discretion of my Executors nothing doubting but at the General Resurrection I shall receive the same again by the mighty Power
of God. And as touching such worldly Estate wherewith it hath
pleased God to bless me in this Life I give devise and dispose of the
Same in the following manner and form, that is to say first
and I do order That in the first place all my just debts and funeral charges
be paid and Satisfied. Item I give & bequeath unto my
dearly beloved Wife the sum of one hundred pounds in Specie
lawful money of the State of Pennsylvania for her use during her life,
and her portion and share of her father Casper Baur which is fifty
✝ pounds she also shall have in her use the Interest thereof during her
life but the principal the said fifty pounds after her decease
Shall be equely devided amongst my Step Children and to my
Youngest son viz: to Jacob Hesler, Elisabeth Hesler, which are prisoners
by the Indians, John Hesler, William Hesler, anna maria Hesler, and
to my said youngest son Israel, and it is my Will that my son
hath received his share and portion in land by the
Maccungie Township for the value of one hundred
which is his portion, and my son Jeremiah hath received his share
and portion also in the land where he lives on in Maccungie Township
for the value of one hundred pounds in Specie which is his portion,
and my son Emanuel hath received of me one hundred pounds
in Specie which shall be his share and portion, and it is my -
Will that my son Ferdenand shall have one hundred pounds in
Specie, and my Daughter Philipina Albrecht shall have one
hundred pounds in Specie, and my Daughter Margaret
Kromer shall have one hundred pounds in Specie, and it is
my Will that John Jarret son of my daughter
deceased shall have sixty pounds in Specie to be recovered out
of a Bond Jeremiah Trexler to me John Trexler Conditioned
for the payment of one hundred pounds, dated the fifth day of Septr.
anno 1786. payable the 27th day of Novr. anno 1804 without Interest
and

and further it is my will that my son Jeremiah Trexler shall give
unto the said John Jarret the sum of forty pounds in Specie which
said sum of forty pounds said Jeremiah received and having the
same in his use for said John Jarret, the said sixty pounds and
the said forty pounds shall be paid unto the said John Jarret
▮▮▮▮▮▮▮▮ to the age of twenty one Years. And it is in
▮▮▮▮▮▮ment that my Youngest son Israel shall have m▮
plantation all and singular the lands mesuages and Tenemen▮
situate partly in Macungie and partly in Lowhill Townships ad▮
ing lands of Henry Haas, Jacob Heilman, Peter sell, Peter ▮
and John Mohr Containing fifty seven acres or thereabouts ▮
the same more or less to him his Heirs and Assigns forever. An▮
is my will that my dearly beloved Wife Susanna shall live on the pl▮
so long she remains a Widow and raise up the Children and far▮
▮▮▮▮▮▮▮ son Israel arives to age twenty one Years
▮▮▮▮▮▮ of all Kind and all the household
goods and Chattels and implements of Husbandrey for her use
towards bringing up the Children, and it is my will that i▮
thirty days after my decease that all my goods and Chattels
shall be Appraised and an appraisement thereof kept in go▮
care But in case my Wife Susanna should marry again the▮
it is my will that she shall have a bed and Chest one Cow and th▮
Kitchen ware for her use and then quit the place; but if she
▮▮▮▮▮▮ widow to live on the place during her life, but if sh▮
▮▮▮▮ ain then the plantation shall be sold and the good▮
Chattels also on public vendue all the goods and Chattels wha▮
then remaining Except what my Wife Susanna shall have,
and the monies ariseing out of the land goods and Chattels shal▮
be put on Interest for my youngest son Israel untill he arive▮
to the age of twenty one Years, and in case my son Israel shal▮
die before he arives to twenty one Years leaving no Heirs then it ▮
▮▮▮ will that his Estate and portion shall be ~~equely~~ equely devi▮
▮▮▮▮▮▮ Children viz to Peter, Jeremiah, Emanuel,
Ferdenand, Philipina, Margaret, and to my Grand Child ▮
Jarret, and in case my Grand Child John Jarret shall die
before he arives to the age of twenty one Years leaving no Hei▮
then it is my will that his portion shall be equely divided amon▮
my

my Children viz to Peter, Jeremiah, Emanuel, Ferdenand,
Philipina, Margaret, and to my Youngest son Israel, and
I do make and ordain my dearly beloved wife Susanna & John Kromer
sole Executors of this my Last Will and Testament, and I do utterly
~~~~~~~~~~~~~~~~~~~ disannul all and every other ~~~~~~~~

~~~~~~~ Willd and bequeathed Ratifying ~~~~~
and no other to be my Last Will and Testament. In Witness
Whereof I have hereunto set my Hand and seal the day and
Year above written ...

Signed Sealed Published Pronounced
and declared by the said John Trexler
as his Last will and Testament in
the presence of us the subscribers --

John Trexler

William Kromer jun.r
Jacob Horner

Transcription of John Trexler's Will

In the name of God, Amen. The twenty-sixth day of January in the year of our Lord one thousand seven hundred and ninety-five, I John Trexler of Macungie County Northampton County and State of Pennsylvania, yeoman, being very sick and weak in Body but of perfect mind and memory thanks be to God therefore calling into mind the mortality of my body and knowing that it is appropriate for all men once to dye, do make and ordain this my Last Will and Testament. That is to say principally and first of all I give and recommend my soul into the Hands of God that gave it and for my body I recommend it to the Earth to be buried in a Christian-like and decent manner at the discretion of my executors, nothing doubting but at the General Ressurection I shall receive the same again by the mighty power of God. And as touching such worldly estate where with it hath pleased God to bless me in this life I give devise and dispose of the same in the following manner and form. (Illegible) and I do order that in the first place all my just debts be paid and satisfied.

Item: I give and bequeath to my dearly beloved Wife the sum of one hundred pounds in specie -- lawful money of the state of Pennsylvania for her use during her life, and her portion and share of her father Casper Baur, which is fifty pounds, she also shall have in her use the Interest thereof during her life but the principal, the said fifty pounds, after her decease shall be equally divided amongst my stepchildren and to my youngest son, viz. to Jacob Hesler, Elisabeth Hesler, which are prisoners by the Indians, John Hesler, William Hesler, Anna Maria Hesler, and to my said youngest son Israel and it is my will that my son Peter hath received his share and portion in land by (illegible) Macungie Township for the value of one hundred (illegible) which is his portion, and my son Jeremiah hath received his share and portion also in the land where he lives on in Macungie Township for the value of one hundred pounds in specie which is his portion, and my son Emanuel hath received of me one hundred pounds in specie which will be his share and portion, and it is my will that my son Ferdenand shall have one hundred pounds in specie, and my daughter Philipina Albrecht shall have one hundred pounds in specie, and my daughter Margaret Kromer shall have one hundred pounds in specie. It is my will that John Jarrett, son of my daughter Maria (illegible) deceased shall have sixty pounds in specie to be recovered out of a bond Jeremiah Trexler to me John Trexler conditioned for the payment of one hundred pounds dated the fifth day of September anno 1786 payable the 27th day of November anno 1804 without interest and further it is my will that my son Jeremiah Trexler shall give unto the said John Jarret the sum of forty pounds in specie which said sum of forty pounds said Jeremiah received and having the same in his use for said John

Jarret, the said sixty pounds and said forty pounds shall be paid unto the said John Jarret when he arrives to the age of twenty one years.

And it is my will and testament that my youngest son Israel shall have my plantation all and singular the lands messuages and tenement situate partly in Macungie and partly in Lowhill townships adjoining lands of Henry Haas, Jacob Heilman, Peter Sell, Peter Hay and John Mohr containing fifty-seven acres or thereabouts be the same more or less to him his heirs and assigns forever. NB: If any money shall remain after all are paid herein named, the same shall pass to my youngest son Israel.

And it is my will that my dearly beloved wife Susanna shall live on the place so long as she remain a widow and raise up the children and farm (illegible) son Israel arrives to age twenty one years. (Illegible) cattle of all kind and all household goods and chattels and implements of husbandry for her use towards bringing up the children and it is my will that thirty days after my decease that all my goods and chattels shall be appraised and an appraisement thereof kept in good care. But in case my wife Susanna should marry again then it is my will that she shall have a bed and chest, one cow and the kitchenware for her use and then quit the place, but if she continues a widow to live on the place during her life, but if she marries again then the plantation shall be sold and the goods and chattels also on public vendue all the goods and chattels what then remaining except what my wife Susanna shall have, and be put on interest for my youngest son Israel until he arrives to the age of twenty one years. And in case my son Israel shall die before he arrives to twenty one years leaving no heirs then it is my will that his estate and portion shall be equally devided among my children, viz. to Peter, Jeremiah, Emanuel, Ferdenand, Philipina, Margaret, and to my grandchild John Jarret. And in case my grandson John Jarret shall die before he arrives to the age of twenty one years leaving no heirs, then it is my will that his portion shall be equally divided among my children Peter, Jeremiah, Emanuel, Ferdenand, Philipina, Margaret, and to my youngest son Israel, and I do make and ordain my dearly beloved wife Susanna and John Kromer sole executors of this my last will and testament and I do utterly revoke and disannul all other and former wills and testaments by one at any time made before this (illegible) willed and bequeathed ratifying and confirming this and no other to be my last will and testament. In witness whereof I have hereunto set my hand and seal the day and year above written.

John Trexler

JANUARY 27, 1802 - EASTON, PA
SIGNATURES OF JOHN KROMER &
SUSANNA BAUER HESSLER TREXLER LEHR
EXECUTORS OF JOHN TREXLER'S WILL

JOHN KROMER IS THE HUSBAND OF
MARGARET TREXLER, AND FATHER OF
CATHERINE KROMER, WHO MARRIED JAMES STRUBING

The Watson Lineage

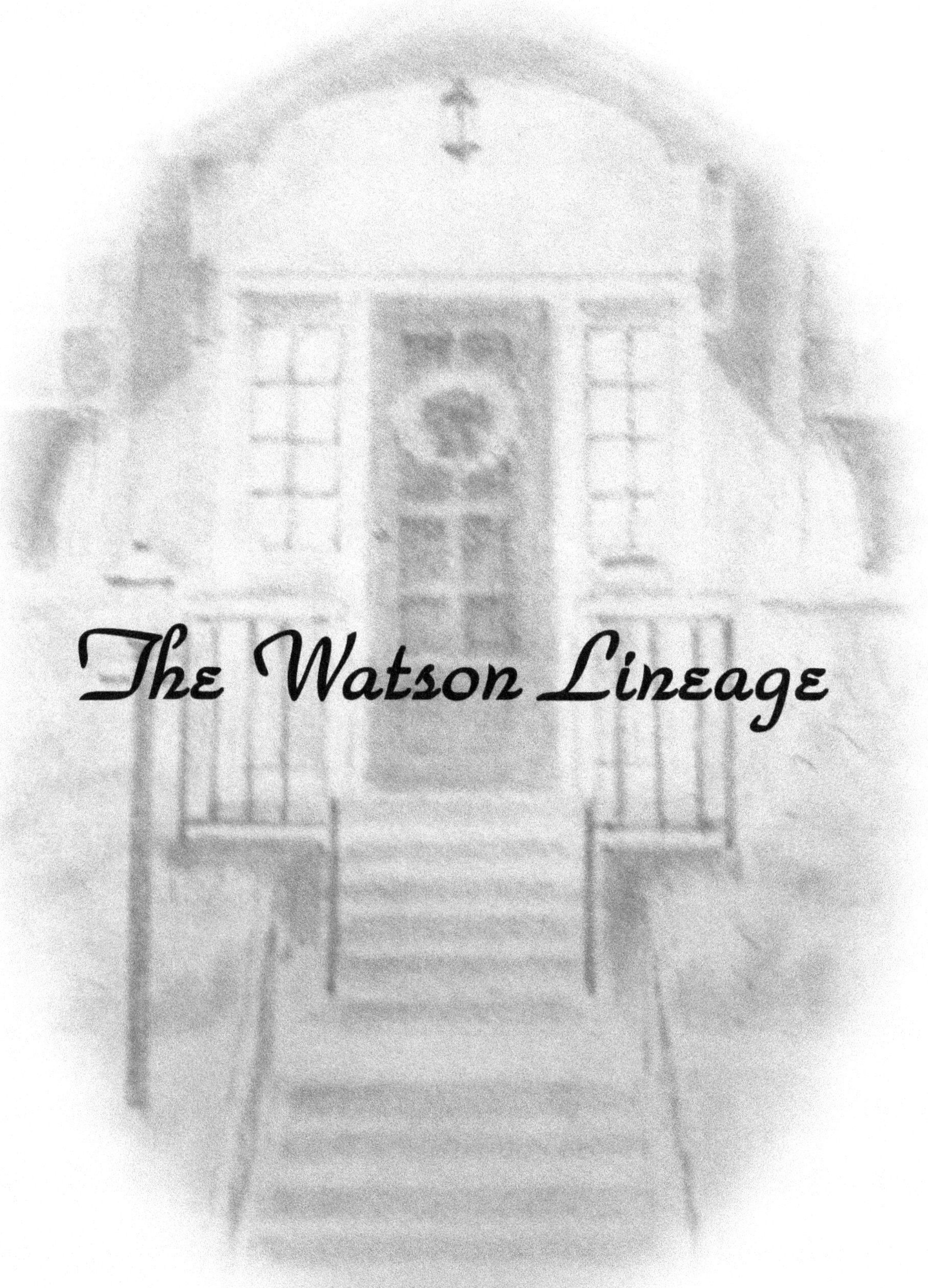

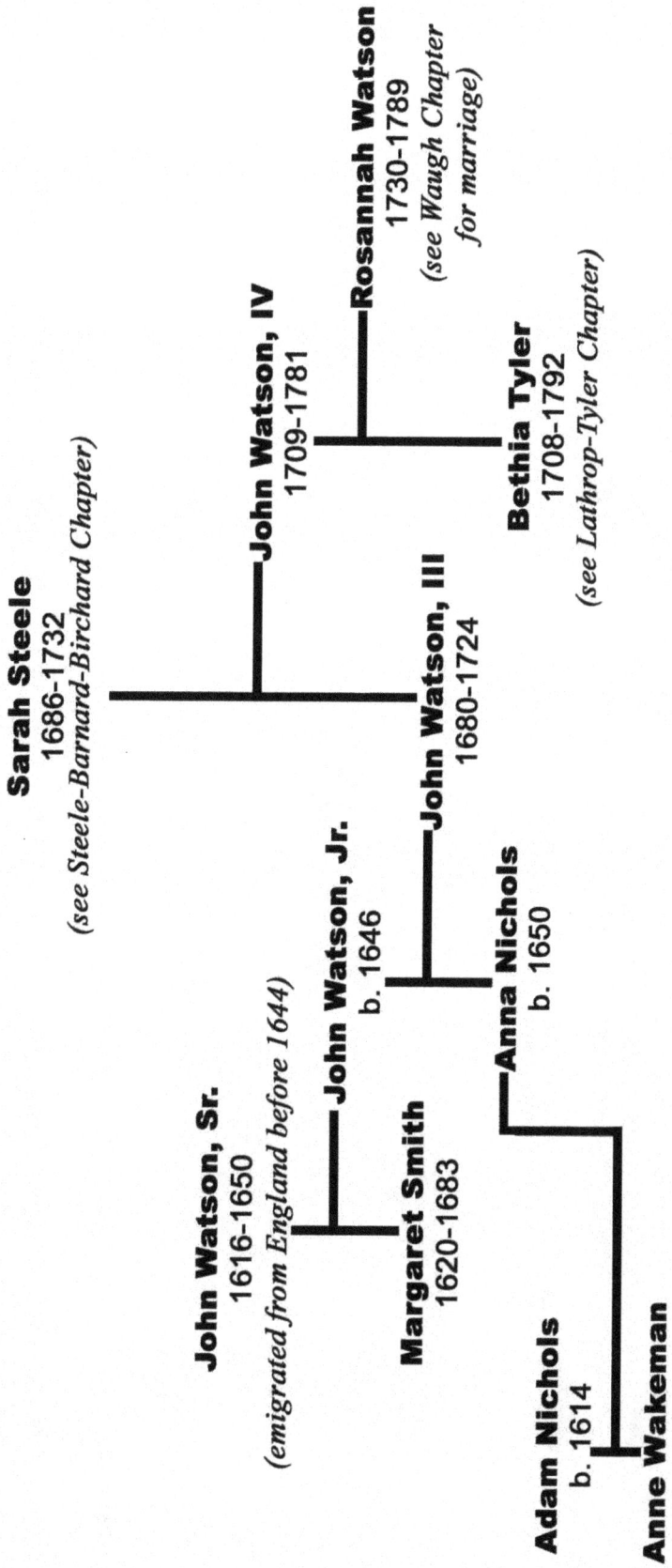

Sarah Steele
1686-1732
(see Steele-Barnard-Birchard Chapter)

John Watson, IV
1709-1781

Rosannah Watson
1730-1789
*(see Waugh Chapter
for marriage)*

John Watson, III
1680-1724

Bethia Tyler
1708-1792
(see Lathrop-Tyler Chapter)

John Watson, Sr.
1616-1650
(emigrated from England before 1644)

John Watson, Jr.
b. 1646

Margaret Smith
1620-1683

Anna Nichols
b. 1650

Adam Nichols
b. 1614

Anne Wakeman

The Watson Lineage

John Watson, Sr., (1616–1650) and Margaret Smith (1620–1683)

John Watson, Sr., was born in 1616 in England.[1] He immigrated to Connecticut sometime before 1644, when he married Margaret Smith.[2] Margaret was born in 1620 in England.[3] John was 28, Mary was 24 when they married.

John and Margaret had at least 1 child:[4]

John, Jr. (b. 1646) – *married Anna Nichols.*

John Watson, Sr., died on 4 June 1650 in Hartford, CT, at age 34.[5] Margaret Smith Watson died on 6 September 1683 in Hartford, CT, at age 63.[6]

John Watson, Jr., (b. 1646) and Anna Nichols (b. 1650)

John Watson, Jr., was born in Connecticut in 1646.[7] He married Anna Nichols, born in 1650 in Connecticut.[8] Anna's parents were Adam Nichols (b. 1614)[9] and Anne Wakeman.[10][11]

John, Jr., and Anna had 1 known child:[12]

John, III (1680–1724) – *married Sarah Steele.*

John Watson, III, (1680–1724) and Sarah Steele (1686–1731)
(see Steele–Barnard–Birchard Lineage chapter)

John Watson, III, was born on 14 November 1680 in Hartford, CT.[13] He married Sarah Steele on 16 February 1706/07.[14] Sarah was born in Hartford, CT, in 1686 to parents James Steele, Jr., and Sarah Barnard.[15] John was 26, Sarah 21 when they married.

John and Sarah had at least 1 child:[16]

John, IV (1709–1781) – *married Bethia Tyler.*

John Watson, III, died in 1724 at age 44.[17] Sarah Steele Watson died on 23 January 1731/32 in Hartford, CT, at age 46.[18]

John Watson, IV, (1709–1781) and Bethia Tyler (1708–1792)
(see the Lathrop–Tyler Lineage chapter)

John Watson, IV, was born 12 June 1709 in Hartford, CT.[19] Bethia Tyler was born 10 November 1708 in Wallingford, New Haven, CT.[20]

John Watson, IV, and Bethia Tyler were married 30 April 1730 in Windsor, Hartford, CT.[21] Bethia was 21; John was 20.

John and Bethia had at least 2 children:[22] [23]

Rosannah (1730–1789) – *married Thomas Waugh.*
James

John Watson, IV, (age 74) died 9 November 1781 in Norfolk, Litchfield, CT.[24] Bethia Tyler Watson (age 87) died on 24 June 1792 in Hartford, CT.[25] [26] If you do the math, their ages at death do not result in their stated birth dates above, but I have no way of knowing what source is incorrect. They are buried in the Footville Burial Grounds, and the inscription on their tombstone reads:

> *In memory of Mr. John Watson*
> *Who died November the 9th 1781*
> *In the 74th Year of his Age*
> *And of Mrs. Bethyah his wife*
> *Who died June the 24th 1792*
> *In the 87th Year of her Age*
> *This monument is respectfully raised*
> *By James Watson*
> *Their youngest son*[27]

Rosannah Watson married Thomas Waugh 11 April 1754.[28] He was 27; she was 23. (*See The Waugh Lineage* chapter.)

---

[1] *US and International Marriage Records, 1560-1900 - Ancestry.com*,[database online] Yates Publishing, The Generations Network Inc., Provo, UT, Source number: 23829.003; Source type: Pedigree chart; Number of Pages: 4.

[2] *US and International Marriage Records, 1560-1900 - Ancestry.com*,[database online] Yates Publishing, The Generations Network Inc., Provo, UT, Source number: 23829.003; Source type: Pedigree chart; Number of Pages: 4.

[3] *US and International Marriage Records, 1560-1900 - Ancestry.com*,[database online] Yates Publishing, The Generations Network Inc., Provo, UT, Source number: 23829.003; Source type: Pedigree chart; Number of Pages: 4.

[4] *Ancestry Family Data Collection.* Edmund West, comp., The Generation Network Inc, 2001 Provo, UT, Edmund West, comp. Family Data Collection - Births [database on-line]. Provo, UT, USA: The Generations Network, Inc., 2001.

[5] *Ancestry Family Data Collection.* Edmund West, comp., The Generation Network Inc, 2001 Provo, UT, Edmund West, comp. Family Data Collection - Deaths [database on-line]. Provo, UT, USA: The Generations Network, Inc., 2001.

[6] *Ancestry Family Data Collection.* Edmund West, comp., The Generation Network Inc, 2001 Provo, UT, Edmund West, comp. Family Data Collection - Deaths [database on-line]. Provo, UT, USA: The Generations Network, Inc., 2001.

[7] *Ancestry Family Data Collection.* Edmund West, comp., The Generation Network Inc, 2001 Provo, UT, Edmund West, comp. Family Data Collection - Births [database on-line]. Provo, UT, USA: The Generations Network, Inc., 2001.

[8] *US and International Marriage Records, 1560-1900 - Ancestry.com*,[database online] Yates Publishing, The Generations Network Inc., Provo, UT, Source number: 1236.000; Source type: Electronic Database; Number of Pages: 1; Submitter Code: RH1.

[9] *US and International Marriage Records, 1560-1900 - Ancestry.com*,[database online] Yates Publishing, The Generations Network Inc., Provo, UT, Source number: 6896.000; Source type: Electronic Database; Number of Pages: 1; Submitter Code: WAY.

[10] *Ancestry Family Data Collection.* Edmund West, comp., The Generation Network Inc, 2001 Provo, UT, Godfrey Memorial Library, comp. American Genealogical-Biographical Index (AGBI) [database on-line]. Provo, UT, USA: The Generations Network, Inc., 1999. Original data: Godfrey Memorial Library. American Genealogical-Biographical Index. Middletown, CT, US.

[11] *US and International Marriage Records, 1560-1900 - Ancestry.com*,[database online] Yates Publishing, The Generations Network Inc., Provo, UT, Source number: 6896.000; Source type: Electronic Database; Number of Pages: 1; Submitter Code: WAY.

[12] *Ancestry Family Data Collection.* Edmund West, comp., The Generation Network Inc, 2001 Provo, UT, Edmund West, comp. Family Data Collection - Births [database on-line]. Provo, UT, USA: The Generations Network, Inc., 2001.

[13] *Ancestry Family Data Collection.* Edmund West, comp., The Generation Network Inc, 2001 Provo, UT, Edmund West, comp. Family Data Collection - Births [database on-line]. Provo, UT, USA: The Generations Network, Inc., 2001.

[14] Research of Bruce Clark. www.bruceclark.net

[15] *Ancestry Family Data Collection.* Edmund West, comp., The Generation Network Inc, 2001 Provo, UT, Edmund West, comp. Family Data Collection - Births [database on-line]. Provo, UT, USA: The Generations Network, Inc., 2001.

[16] *Ancestry Family Data Collection.* Edmund West, comp., The Generation Network Inc, 2001 Provo, UT, Edmund West, comp. Family Data Collection - Births [database on-line]. Provo, UT, USA: The Generations Network, Inc., 2001.

[17] *Ancestry Family Data Collection.* Edmund West, comp., The Generation Network Inc, 2001 Provo, UT, Edmund West, comp. Family Data Collection - Deaths [database on-line]. Provo, UT, USA: The Generations Network, Inc., 2001.

[18] *Ancestry Family Data Collection.* Edmund West, comp., The Generation Network Inc, 2001 Provo, UT, Edmund West, comp. Family Data Collection - Deaths [database on-line]. Provo, UT, USA: The Generations Network, Inc., 2001.

[19] *Ancestry Family Data Collection.* Edmund West, comp. Family Data Collection - Births [database on-line]. Provo, UT, USA: The Generations Network, Inc., 2001.

[20] Jacobus, Donald Lines. *Families of Ancient New Haven.* Baltimore: Genealogical Publishing Company, Inc., 1997. Originally published as *New Haven Genealogical Magazine, Vol. I-VIII*, Rome, NY, 1922-32.; p. 1922.

[21] Hartford, CT Vital Records, p. 421.

[22] Hartford, CT Vital Records, p. 433.

[23] Payne, Charles Thomas. *Litchfield & Morris Inscriptions: A record of inscriptions upon the tombstones in the towns of Litchfield & Morris, CT.* Litchfield, CT: Dwight C. Kilbourne, 1905.

[24] *Ancestry Family Data Collection.* Edmund West, comp. Family Data Collection - Deaths [database on-line]. Provo, UT, USA: The Generations Network, Inc., 2001.

[25] Research of Bruce Clark. www.bruceclark.net

[26] Payne, Charles Thomas. *Litchfield & Morris Inscriptions: A record of inscriptions upon the tombstones in the towns of Litchfield & Morris, CT.* Litchfield, CT: Dwight C. Kilbourne, 1905.

[27] Payne, Charles Thomas. *Litchfield & Morris Inscriptions: A record of inscriptions upon the tombstones in the towns of Litchfield & Morris, CT.* Litchfield, CT: Dwight C. Kilbourne, 1905.

[28] *Connecticut Town Marriage Records, pre-1870* (Barbour Collection) by Lucious Barnes Barbour. [database online] Original data: White, Lorraine Cook, ed. *The Barbour Collection of Connecticut Town Vital Records. Vol. 1-55.* Baltimore, MD, USA: Genealogical Publishing Co., 1994-2002. Found on Ancestry.com.

The Waugh Lineage

John Waugh
1687-1781
(emigrated from Scotland to Ireland;
emigrated from Ireland 1718)

Thomas Waugh
1727-1801

Margaret Unknown
1699-1772

Asa Waugh
1772-1817

Rosannah Watson
1730-1789
(see Watson Chapter)

Cecelia Waugh
1815-1900

Sarah Cordray
b. 1786

Elizabeth Huhn
1834-1916
(see Godshall Chapter
for marriage)

Charles Huhn
1806-1872

The Waugh Lineage

John Waugh (1687–1781) and Margaret Unknown (1699–1772)

Much of John's pre–Connecticut history must be taken with a grain of salt, as there is no documentation.

The Waughs, like many other Scottish families, moved to Londonderry, Ireland, to escape religious oppression in Scotland from the authorities of the Church of England. In 1718, large numbers of this group moved to America, to New England. Three brothers Waugh immigrated with them. William Waugh settled in Londonderry, New Hampshire. Robert Waugh moved to Maine and became a Baptist minister.[1]

The third brother, our John Waugh (aged 31 at immigration), lived in eastern Massachusetts; in Windham County, Connecticut,[2] and finally in Litchfield, CT. John (58) took possession of the old Waugh Farm in Litchfield on 19 June 1745.[3] Deeds show that he could not sign his name (making his "mark" instead), and was therefore not literate.

There are deeds to prove that John Waugh lived in Connecticut. On 10 June 1745, he bought his original farm from Samuel Tyler. On 4 November 1748, he bought more land from Amos Morris. On 16 November 1751, he purchased more land from Pelitiah Buck, Jr. The first 2 deeds had John living in Lebanon, Windham, CT, while the third has his address as Litchfield, so he probably did not move to the farm until after 1748.[4]

John was married to a woman named Margaret, although it is unknown when they married or where. Given that their oldest recorded child was born in 1724, it is likely they married in New England, after John's 1718 immigration.

John and Margaret had 4 children:[5]

Robert (b. 1724)
Joseph (b. 1726)
Thomas (b. 1727) – *married Rosannah Watson.*
Alexander (b. 1729)

Margaret died at age 74, on 15 February 1772.[6] John Waugh died at age 95. There is a discrepancy in the date of death. Local records date it at 31 August 1781, but the tombstone reads 6 September 1781.[7] Both are buried in the Morris Burying Ground.

Margaret's inscription:[8]

> *In Memory of Mrs. Margaret, wife of John Waugh,*
> *Who departed this life Feb 15, 1772 aged 74.*
> *Here lies interned on house of clay*
> *That yields to worms and easy prey*
> *Yet Christ my Lord this tomb shall burst*
> *And raise again the sleeping dust.*

John's inscription:[9]

> *In Memory of Mr. John Waugh, who departed this life September 6, 1781,*
> *in the 95th year of his age.*
> *When ere the _____ reigns his big _____*
> *Though young, finds inward peace in death*
> *And life itself can yield no more,*
> *Though lengthen'd out to ninety four*

Thomas Waugh (1727–1801) and Rosannah Watson (1730–1789)
(see the Watson Lineage chapter)

Thomas Waugh was born in 1727.[10] His father, John, divided up his farm among his 4 sons prior to his death. Thomas lived in Litchfield, CT, all of his adult life. Unlike his father, he was literate—at least he could sign his name, as could his brothers. He married Rosannah W. Watson (b. 8 February 1730/31)[11] on 11 April 1754 at New Haven Second Church.[12] He was 27; Rosannah was 23.

Thomas is a listed Patriot with the Daughters of the American Revolution. At a Litchfield town meeting on 10 December 1777, Thomas (50) was appointed a member of the committee to provide food for soldiers of the Continental Army and their families.[13][14]

Thomas and Rosanna had 8 children:[15]

John (b. 1756) – *married Olive Stone.*
Samuel (b. 1758) – *married Elizabeth Goodwin.*
Anne (b. 1760) – *married Samuel Goodwin.*
Tryphena (b. 1761) – *married Obediah Lovejoy.*
Thomas, Jr. (b. 1766)
Elizabeth "Polly" – *married Israel Brainard Spencer.*
Asa – *married Sarah Cordray.*
Lucy – *married Gideon Gallop.*

Thomas appears on the 1790[16] and 1800[17] Litchfield, CT, Census forms. After the death of his first wife, Thomas married Elizabeth (Bernard) Lewis.[18]

Rosannah Watson Waugh died 4 August 1789, at age 60. Thomas Waugh died 24 February 1801, aged 76.[19] Both are buried at the Footville Burying Ground in Connecticut.[20]

Asa Waugh (1772–1817) and Sarah "Sally" Cordray/Cowdrey (b. 1786)

This couple has proved quite elusive. The birth dates are unproven, so all ages listed below are estimates. It seems that Asa Waugh moved from Connecticut to New York City. I would like to point out that as of this writing, there is no proof that the New York Asa Waugh is in fact the same Asa Waugh, son of Thomas Waugh. Other researchers have assumed he is, since his name is quite distinctive.

There is an Asa Waugh listed on the 1800 United States Census for New York City's 5th Ward. He owned 1 slave. Other members of his family were: Free White Males: 1 aged 16–25 and 2 aged 26–44; Free White Females: 1 under age 10, 1 aged 10–15, and 1 aged 26–44. Asa would have been about 28 at this time.[21]

In the 23 or 30 October 1802 Saturday edition of the *New York Weekly Museum and The Telescope*, it says, "On Saturday eve last, by the Reverend Mr. Pilmore, Mr. Asa Waugh to Miss Sally Cowdrey, both of this city." The Rev. Joseph Pilmore was a Methodist who converted to the Protestant Episcopal Church, and was stationed in New York's Christ Church in 1802. At the time of their marriage, Asa would have been about 30, and Sally about 16.[22]

The couple had 4 known children, all christened at Christ Episcopal Church at Broadway and 71st Street, New York, NY:[23]

Juliann (b. 1803)
Mary Louisa (1806–1881) – *married Joseph Kerr.*
Eliza Bell (b. 1813)
Cecelia Waugh (1815–1900) – *married Charles Huhn.*

In 3 articles from New York City papers, we glean the following information:

In 1806, Asa Waugh (34) rented a property at 8 Barley St.[24] He rented out the upper part of the building, and lived or worked at 119 Front Street.[25]

In 1808, Asa Waugh (36) was listed as insolvent.[26]

The 1810 Census has an Asa Wall listed in New York's 10th Ward. This Asa, assuming he is ours, was aged 26–44 (Asa would have been about 38), with his probable wife listed as aged 16–25 (Sarah would have been about 24). Also in the household were 2 males and 2 females under age 10; one female aged 10–15; and 3 females aged 45 and over.[27]

Asa Waugh was an accountant, and seemed to move frequently. The New York City Directories trace his path:

Longworth's NY Directory 1810: Waugh, Afa (Asa), accountant, 48 Second St.[28]

Longworth's NY Directory 1811: Waugh, Asa, accountant, 69 First St.[29]

Longworth's NY Directory 1812: Waugh, Asa, accountant, 59 Stone St.[30]

War of 1812 Service Records: Asa Waugh – Company: 1 Reg't Art'y (Sticher's) New York Vols; Rank: Private; Discharge: Matross; Roll/Box 220.[31] It is unknown if this Asa Waugh is the same Asa Waugh we are tracking here. Our Asa would have been 40.

In 1813, he lived at 14 Roosevelt,[32] in 1814 at 22 White, [33] in 1815 and 1816 at 41 Chamber,[34] [35]and in 1817 at 114 Liberty.[36]

On 7 May 1817, Asa Waugh drowned at age 45 and was buried in Methodist's Cemetery, 2nd Street.[37] At the time of his death, he resided at the Almshouse. It is unknown why he lived at the Almshouse – he may have been a staff accountant, or he may have had some physical, mental, or financial problem.[38] It also stated that this Asa Waugh was born in New York, which conflicts with the notion that all of Thomas Waugh's children were born in Connecticut. But birth information was often inaccurate in records of those times.

The 1817 death date conflicts with the 1820 death date given in the DAR records. However, since no source was cited for the DAR records, they could well be incorrect. If we accept that the New York Asa Waugh is Thomas Waugh's son, then the 1817 date is well proven as the correct death date for this individual.

Sarah Cordray Waugh was left a 31–year–old widow at that time, and lived in boardinghouses until she disappears from the records.

In 1818 she lived at 156 William.[39] From 1819 to 1822 she lived at 174 Broadway.[40] [41] [42]

The 1820 Census for New York's 2nd Ward also lists Sarah (who would have been about 34). Her household includes: Males: 1 aged 10–16; 2 aged 16–26; 2 aged 26–45, and Females: 2 under age 10; 4 aged 10–16; and 2 aged 26–45.[43] This has too many children, but some could belong to the other 26–45-year-old woman and man. Sarah ran a boardinghouse, so this is likely to be the correct explanation.

Longworth's NY Directory 1822–1823: Waugh, Sarah, boardinghouse, 338 Pearl.[44]

It is unknown what happened to Sarah Cordray Waugh after this time. She could have moved, remarried, or died. No death records were found, nor were any records of her found on the 1830 Census or beyond in any state.

Cecelia Waugh (1815–1900) and Charles Huhn (1806–1872)

Cecelia Waugh is Asa and Sarah's daughter, born September 1815.[45] We are unsure of where she was born – sources have her birthplace as New York, New Jersey, and Maryland. The New York City location seems most likely, as her parents seem to have resided in New York City consistently. She married Charles Huhn (b. 1806)[46] at some unknown time, probably around 1832.[47] Cecelia would have been 18; Charles aged 27.

Cecelia and Charles had at least 10 children:[48]

Elizabeth "Lizzie" (1834–1916) – *married Henry Stites Godshall.*
Mary (b. 1837)
Cecelia M. (b. 1839) – *married Charles Brady.*
Sarah "Sally" (1840–1922) – *married George R.R. Bean.*
Emeline "Emily" Dallas (1844–1904) – *married William Aiken Johnson.*
Kate (1846–1853)
Louisa (b. 1848) – *married William P. Henderson.*
George (1850–1929) – *married Emma Parham, then Alice Janney.*
Edward C. (1856–1937)
Margaret J. "Maggie" (b. 1858) – *married Horace Rhawn.*

Two young children, both named Charles Huhn, are buried in the Woodlands Cemetery lot with Charles and Cecelia. One young Charles died at age 10 months of scarlet fever in 1844. The other young Charles died of convulsions at age 9 months in 1853.[49]

In 1839, brickmaker Charles Huhn makes his first appearance in the Philadelphia City Directory, living at 7th above Poplar.[50] He is 34–35 at this time, and has been married for about 7 years, and has several children. I do not think that if he already had a family he would not have been working, or that the Directory people would have "missed" him for 7 years. So I believe he was living somewhere else until that date. His wife was from New York, so I speculate he may have been living there.

One line of ancestry for Charles is thought to be Daniel Huhn, brickmaker of Philadelphia, PA, as his father. But again, why would Charles have been absent all those productive years (some 15 years)? Although his death certificate states he was born in Philadelphia, PA, I am suspicious. Also, there seems no relation between him and the other Huhn brickmakers as far as locality of address.

From 1840 through 1846, Charles and family lived at 17 Union Square in Philadelphia, PA.[51]

In 1847, the family was at the corner of 10th and Melon.[52] In 1848, Charles was on Wistar below 11th,[53] and in 1849–1850, they lived on 7th below Pine.[54]

In 1850, the Huhn family lived in the Lombard Ward of Philadelphia, PA. Charles (45) was a brickmaker. Although there is a Silas listed on the Census, I believe this was Cecelia (34) mislabeled. Eight children were listed, all born in Pennsylvania: Elizabeth, 16; Mary, 13; Cecelia, 11; Sarah, 9; Emeline, 6; Kate, 4; Louisa, 2, and George, 5 months. Margaret Beaty, 38, was an Irish servant who lived with them, no doubt to help with all the children![55]

In 1852[56], Charles lived on 7th above Lombard. In 1857[57], he has 2 addresses listed—one is likely his home and the other his business, but neither is designated with an "H" to denote home: Lombard above Pine and 20th above Locust. In 1858,[58] he was on Poplar below 7th. In both 1859 and 1860,[59] Charles' family resided at 1941 Callowhill.

In 1860, Charles and Cecelia lived with their family in the 15th Ward of Philadelphia, PA. Charles, still a brickmaker, was 55; Cecelia, 44. Children living with them: Cecelia, 21; Sally (Sarah), 19; Emily, 16; Louisa, 12; George, 10; Edward, 4, and Maggie, 2. Charles' personal property was valued at $500. Oldest daughter *Elizabeth* had married Henry Stites Godshall in 1851.[60]

Charles and Cecelia married off 2 more daughters: Sarah married George R.R. Bean in 1860, and Cecelia married Charles Brady in 1863.[61]

In 1861, Charles and family lived at 2022 Brandywine.[62] In 1862–1863, they were at 1812 Christian.[63] From 1864 until 1867, the Huhn family was at 2018 Christian.[64]

In 1870, Charles and Cecelia lived in the 9th Precinct of the 26th Ward of Philadelphia, PA. Charles was 65 years old; Cecelia was 50. As you can see, there are sometimes discrepancies in age from Census to Census. Still living at home were the 2 youngest children: Edward (14) and Maggie (12). They also had a servant, Margaret Briggs (35). Charles valued his personal property at $800.[65]

On 7 November 1872, Charles Huhn died of Bright's disease (a vague term for then little–understood kidney disease).[66] He was 66 years old, and was buried at the Woodlands Cemetery in Philadelphia, PA, Section C, Lot 190.[67] At this time, he lived at 3036 Christian Street in Philadelphia's 26th Ward.[68]

In 1900, 85-year-old Cecelia Huhn was living with her youngest daughter, Maggie, at 3223 Winter St. in the 24th Ward of Philadelphia, PA. Maggie was married to Horace Rhawn, and had 3 children: George W. (18), Cecelia M. (13), and Charles H. (9). There are also 3 servants: Anna Nolan (nurse) (25), Constance Archer (29), and Josephine Todd (25). Cecelia's birth date was listed as August 1814, and she is listed as having borne 13 children, although we have names of only 12.[69]

On 23 November 1900, Cecelia Waugh Huhn died at age 85 of senile debility. She resided at 3223 Spencer Terrace, Philadelphia Ward 27. She is also buried at the Woodlands Cemetery in Philadelphia, PA, Section C, Lot 190.[70]

Her daughter ***Elizabeth Huhn*** married Henry Stites Godshall in 1851.[71] She was 17; he was 22. (*See The Godshall Lineage chapter.*)

---

[1] Waugh, Patricia. *Waugh Family History* (1986), p. 3. From a letter written by Robert Waugh of Sangerville, Maryland on 12/26/1922 sent to Mrs. John Husen.

[2] Waugh, Patricia. *Waugh Family History* (1986), p. 6.

[3] Waugh, Patricia. *Waugh Family History* (1986), p. 3.

[4] Waugh, Patricia. *Waugh Family History* (1986), p. 3.

[5] Dittenhafer, Miriam Marcy. *Godshall Family History,* p. 137.

[6] Waugh, Patricia. *Waugh Family History* (1986), p. 6.

[7] Dittenhafer, Miriam Marcy. *Godshall Family History,* p. 137.

[8] Payne, Charles Thomas. *Litchfield & Morris Inscriptions: A record of inscriptions upon the tombstones in the towns of Litchfield & Morris, CT.* Litchfield, CT: Dwight C. Kilbourne, 1905. p. 234.

[9] Payne, Charles Thomas. *Litchfield & Morris Inscriptions: A record of inscriptions upon the tombstones in the towns of Litchfield & Morris, CT.* Litchfield, CT: Dwight C. Kilbourne, 1905. p. 234.

[10] Daughters of the American Revolution application, Ethel Warren Castle #186114. Originals housed with National Society Daughters of the American Revolution, 1776 D Street, NW, Washington, DC, 20006-5303.

[11] Hartford, CT, Vital Records, p 433.

[12] *Connecticut Town Marriage Records, pre-1870* (Barbour Collection) by Lucious Barnes Barbour. [database online] Original data: White, Lorraine Cook, ed. *The Barbour Collection of Connecticut Town Vital Records. Vol. 1-55.* Baltimore, MD, USA: Genealogical Publishing Co., 1994-2002. Found on Ancestry.com.

[13] Daughters of the American Revolution application, Ethel Warren Castle #186114. Originals housed with National Society Daughters of the American Revolution, 1776 D Street, NW, Washington, DC, 20006-5303.

[14] Payne Kenyon Kilbourne, M.A, *Sketches and Chronicles of the Town of Litchfield, Connecticut: Historical, Biographical & Statistical; together with a complete official register of the town.* (Hartford: Press of Case, Lockwood, and Company, 1859), p. 119.

[15] Dittenhafer, Miriam Marcy. *Godshall Family History,* p. 139.

[16] *1790 United States Census*, Litchfield, CT. Year: 1790; Census Place: Litchfield, Litchfield, Connecticut; Series: M637; Roll: 1; Page: 337; Image: 327; Family History Library Film: 0568141.

[17] *1800 United States Census*, Litchfield, CT. Year: 1800; Census Place: Litchfield, Litchfield, Connecticut; Roll: 2; Page: 630; Image: 18; Family History Library Film: 205619.

[18] Waugh, Patricia. *Waugh Family History* (1986), p. 339.

[19] Woodruff, George C. *A Genealogical Register of the Inhabitants of the town of Litchfield, Connecticut* (published 1845), p 230.

[20] Dittenhafer, Miriam Marcy. *Godshall Family History,* p. 137.

[21] *1800 United States Census*, New York, New York. Year: 1800; Census Place: New York Ward 5, New York, New York; Roll: 23; Page: 755; Image: 136; Family History Library Film: 193711.

[22] Dittenhafer, Miriam Marcy. *Godshall Family History,* p 139.

[23] Dittenhafer, Miriam Marcy. *Godshall Family History,* p. 143.

[24] *American Citizen*, 1806-03-10; Vol. 6; Iss: 1850; p 3.

[25] *Commercial Advertiser*, 1806-03-26; Vol. IX; Iss: 3415; p. 2.

[26] *American Citizen*, 1808-08-26; Vol. 9; Iss: 2613; p. 4.

[27] *1810 United States Census*, New York, New York. Year: 1810; Census Place: New York Ward 10, New York, New York; Roll: 32; Page: 647; Image: 0181386; Family History Library Film: 00325.

[28] *New York City Directory, Longworth's*; Year: 1810; p. 384.

[29] *New York City Directory, Longworth's*; Year: 1811; p. 315.

[30] *New York City Directory, Longworth's*; Year: 1812; p. 335.

[31] Ancestry.com, U.S., War of 1812 Service Records, 1812-1815. Direct Data Capture, comp. *U.S., War of 1812 Service Records, 1812-1815* [database on-line]. Provo, UT, USA: Ancestry.com Operations Inc, 1999. Original data: National Archives and Records Administration. *Index to the Compiled Military Service Records for the Volunteer Soldiers Who Served During the War of 1812.* Washington, D.C.: National Archives and Records Administration. M602, 234 rolls.

[32] *New York City Directory, Longworth's*; Year: 1813; p. 329.

[33] *New York City Directory, Citizen's Directory & Strangers Guide*; Year: 1814; p. 425.

[34] *New York City Directory, Longworth's*; Year: 1815; p. 431.

[35] *New York City Directory, Longworth's*; Year: 1816; p. 443.

[36] Dittenhafer, Miriam Marcy. *Godshall Family History,* p. 141; Original data: Longworth's New York City Directory, 1817.

[37] Dittenhafer, Miriam Marcy. *Godshall Family History,* p. 139.

[38] Dittenhafer, Miriam Marcy. *Godshall Family History,* p. 141.

[39] *New York City Directory, Longworth's*; Year: 1818; p. 346.

[40] *New York City Directory, Longworth's*; Year: 1819; p. 415.

[41] *New York City Directory, Longworth's*; Year: 1820; p. 463.

[42] *New York City Directory, Longworth's*; Year: 1821-22; p. 458.

[43] *1820 United States Census*, New York, New York. 1820 U S Census; Census Place: New York Ward 2, New York, New York; Page: 93; NARA Roll: M33_77; Image: 59.

[44] *New York City Directory, Longworth's*; Year: 1822-23; p. 468.

[45] Dittenhafer, Miriam Marcy. *Godshall Family History,* p. 90.

[46] 1850 United States Census, Year: 1850; Census Place: Philadelphia Lombard Ward, Philadelphia, Pennsylvania; Roll: M432_812; Page: 197B; Image: 402.

[47] Dittenhafer, Miriam Marcy. *Godshall Family History,* p. 90.

[48] Dittenhafer, Miriam Marcy. *Godshall Family History,* p. 93-95.

[49] Dittenhafer, Miriam Marcy. *Godshall Family History,* p. 95.

[50] *McElroy's Philadelphia City Directory 1839.* Philadelphia: A. McElroy & Co., 1839; p. 121.

[51] *McElroy's Philadelphia City Directory 1840.* Philadelphia: A. McElroy & Co., 1840, p. 121; Year: 1841, p. 128; Year: 1842, p. 127; Year: 1843, p. 133; Year: 1844, p. 150; Year: 1845, p. 172; Year: 1846, p. 170.

[52] *McElroy's Philadelphia City Directory 1847.* Philadelphia: A. McElroy & Co., 1847; p. 166.

[53] *McElroy's Philadelphia City Directory 1848.* Philadelphia: A. McElroy & Co., 1848; p. 171.

[54] *McElroy's Philadelphia City Directory 1849.* Philadelphia: A. McElroy & Co., 1849, p. 179; Year: 1850, p. 198.

[55] *1850 United States Census*, Philadelphia, PA. Year: 1850; Census Place: Philadelphia Lombard Ward, Philadelphia, Pennsylvania; Roll: M432_812; Page: 197B; Image: 402.

[56] *McElroy's Philadelphia City Directory 1852.* Philadelphia: A. McElroy & Co., 1852; p. 213.

[57] *McElroy's Philadelphia City Directory 1857.* Philadelphia: A. McElroy & Co., 1857, p. 319.

[58] *McElroy's Philadelphia City Directory 1858.* Philadelphia: A. McElroy & Co., 1858; p. 322.

[59] *McElroy's Philadelphia City Directory 1859.* Philadelphia: A. McElroy & Co., 1859, p. 339; Year: 1860, p. 465.

[60] *1860 United States Census*, Philadelphia, PA. Year: 1860; Census Place: Philadelphia Ward 15, Philadelphia, Pennsylvania; Roll: M653_1165; Page: 684; Image: 690; Family History Library Film: 805165.

[61] Dittenhafer, Miriam Marcy. *Godshall Family History,* p. 93.

[62] *McElroy's Philadelphia City Directory 1861.* Philadelphia: A. McElroy & Co., 1861; p. 467.

[63] *McElroy's Philadelphia City Directory 1862.* Philadelphia: A. McElroy & Co., 1862, p. 318; Year: 1863, p. 370.

[64] *McElroy's Philadelphia City Directory 1864.* Philadelphia: A. McElroy & Co., 1864, p. 353; Year: 1865, p. 337; Year: 1866, p. 353; Year: 1867, p. 445.

[65] *1870 United States Census*, Philadelphia, PA. Year: 1870; Census Place: Philadelphia Ward 26 Precinct 9 (2nd Enum), Philadelphia, Pennsylvania; Roll: M593_1442; Page: 338A; Image: 289; Family History Library Film: 552941.

[66] Dittenhafer, Miriam Marcy. *Godshall Family History,* p. 90, 92.

[67] Dittenhafer, Miriam Marcy. *Godshall Family History,* p. 90.

[68] Obituary of Charles Huhn. *Philadelphia Inquirer,* 8 Nov 1872.

[69] *1900 United States Census*, Philadelphia, PA. Year: 1900; Census Place: Philadelphia Ward 24, Philadelphia, Pennsylvania; Roll: 1466; Page: 5A; Enumeration District: 0578; FHL microfilm: 1241466.

[70] Dittenhafer, Miriam Marcy. *Godshall Family History,* p. 90, 92.

[71] Marriages 1826-1875, p. 54. Originals housed at the Presbyterian Historical Society, 425 Lombard St Philadelphia, PA 19147.

1752 petition to the General Assembly asking permission to pay the annual ecclesiastical taxes to Bethlem rather than to Litchfield.

THOMAS WAUGH AND HIS BROTHERS SIGNED THIS

The Wooldridge Lineage

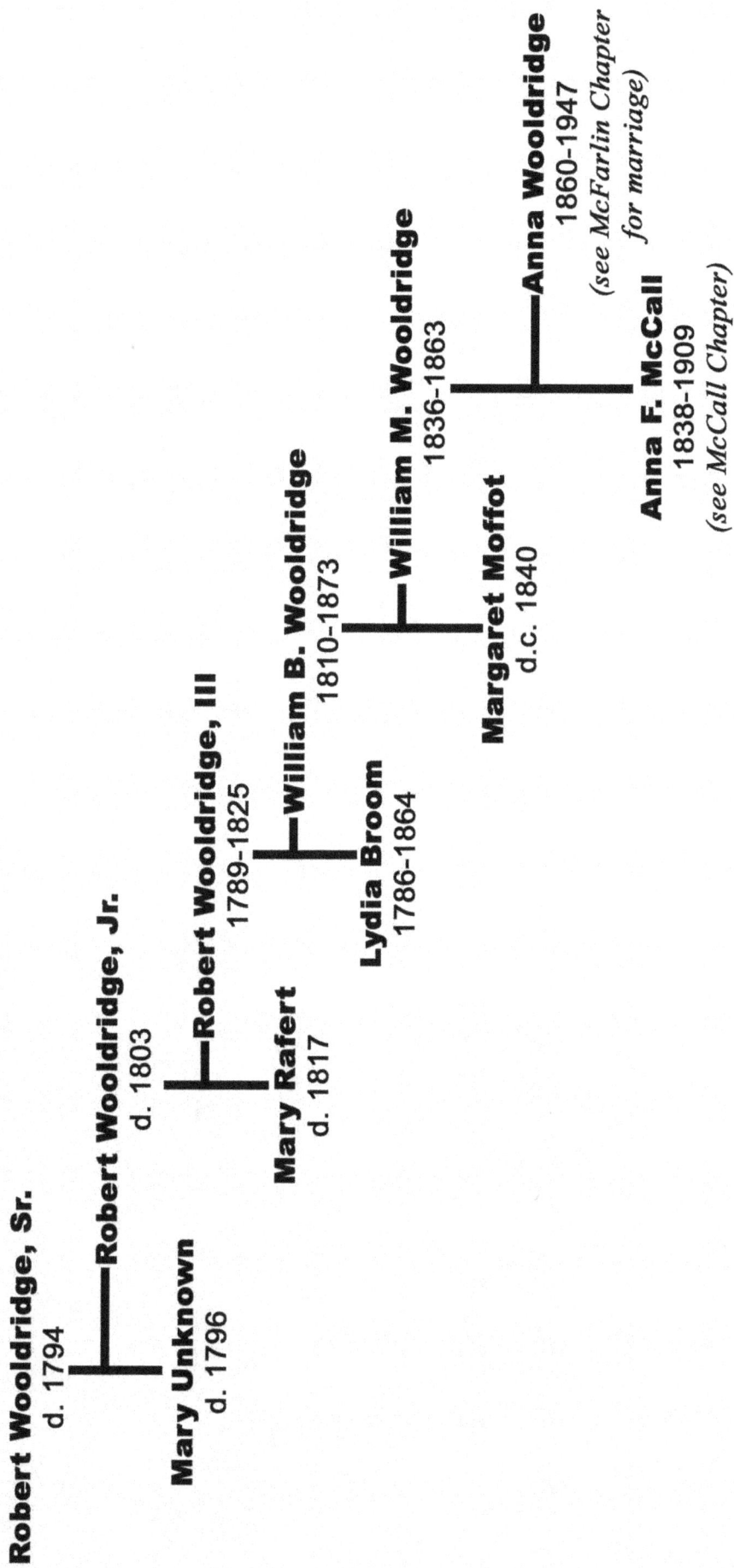

Robert Wooldridge, Sr.
d. 1794

Robert Wooldridge, Jr.
d. 1803

Mary Unknown
d. 1796

Robert Wooldridge, III
1789-1825

Mary Rafert
d. 1817

William B. Wooldridge
1810-1873

Lydia Broom
1786-1864

William M. Wooldridge
1836-1863

Margaret Moffot
d.c. 1840

Anna Wooldridge
1860-1947
(see McFarlin Chapter
for marriage)

Anna F. McCall
1838-1909
(see McCall Chapter)

The Wooldridge Lineage

In the beginning, there was confusion...

The earliest known Wooldridge in Philadelphia, PA, is a Robert Wooldridge, who was a mariner captured by the British on 8 January 1777 during the Revolutionary War. He was released by the British only after he swore to never take up arms against them again. To this end, he petitioned the Continental Congress in 1778 to allow him to serve the United States in a non–mariner capacity, that he might not break his word. They allowed him to do so, and he was at that time employed by McAndrew helping to clean the river.[1]

Fast forward to 1793. There is a Thomas Wooldridge, also a mariner, living on 5th near Lombard in Philadelphia, PA.[2]

In 1794, there is a Robert Wooldridge, laborer, living at 120 South 5th Street, Philadelphia, PA.[3]

The vagueness of Thomas' address means that he and Robert could very well have lived at the same address, since they both lived on 5th Street. Some questions that need to be answered:

- Are Thomas and Robert brothers? Since Thomas does not appear after 1793, and Robert does not appear after 1794, it is likely they both passed away. In which case they were likely of an age, implying that they could have been brothers—especially if they were residing at the same address.

- How are they related to 1778 Robert Wooldridge, mariner turned laborer, if at all? Robert 1778 could be their father, of course. But the fact that Thomas and Robert the Laborer both died in the 1790s says they were probably around 50–60 at that time, which would make their births closer to 1740, or even 1730. What makes this interesting is that one would assume a mariner during the Revolutionary War to be in his 20s or 30s—the prime of life. Which means that Robert of 1778 and Robert the Laborer would have been about the same age. Are they, in fact, the same person? Were Thomas and Robert 1778 brothers who both were mariners, but Robert forsook it to keep his word and never returned, staying employed as a laborer until his death in 1794?

- I could not locate either Thomas or Robert on the 1790 Philadelphia Census. Perhaps they had not arrived in Philadelphia at this time, or were away working?

In 1795, both Thomas and Robert were gone, leaving a widowed Mary Wooldridge, a huckster, living "near 98 South 5th Street."[4] Robert's 1794 address, 120 South 5th, could be considered near 98 South 5th. I believe this Mary is Robert the Laborer's widow, because had she been Thomas' widow, she would have appeared in 1794, when he disappeared. 1796 found her still "near 98 South 5th" still working as a huckster.[5] She does not appear after this time.

This brings us to the first certain couple in our Wooldridge lineage:

Robert Wooldridge, Jr., (d.c. 1803) and Mary Rafert (d.c. 1817)

Robert the Mariner makes his first appearance in the 1798 Philadelphia City Directory. His address was "between Lombard and South Streets on 5th."[6] That address leaves us with a little gray as to who his father was—Thomas or Robert. Thomas was a mariner, and he did live on 5th near Lombard. Robert was not a mariner, but he also lived on 5th Street, at 120 South 5th. Because the name Thomas does NOT carry down this line, but the name Robert occurs regularly, I believe Robert the Mariner to be Robert the Laborer's son.

Robert married Mary Rafert on 9 September 1777 in Gloria Dei Church (now Old Swedes' Church).[7]

The 1800 Census found Robert Wooldridge, Jr., and family living in the Cedar Ward of Philadelphia, PA. In the household there were 2 boys under age 10, 2 males over 45 (one is Robert, the other perhaps a brother?), 1 girl 10–16, 1 woman 25–44, and 1 woman over 45 (probably Robert's wife, Mary). Another possibility is that 1 man and 1 woman 45+ were Mary's parents, and Robert was 45+ and Mary was in her early 40s, not yet 45.[8]

The 1801 City Directory found Robert the Mariner living at "the next house after 118 South 5th Street."[9] The next house after 118 would be 120 South 5th Street—the exact address of Robert the Laborer and his widow Mary. This is why I believe Robert to be their son.

In 1802, Robert and family lived at 154 South 5th Street.[10]

Robert Wooldridge, Jr., does not appear again in any City Directory. Instead, 1805 found his widow, Mary, living at 154 South 5th Street.[11]

In the 1807 Directory, we meet **Robert Wooldridge, III,** an oak cooper, who resides at 154 South 5th Street.[12]

Mary Rafert Wooldridge, Robert the Mariner's widow, made her final appearance in the City Directory in 1817, still living at 154 South 5th.[13] Therefore her death was probably around 1817.

Robert Wooldridge, III, (c. 1789–c. 1825) and Lydia Broom (1786–1864)

Robert the Oak Cooper was one of the boys under age 10 on the 1800 Census, which could have put his birth as early as 1789 or 1790. For him to be listed in the Directory in 1807,[14] he would have had to be of age, which makes the 1789 date more likely (as he would have been 18 in 1807).

There was a Wooldridge and Ellis Oak Coopers business, located at 13 Little Water from 1806 to 1811.[15] This was likely to be Robert's business, as there were no other Wooldridge oak coopers in the Directory—and in 1811 Thomas Ellis lived at the same address as Robert, 15 Swanson St.[16] That would mean Robert went into business at age 17, believable for the time period—teenagers were considered adults back then, especially so when the father had died.

So, in 1807 Robert the Oak Cooper lived with his mother, Mary, at 154 South 5th Street.[17] By 1811 he lived with his family and his business partner at 15 Swanson Street.[18]

On 18 December 1806, Robert married Lydia Broom in Old Saint Paul's Catholic Church in Philadelphia, PA.[19] Robert and Lydia had 5 known children:[20] [21]

Robert, IV (1808–1840) – *married Margaret Watt.*
William B. (1810–1873) – *married Margaret Moffot, then Rachel Clarke, then Mary Unknown.*
Mary (1814–1839) – *married Parker Smith.*
James W. (b. 1815) – *married Catherine Unknown.*
Jane (c. 1820–1836)

In 1813,[22] 1814,[23] 1816,[24] and 1818,[25] Robert lived at 11 Elmslie's Alley.

In 1820, he lived at Chestnut above 13th. The 1820 Census finds Robert and family in the Middle Ward of Philadelphia, PA. Robert's household consisted of 1 male under 10 (James, 5), 2 males 10–15 (William B., 10, and Robert, 12), 2 males 26–44 (Robert, ~31), 2 females under 10 (Jane, < 1, Mary, 9), 1 female 16–25, and 1 female 26–44 (wife Lydia, 34).[26]

The other male 26–44 could be a brother or brother–in–law, and the female 16–25 could be the other male's wife. Or they could both be siblings of Robert or Lydia.

In 1821[27] and 1822,[28] the family still lived on Chestnut above 13th Street, but in 1823[29] and 1824[30] they lived on 11th above Filbert.

1824 is the last time Robert the Oak Cooper is listed in a Directory, meaning he died in either 1823 or 1824 (sometimes a deceased person is listed the year after he died, depending on the printing schedule). He would have been about 36 years old.

Widow Lydia and her family dropped out of sight from 1824 until they reappeared in the Directory in 1829.[31] At that time, they lived at 75 Christian St., Philadelphia, PA, where they resided until at least 1833.[32]

At some point between 1833 and 1836, the family moved to 3 Boyd's Avenue .[33]

Lydia then vanished until 1850, when she appears on the 1850 Census. Lydia (66) was in the home of Benjamin (68) and Jane Crozier (70).[34] I have no idea why she is living with this couple, rather than with one of her children. Lydia lived with Benjamin and Jane Crozier at 180 Queen at least until 1853, when she again disappeared.[35]

Lydia resurfaced in 1860, living with Henry and Anna McIntyre.[36] Anna is 21, born c. 1839, so not a daughter. Perhaps a granddaughter? Anna and Henry have a 2–year–old daughter, Anna L. Might the L stand for Lydia, her great–grandmother? Lydia's daughter Mary (married to Parker Smith) did have a daughter Ann Smith (b.c. 1838). Mary died in 1839 – perhaps giving birth to Ann?

Lydia Broom Wooldridge died 24 May 1864 at age 78. The funeral was held at the residence of her son William B. Wooldridge.[37]

William B. Wooldridge (1810–1873) and Margaret Moffot (d.c. 1840)

William B. Wooldridge was born on 9 July 1810. He was christened at Old Saint Paul's Catholic Church on 29 March 1815.[38] He and his first wife, Margaret Moffot, married at Trinity Episcopal Church, Philadelphia, PA, on 26 April 1832.[39]

William and Margaret had 4 known children, all born in Pennsylvania:[40] [41]

Emma V. (b. 1834) – *married Henry A. Jones.*
William M. (1836–1863) – *married Anna F. McCall.*
Marietta (b. 1838)
Sarah Jane (b. 1840) – *married Henry W. Buchanan.*

I found an entry in the Church of the Evangelist (Catholic) for William B. Wooldridge. The notation says (W number 186). The W seems to mean Wedding, based on other entries. The date was 7 March 1841. This could be his marriage to Rachel Clarke, who appears in the 1850 Census. If this chronology is correct, Margaret may have died giving birth to Sarah Jane in 1840.[42]

His second wife Rachael Clarke was born in 1811. He was born in Pennsylvania, she in New Jersey. They had at least 4 children together:[43]

Rachael (b. 1843)[44]
Elizabeth (1845–1850)
George (b. 1848)
Rebecca (b.c. 1851)

William B. makes his first appearance in the City Directories in 1835,[45] as a painter living on Christian at Front Street. This might be 75 Christian, where his mother, Lydia, lived, but more likely 76 Christian, where William and his family lived for many years. William's occupation and address were the same in 1836,[46] when we know his mother lived elsewhere.

A *Philadelphia Inquirer* article on 12 January 1837[47] lists William among those who gave a toast at the Typographic Festival marking the Fifth Anniversary of the Philadelphia Typographical Society. So it is clear that by this time he has moved into the profession he holds the rest of his life—a printer (also known as a compositor).

In 1839,[48] William and his family still resided at 76 Christian St., where they lived until 1843.[49]

In the 1840 Census, William B. Wooldridge lived in Philadelphia's 2nd Ward, Southwark. His household consisted of: 1 white male under age 6 (William M., 4), 1 white male between 20–29 (William B., 29), 1 white female under age 6 (Marietta, 2), 1 white female between 5–9 (Emma, 7), and 1 white female between 20–29 (Margaret, 29).[50]

In 1843, the Wooldridges left 76 Christian and lived at 22 Beck St.[51] This was only temporary, as in 1844[52] they moved to 148 Carpenter St., where they lived until 1849,[53] when they moved to 439 South 6th Street.

In 1850, William (39) and family lived in the Southwark 4th Ward in Philadelphia, PA. William was a printer. The large household consisted of wife Rachael (39), and children Emma (16), William (14), Marietta (12), Sarah (10), Rachael (7), Elizabeth (4), and George (2), as well as William's mother–in–law, Rachael Clarke (65). Children William, Marietta, Sarah, and Rachael were all attending school.[54]

William was in the *Philadelphia Inquirer* on 18 January 1853. In the Column: "LOCAL ITEMS":

"Beautiful Daguerreotype – One of the most perfect pictures ever taken by the Daguerrean process has just been exhibited to us. It consists of the photographs of William B. Wooldridge, an active member of the association of Printers, together with the likenesses of his entire family, making nine persons, all told. It is a beautiful family group, artistically taken by Mr. M. A. Root, and it may well be considered another proud triumph of his superior skill."[55]

I am trying to locate a copy of this daguerreotype, but it is like searching for a needle in a haystack.

The Wooldridge family lived at 439 South 6th Street until 1852,[56] when they moved to "SW corner of Parker and Carpenter," where they lived until at least 1858.[57] This may also be their residence in 1860, listed as 1000 Parker.[58]

Rachael Clarke Wooldridge died in September 1853. Her funeral was at the Church of the Evangelist (Catholic) on 25 September 1853, and she was buried at Philanthropic Cemetery.[59]

In 1860, William (49) appeared with third wife, Mary (45), and 4 children: Marietta (21), Sarah J. (19), George W. (12), and Rebecca (9). After Rachael's death in 1853, William married Mary from Massachusetts. Minor daughters Elizabeth and Rachael are also missing. Rachael would have been 17, so it is possible she had married. Elizabeth, however, would have only been 14, so it seems likely she died.[60]

In 1861[61] and 1862,[62] William and family lived at 206 Stamper's Alley. At some time before 25 July 1862,[63] William moved to 310 Union St., where the family lived until at least 1867.[64]

The 1870 Census lists a James Wooldridge, printer, living with daughter Rebecca in Ward 4, District 14 of Philadelphia, PA.[65] Although the name is wrong, I believe this is Rebecca and her father, William B. Wooldridge. William did have a brother James, but James was a painter and did not have a daughter Rebecca.

William B. Wooldridge died 5 March 1873 at age 62.[66] The funeral was at daughter Emma's house, 309 Pine. It was usual to have a funeral from the residence of the deceased, so possibly he lived there in his last few years. The death certificate said he was married, so perhaps his third wife was still alive—or it was incorrect, as they so often were. He was buried 8 March 1873 at Philanthropic Cemetery in Philadelphia, PA.[67]

William M. Wooldridge (1836–1863) and Anna McCall (1838–1909)
(see the McCall Lineage chapter)

William M. Wooldridge was born in Pennsylvania in July 1836.[68] In 1854, William made the newspaper for using a pocket knife to carve a handsaw cross, a square and compass, several rings, miniature chairs, links of a chain, and other articles out of a coconut shell.[69] One assumes this was for an art contest of some kind, although this was not stated in the part of the article that was clipped.

At some point prior to 1856, William moved to Baltimore, MD. While living there in 1856, he remodeled the City Hotel, run by David Baraum.[70] In 1857, William exhibited some of his drawings in Baltimore: the country residence of Edwin M. Taylor, Staunton, VA; the villa for William E. Pratt, Charlotte County, VA, and the villa for Col. Charles S. Dorsey, of Ellicott's Mills, MD.[71]

By August 1857, William was back in Philadelphia, PA, as architect for the Olivet Baptist Church at 6th and Federal Streets, "presided over by the Rev. N.B. Baldwin. William's design was in the American style of architecture (lately introduced), will be 58 feet front by 115 feet deep, the audience room will seat from 1,000 to 1,100 people. The spire will be an octagon supported by Ionic columns, 24 feet at the base, and rising to a tapering 205 feet."[72] The *Baltimore American* also ran a piece about this church, adding that the "chaste" pulpit "was covered by a neat pediment supported by 8 columns and pilasters and surmounted by a very rich and graceful scroll ornament. The Sunday school, session, and classrooms are in the basement story." This article has the dimensions of the building as 56 feet by 102 deep. They call William "of Baltimore."[73] Unfortunately, this church is no longer standing.

William married Anna McCall 29 November 1857.[74][75] He was 21; she was 19.

William and Anna moved a great deal, as can be seen in the birthplaces of their children:[76] [77]

Charles (b. 1859) – *born in Maryland.*
Anna (1860–1947) – *born in Ohio. Married Edward Arthur McFarlin, Jr.*
William C. (b. 1862) – *born in Maryland.*

William lived with his father until his marriage to Anna. In 1859, he and Anna were in Maryland, where their oldest son, Charles, was born.[78]

In 1860, William was in Cincinnati, Ohio, to try to sell his public fountain design. William designed a letter box, public hydrant, and lamppost all in one. This was examined by Cincinnati's City Council, although the newspaper article about it does not say if the Council adopted William's fountains.[79]

In June 1860, just 6 weeks after young Anna was born in Cincinnati, OH, the Wooldridge family was living in Edgefield, Tennessee. William (24) was an architect. Anna (22) was busy with Charles (1) and 2–month–old Anna. To help her, there was 20–year–old Mary Rone, a domestic from Ireland.[80]

William M. Wooldridge is our only Civil War ancestor. Originally, Capt. William M. Wooldridge was part of the Sappers and Miners Fire Zouaves corps, attached to Col. Baker's Brigade out of Philadelphia, PA. The entire corps was made up of practical mechanics, except the officers, who were all civil engineers. With William were officers First Lt. James Patterson and Second Lt. William Carman.[81] A few days later an article reprinted from the *Baltimore American* stated that Baker's Brigade's Fifth Regiment had arrived in Washington, DC, along with the attached engineering corps headed by Capt. William M. Wooldridge. This article states that Wooldridge is "well known in this city as a practical architect in the office of R. Snowden Andrews, who is now a State prisoner in Fort Lafayette."[82] (Andrews was apparently released, for he went on to a distinguished career with the Confederate artillery.)

On 24 July 1862, William was made a captain of Philadelphia Light Guards, Company F.[83] He is mentioned in a newspaper recruitment advertisement for the Light Guards on 25 July 1862.[84]

In September 1862, William transferred to Company G, 121st PA Infantry under Col. Biddle.[85] He mustered in on 30 August 1862 in Washington, DC. He appears also on the muster–in roll of 12 September 1862 in Washington, DC. On 31 October 1862, his unit was still in Washington, DC, and William was listed as "present." He appears on the November–December 1862 Washington, DC, muster-in roll, listed as "absent with leave: sick leave at Clarion Hotel in Washington, DC". The muster roll was for both November and December.[86]

William and Anna's youngest child, William C., was born in Maryland in 1862, probably during Capt. William's time stationed in Washington, DC.

William was with his unit until injured 13 December 1862 at Fredericksburg, VA. A newspaper article about the Fredericksburg engagement states that William was injured but still on duty.[87] William applied for a leave of absence on 5 January 1863. He was granted this leave by the medical officer, due to the doctor's finding him "suffering from enlargement and tenderness of the liver. Inflammation of kidneys and Neuralgia. Also, gunshot wound (flesh) of right elbow received in action at Fredericksburg, VA, Dec 13, 1862."[88]

William returned to Philadelphia, PA, while on leave. On 12 February 1863, an Army medical officer examined William at William's home at 1443 South 5th Street. William was found to have chronic bronchitis and general debility and therefore was unfit to return to duty and should resign.[89]

On 24 February 1863, Capt. William M. Wooldridge sent a letter of resignation to his superiors, which was duly accepted.[90]

On 2 July 1863, at age 27, William. M. Wooldridge died of typhoid fever (likely contracted during the war). The funeral was out of his home at 1443 South 5th Street.[91] His occupation was described as a draftsman. William was buried 5 July 1863 in the Wharton Street ME Church Vault in Philadelphia, PA.[92]

In 1863, Anna McCall Wooldridge was widowed with 3 very young children. However, as a single mother she got a job in millinery. Their address was 209 North 9th Street,[93] but that may have been the shop where she worked, because 1864 finds her running a boardinghouse out of 1443 South 5th Street—William's post–war address.[94]

Anna married George Nitzky 5 April 1866 in St. Paul's Episcopal Church in Philadelphia, PA.[95] Anna and George had 4 known children:[96] [97]

George, Jr. (b. 1867)
Francis (1869–bef. 1880)
Carrie (b. 1871)
Elsie G. (b. 1884) – *married James F. Brubaker.*

In 1870, in Ward 26, District 84 of Philadelphia, PA, Anna F. McCall Wooldridge Nitzky (33) and second husband George A. Nitzky (24) lived with her 2 sons Charles (12) and William (8), and their sons George A. (2) and Francis (9 months). Also living with them were Anna's sister Ida McCall (18) and George's brother Wilhelm (21). There was also a George Clegg (28). Missing was 10-year-old Anna Wooldridge, who we know lived because she is our direct ancestor! So where was she?[98]

Given young Anna's age and the fact that I cannot find her listed elsewhere on the 1870 Census, I believe that she did live with the Nitzky family but was somehow overlooked when the Census was taken – perhaps by human error on the part of the Census taker. Censuses can be wildly incorrect on some very basic information.

In 1880, Anna McCall Wooldridge Nitzky (38) and George Nitzky (34) lived at 649 Federal Street in Philadelphia. He was a retail grocer, and their children together were: George (13) and Carrie (9). Also living with them at the house at 649 Federal St. in Philadelphia were Anna Wooldridge (20), who worked as a milliner, and William Wooldridge (18), who was an apprentice upholsterer.[99]

The 1900 Census found Anna McCall Wooldridge Nitzky (61) living in Sharon Hill, PA, on Woodland Avenue. She had been married for 33 years to George Nitzky (54), who had emigrated from Germany in 1858. He was a butcher who owned (with a mortgage) the house they lived in. Another daughter, Elise (15), lived with them, as did a niece, Amy Wilshire (22). This Census also states that Anna had borne 14 children, although only 5 of them were still living in 1900.[100] I only have the names of 7 children.

It is unknown when George Nitzky died. Anna F. McCall Wooldridge Nitzky died at age 71 on 22 March 1909. She died of what appears to read "congestion of brain." She lived at 619 West Chestnut in Lancaster, PA, at the time of her death.[101] It may be of interest to note that on her death certificate, her mother's name is not listed as Margaret Strubing. It is Margaret, but the last name is Ferguson. The mistake of calling her mother Ferguson adds to my circumstantial evidence that the parents of her father, Charles, were Beekman McCall and Anna Ferguson. I believe the F. in Anna F. McCall is Anna Ferguson McCall. It was common for women to have their mother's maiden names as middle names, so it would have been natural for someone to assume that the Ferguson was her MOTHER's maiden name, rather than her GRANDMOTHER's. The death certificate also says her father was born in North Carolina, not South Carolina, so this document is riddled with human error. The death certificate seems to indicate she was to be buried in Philadelphia, PA, but no clear cemetery is listed.

Her daughter *Anna Wooldridge* married Edward Arthur McFarlin, Jr. They married in 1884.[102] He was 22; she was 24. (*See The McFarlin Lineage chapter.*)

[1] Copy of Robert Wooldridge's Petition to Congress, 1778.

[2] *Hardie's Philadelphia City Directory, 1793.* James Hardie, ed., Philadelphia: T. Dobson, 1793; p. 160.

[3] *Hardie's Philadelphia City Directory, 1794.* James Hardie, ed., Philadelphia: Jacob Johnson & Co., 1794; p. 170.

[4] *Hogan's Philadelphia City Directory, 1795.* Edmund Hogan, ed., Philadelphia: Francis & Robert Bailey, 1795; p. 134.

[5] *Stephens's Philadelphia City Directory, 1796.* Thomas Stephens, ed., Philadelphia: W. Woodward, 1796; p. 203.

[6] *Stafford's Philadelphia City Directory, 1798.* Cornelius William Stafford, ed., Philadelphia: William W. Woodward, 1798; p. 156.

[7] Old Swedes Church (Gloria Dei) church records. Ancestry.com. *Pennsylvania, Marriage Records, 1700-1821* [database on-line]. Provo, UT, USA: Ancestry.com Operations Inc, 2011. Original data: *Pennsylvania Marriage Records.* Harrisburg, PA: Pennsylvania Archives Printed Series, 1876. Series 2, Series 6.

[8] *1800 United States Census*, Philadelphia, PA. Year: 1800; Census Place: Philadelphia Cedar Ward, Philadelphia, Pennsylvania; Roll: 43; Page: 290,291; Image: 123; Family History Library Film: 363346.

[9] *Stafford's Philadelphia City Directory, 1801.* Cornelius William Stafford, ed., Philadelphia: William W. Woodward, 1801; p. 66.

[10] *Robinson's Philadelphia City Directory, 1802.* James Robinson, ed., Philadelphia: William W. Woodward, 1802; p. 266.

[11] *Robinson's Philadelphia City Directory, 1817.* Philadelphia: James Robinson, 1805; p. 261.

[12] *Robinson's Philadelphia City Directory, 1807.* James Robinson, ed., Philadelphia: W. Woodhouse, 1807; p. 314.

[13] *Robinson's Philadelphia City Directory, 1817.* Philadelphia: James Robinson, 1817; p. 478.

[14] *Robinson's Philadelphia City Directory, 1807.* James Robinson, ed., Philadelphia: W. Woodhouse, 1807; p. 314.

[15] *Robinson's Philadelphia City Directory, 1806.* Philadelphia: James Robinson, 1806, p. 291; Year: 1807, p. 314; Year: 1808, p. 326; Year: 1809, p. 319; Year: 1810, p. 312; *Aitken's,* Year: 1811, p. 360.

[16] *Aitken's Philadelphia City Directory, 1811.* Philadelphia: Jane Aitken, 1811; p. 360.

[17] *Robinson's Philadelphia City Directory, 1807.* James Robinson, ed., Philadelphia: W. Woodhouse, 1807; p. 314.

[18] *Aitken's Philadelphia City Directory, 1811.* Philadelphia: Jane Aitken, 1811; p. 360.

[19] Old Saint Paul's Roman Catholic Church records. Historical Society of Pennsylvania; *Historic Pennsylvania Church and Town Records*; Reel: *240.*

[20] Church Baptismal Records, Old St. Paul's Roman Catholic Church, Philadelphia, PA. Historical Society of Pennsylvania; *Historic Pennsylvania Church and Town Records*; Reel: *240.*

[21] Obituary of Jane Wooldridge. *Philadelphia Inquirer*, March, 25, 1836.

[22] *Paxton's Philadelphia City Directory, 1813.* John A. Paxton, ed., Philadelphia: B & T Kite, 1813; p. 463.

[23] *Kite's Philadelphia City Directory, 1814.* Philadelphia: B & T Kite, 1814; p. 511.

[24] *Robinson's Philadelphia City Directory, 1816.* Philadelphia: James Robinson, 1816; p. 464.

[25] *Paxton's Philadelphia City Directory, 1818.* John Adems Paxton, ed. Philadelphia: E & R Parker, 1818; p. 383.

[26] *1820 United States Census*, Philadelphia, PA. 1820 U S Census; Census Place: Philadelphia Middle Ward, Philadelphia, Pennsylvania; Page: 74; NARA Roll: M33_108; Image: 86.

[27] *McCarty & Davis' Philadelphia City Directory, 1821.* Philadelphia: McCarty & Davis, 1821; p. 489.

[28] *McCarty & Davis' Philadelphia City Directory, 1822.* Philadelphia: McCarty & Davis, 1822; p. 527.

[29] *DeSilver's Philadelphia City Directory, Desilver's, 1823.* Philadelphia: Robert DeSilver, 1823; p. 385.

[30] *DeSilver's Philadelphia City Directory, Desilver's, 1824.* Philadelphia: Robert DeSilver, 1824; p. 405.

[31] *DeSilver's Philadelphia City Directory, Desilver's, 1829.* Philadelphia: Robert DeSilver, 1829; p. 216.

[32] *DeSilver's Philadelphia City Directory, Desilver's, 1833.* Philadelphia: Robert DeSilver, 1833; p. 237.

[33] Obituary of Jane Wooldridge, *Philadelphia Inquirer*, 25 March 1836.

[34] *1850 United States Census*, Philadelphia, PA. Year: 1850; Census Place: Southwark Ward 4, Philadelphia, Pennsylvania; Roll: M432_822; Page: 281B; Image: 87.

[35] *McElroy's Philadelphia City Directory 1853.* Philadelphia: A. McElroy & Co., 1853; p. 455.

[36] *1860 United States Census*, Philadelphia, PA. Year: 1860; Census Place: Philadelphia Ward 1 Precinct 4, Philadelphia, Pennsylvania; Roll: M653_1151; Page: 260; Image: 264; Family History Library Film: 805151.

[37] Obituary of Lydia Wooldridge. *Philadelphia Inquirer*, May 25, 1864.

[38] Church Records, Old St. Paul's Roman Catholic Church, Philadelphia, PA. Historical Society of Pennsylvania; *Historic Pennsylvania Church and Town Records*; Reel: *240*.

[39] Trinity Episcopal Church records. Historical Society of Pennsylvania; *Historic Pennsylvania Church and Town Records*; Reel: *977*.

[40] *1850 United States Census*, Philadelphia, PA. Year: 1850; Census Place: Southwark Ward 4, Philadelphia, Pennsylvania; Roll: M432_822; Page: 336A; Image: 198.

[41] *1860 United States Census*, Philadelphia, PA. Year: 1860; Census Place: Philadelphia Ward 2, Philadelphia, Pennsylvania; Roll: M653_1152; Page: 168; Image: 172; Family History Library Film: 805152.

[42] Church of the Evagelist (Catholic) records. Historical Society of Pennsylvania; *Historic Pennsylvania Church and Town Records*; Reel: *228*.

[43] *1850 United States Census*, Philadelphia, PA. Year: 1850; Census Place: Southwark Ward 4, Philadelphia, Pennsylvania; Roll: M432_822; Page: 336A; Image: 198.

[44] Church of the Evangelist (Catholic) records. This baptismal record lists Rachel's parents as William and Rachel, and her sponsor as her grandmother Lydia.

[45] *DeSilver's Philadelphia City Directory, Desilver's, 1835-36*. Philadelphia: Robert DeSilver, 1835-36; p. 197.

[46] *DeSilver's Philadelphia City Directory, Desilver's, 1835-36*. Philadelphia: Robert DeSilver, 1835-36; p. 197.

[47] *Philadelphia Inquirer* article, 12 January 1837.

[48] *McElroy's Philadelphia City Directory 1839*. Philadelphia: A. McElroy & Co., 1839; p. 281.

[49] *McElroy's Philadelphia City Directory 1842*. Philadelphia: A. McElroy & Co., 1842; p. 296.

[50] *1840 United States Census*, Philadelphia, PA. Year: 1840; Census Place: Southwark Ward 2, Philadelphia, Pennsylvania; Roll: 486; Page: 72; Image: 633; Family History Library Film: 0020555.

[51] *McElroy's Philadelphia City Directory 1843*. Philadelphia: A. McElroy & Co., 1843; p. 310.

[52] *McElroy's Philadelphia City Directory 1844*. Philadelphia: A. McElroy & Co., 1844; p. 347.

[53] *McElroy's Philadelphia City Directory 1849*. Philadelphia: A. McElroy & Co., 1849; p. 415.

[54] *1850 United States Census*, Philadelphia, PA. Year: 1850; Census Place: Southwark Ward 4, Philadelphia, Pennsylvania; Roll: M432_822; Page: 336A; Image: 198.

[55] *Philadelphia Inquirer*, 18 Jan 1853.

[56] *McElroy's Philadelphia City Directory 1852*. Philadelphia: A. McElroy & Co., 1852; p. 485.

[57] *McElroy's Philadelphia City Directory 1858*. Philadelphia: A. McElroy & Co., 1858; p. 749.

[58] *McElroy's Philadelphia City Directory 1860*. Philadelphia: A. McElroy & Co., 1860; p. 1094.

[59] Church of the Evangelist (Catholic) records. Historical Society of Pennsylvania; *Historic Pennsylvania Church and Town Records*; Reel: *227*.

[60] *1860 United States Census*, Philadelphia, PA. Year: 1860; Census Place: Philadelphia Ward 2, Philadelphia, Pennsylvania; Roll: M653_1152; Page: 168; Image: 172; Family History Library Film: 805152.

[61] *McElroy's Philadelphia City Directory 1861*. Philadelphia: A. McElroy & Co., 1861; p. 1087.

[62] *McElroy's Philadelphia City Directory 1862*. Philadelphia: A. McElroy & Co., 1862; p. 735.

[63] *Philadelphia Inquirer* obituary for Sarah Jane Wooldridge Buchanan, 25 July 1862.

[64] *McElroy's Philadelphia City Directory 1867*. Philadelphia: A. McElroy & Co., 1867; p. 993.

[65] *1870 United States Census*, Philadelphia, PA. Year: 1870; Census Place: Philadelphia Ward 4 District 14, Philadelphia, Pennsylvania; Roll: M593_1390; Page: 357A; Image: 719; Family History Library Film: 552889.

[66] Death certificate of William B. Wooldridge. Ancestry.com. *Philadelphia, Pennsylvania, Death Certificates Index, 1803-1915* [database on-line]. Provo, UT, USA: Ancestry.com Operations, Inc., 2011. Original data: "Pennsylvania, Philadelphia City Death Certificates, 1803–1915." Index. FamilySearch, Salt Lake City, Utah, 2008, 2010. (https://familysearch.org/pal:/MM9.1.1/J6YT-9ZJ : accessed 11 Nov 2012) From originals housed at the Philadelphia City Archives.

[67] *Philadelphia Inquirer* obituary of William B. Wooldridge, March 7, 1873.

[68] *1860 United States Census*, Edgefield, TN. Year: 1860; Census Place: Edgefield, Davidson, Tennessee; Roll: M653_1246; Page: 496; Image: 797; Family History Library Film: 805246.

[69] *Philadelphia Inquirer*, 2 December 1854.

[70] Captain William M. Wooldridge Papers Scrapbook – photo dated 1856.

[71] *Baltimore American*, 26 October 1857.

[72] *Philadelphia Public Ledger*, 26 August 1857.

[73] *Baltimore American*, 26 November 1857.

[74] Daughters of the American Revolution application - Marjorie Warren Gondolf #533004. Original in possession of Kerry Gans Douglas.

[75] *Philadelphia Bulletin*, 7 December 1857.

[76] *1860 United States Census*, Edgefield, TN. Year: 1860; Census Place: Edgefield, Davidson, Tennessee; Roll: M653_1246; Page: 496; Image: 797; Family History Library Film: 805246.

[77] *1880 United States Census*, Philadelphia, PA. Year: 1880; Census Place: Philadelphia, Philadelphia, Pennsylvania; Roll: 1167; Family History Film: 1255167; Page: 187B; Enumeration District: 044

[78] *1860 United States Census*, Edgefield, TN. Year: 1860; Census Place: Edgefield, Davidson, Tennessee; Roll: M653_1246; Page: 496; Image: 797; Family History Library Film: 805246.

[79] *Cincinnati Times*, 10 July 1860.

[80] *1860 United States Census*, Edgefield, TN. Year: 1860; Census Place: Edgefield, Davidson, Tennessee; Roll: M653_1246; Page: 496; Image: 797; Family History Library Film: 805246.

[81] *Philadelphia Press*, 1 October 1861.

[82] *Philadelphia Inquirer*, 4 October 1861.

[83] *Philadelphia Inquirer*, 24 July 1862.

[84] *Philadelphia Inquirer*, 25 July 1862.

[85] *Philadelphia Press*, 10 September 1862.

[86] National Archives of the USA, Civil War records, Card #s: 22204389, 22211999, 22212070, 22212141, 22212213, 22212816.

[87] *Philadelphia Inquirer*, 25 December 1862.

[88] National Archives of the USA, Civil War records, Card #s: 22204389, 22211999, 22212070, 22212141, 22212213, 22212816.

[89] National Archives of the USA, Civil War records, Card #s: 22204389, 22211999, 22212070, 22212141, 22212213, 22212816.

[90] National Archives of the USA, Civil War records, Card #s: 22204389, 22211999, 22212070, 22212141, 22212213, 22212816.

[91] Death Notice of William M. Wooldridge. *Philadelphia Public Ledger*, 6 July 1863.

[92] Death Certificate of William M. Wooldridge. FamilySearch.org (LDS records), "Pennsylvania, Philadelphia City Death Certificates, 1803-1915," index and images, FamilySearch (https://familysearch.org/pal:/MM9.1.1/J6YT-9ZJ : accessed 11 Nov 2012), Wm. M. Wooldridge, 1863.

[93] *McElroy's Philadelphia City Directory 1863*. Philadelphia: A. McElroy & Co., 1863; p. 825.

[94] *McElroy's Philadelphia City Directory 1864*. Philadelphia: A. McElroy & Co., 1864; p. 818.

[95] St. Paul's Episcopal Church records. Historical Society of Pennsylvania; *Historic Pennsylvania Church and Town Records*; Reel: *373*.

[96] *1870 United States Census*, Philadelphia, PA. Year: 1870; Census Place: Philadelphia Ward 26 District 84, Philadelphia, Pennsylvania; Roll: M593_1413; Page: 156A; Image: 13; Family History Library Film: 552912.

[97] *1880 United States Census*, Philadelphia, PA. Year: 1880; Census Place: Philadelphia, Philadelphia, Pennsylvania; Roll: 1167; Family History Film: 1255167; Page: 187B; Enumeration District: 044

[98] *1870 United States Census*, Philadelphia, PA. Year: 1870; Census Place: Philadelphia Ward 26 District 84, Philadelphia, Pennsylvania; Roll: M593_1413; Page: 156A; Image: 13; Family History Library Film: 552912.

[99] *1880 United States Census*, Philadelphia, PA. Year: 1880; Census Place: Philadelphia, Philadelphia, Pennsylvania; Roll: 1167; Family History Film: 1255167; Page: 187B; Enumeration District: 044

[100] *1900 United States Census*, Philadelphia, PA. Year: 1900; Census Place: Sharon Hill, Delaware, Pennsylvania; Roll: 1405; Page: 3B; Enumeration District: 166; FHL microfilm: 1241405.

[101] Death Certificate of Anna F. McCall Wooldridge Nitzky, File # 24282; Registered # 167. Original housed at PA Department of Health, Division of Vital records, PO Box 1528, New Castle, PA 16103.

[102] Edward McFarlin & Anna Wooldridge, 25th Wedding Anniversary Invitation. Original in possession of Kerry Gans Douglas.

1778 - ROBERT WOOLDRIDGE
PETITION TO THE CONTINENTAL CONGRESS

179

To the Right Honourable

Henry Laurance President of Congress.

The Humble Petition of Robert Wooldridge

Sheweth.

That your Petitioner was taken by
the Enemie Jan 8th 1777 in a Vessel belonging to The Hon:
Robert Morris, Robison Commander When they had brought
petitioner to New York he was put on board the prison Ship
after he Had Laid Some time in that Miserable Situation
they told him he must go on board of Man of War to Serve
the King Which he absolutely Refused being Resolved
never to Lift arms against the united States upon which
they told him if he would not Swear Never to Lift arms
against Great Britton they would force him on board Man
War, Wherefore Hon Mr Petitioner thought it his duty to
chuse the Least Evil, Aug.t 2d 1777 your Petitioner arrived
in Philadelphia & the 3 Inst. was taken by Comodore Hazzel
to the City Tavern and Sworn before his Excellency Gen'l
Washington Concerning the true Situation of the enemies
army Petitioner is now Imployed by Mr Andrew deloss
in the Service of this State helping to Clear the River
Your Petitioner Humbly prays your Honour to save
him from being Compel'd to break his oath as Petitioner
is moast willing to Serve the States to the utmoast of his
power in every way & means he is capable of
And as Im duly bound will ever pray

1778 Robert Wooldridge
Petition to the Continental Congress

To the Right Honourable Henry Laurance, President of Congress

The humble petition of Robert Wooldridge showeth:

That the petitioner was taken by the Enemie Jan 8th 1777 in a vessel belonging to the Honorable Robert Morris, Mr. Robinson Commander. When they had brought petitioner to New York he was put on board the prison ship. After he had laid some time in that miserable situation, they told him he must go on board of Man of War to serve the king. Which he absolutely refused, being resolved never to lift arms against the United States. Upon which they told him if he would not swear never to lift arms against Great Britton, they would force him on board Man of War. Wherefore Honourable Petitioner thought it his duty to choose the least evil. August 2nd 1777 your petitioner arrived in Philadelphia and the 3rd instant was taken by Commander Harrel?? To the City Tavern and sworn before this Excellency General Washington concerning the true situation of the British army. Petitioner is now employed by McAndrew ???? in the service of this state helping to clean the river. Your Petitioner humbly prays your Honour to save him from being compelled to break his oath as Petitioner is most willing to serve the states to the utmost of his power in every way & means he is capable of
And as in duty bound will ever ????

WILLIAM B. WOOLDRIDGE
(1810-1873)

(DATE OF PHOTO UNKNOWN)

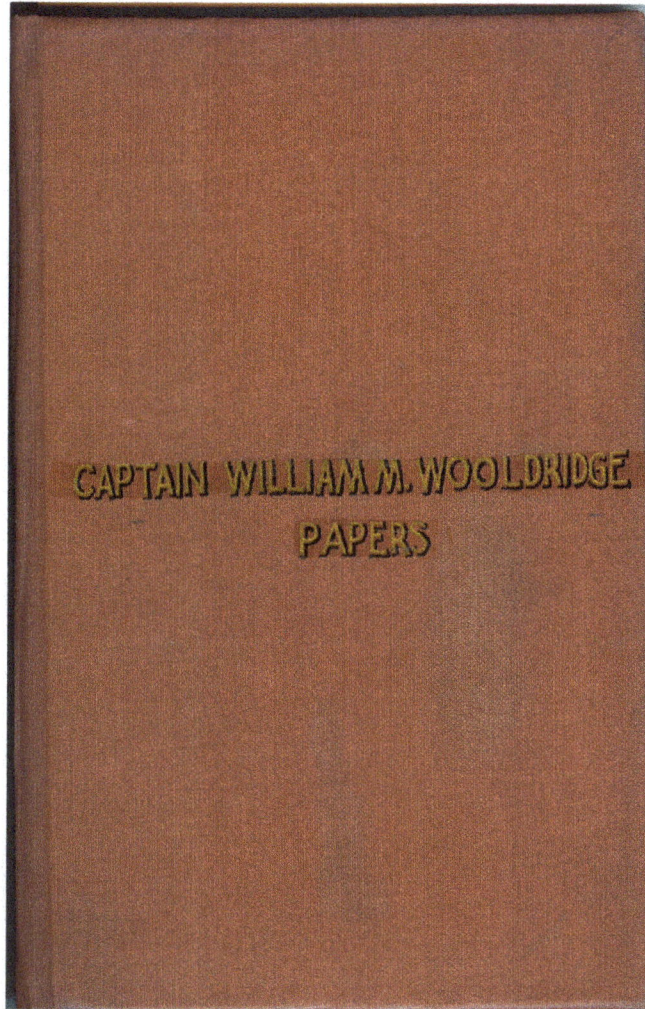

COVER OF BOOK CONTAINING
NEWSPAPER CLIPPINGS OF
CAPT. WILLIAM M. WOOLDRIDGE

BELOW IS THE CITY HOTEL
IN BALTIMORE, MD, 1856
WILLIAM WAS THE LEAD
ARCHITECT FOR THE RENOVATION

CAPT. WILLIAM M. WOOLDRIDGE
UNION SOLDIER IN 121ST PA
INJURED AT FREDERICKSBURG DEC 1862
DIED OF TYPHOID JULY 1863

CAPT. WILLIAM M. WOOLDRIDGE
CASUALTY SHEET & LEAVE OF ABSENCE · 1862
CASUALTY SHEET.

Name, *Wm H Woolridge*

Rank, *Capt.*, Company "*G*", Regiment, *121*

Arm, *Infy.*, State, *Penn.*

Place of casualty, *near Fredericksburg, Va.*

Nature of casualty, *Wounded*

Date of casualty, *Dec. 13· 1862.*

FORM OF A MEDICAL CERTIFICATE.

Capt G. M. Wooldridge, of the *121st* Regiment of *Penn.a Vols*, having applied for a certificate on which to ground an application for leave of absence, I do hereby certify that I have carefully examined this officer, and find ~~that~~ him suffering from *enlargement and tenderness of liver, Inflamation of kidneys & Neuralgia, Also Gun shot Wound (flesh) of right elbow received in action at Fredericksburg Va. Dec. 13th 1862.*

And that, in consequence thereof, he is, in my opinion, unfit for duty. I further declare my belief that he will not be able to resume his duties in a less period than *twenty* days without risk of permanent disability.

Dated at *Washington D.C.*, this *Fifth* day of *January*, 186*3*.

Meredith Clymer

Surgeon, U. S. A.

CAPT. WILLIAM M. WOOLDRIDGE
MEDICAL RESIGNATION NOTE - 1863

Resignation

~~LEAVE OF ABSENCE.~~

Captain Wm M Wooldridge of the 121st regiment of P.V. having

applied for a certificate on which to ground ~~an application for leave of absence~~ *his resignation*, I do hereby

certify that I have carefully examined *this Officer* and find that

he is suffering from Chronic Bronchitis, with general debility

And that, in consequence thereof, he is, in my opinion, unfit for duty. I further declare my

belief that he will not be able to resume his duties in a less period than ——————— days.

Dated at *Philada* this *12th* day of *February* 1863.

Francis G Smith Jr.
—— " —— Medical Officer.

CAPT. WILLIAM M. WOOLDRIDGE
LETTER OF RESIGNATION - 1863

Philada Feb 13th 1863

S. Thomas,
Adj't General.
U.S. Army -

General -

Owing to my continued ill health, and believing with my Surgeon, that I will not again be able to resume my duties in the field, I am compelled to offer my resignation from the U.S. Army -

I have been absent from duty, since the 14th day of December 1862, and although I have been under the constant treatment of a skillful Surgeon (whose certificate please find enclosed) yet my complaint, Chronic Bronchitis, has been gradually growing worse -

I offer my resignation not only in justice to myself, but to the service; trusting that my position will be filled by some one who is blessed with better health than

Your Most Ob't Serv't
Wm M Wooldridge
Capt. Co G. 121st Regt. Pa. Vols.
(1443 South 5th St. Phila)
Pa.)

CAPTAIN WILLIAM M. WOOLDRIDGE
(photo courtesy Warren Gondolf)

Anna McCall Wooldridge Nitzky (1838-1909)

(photo date unknown)

Anna McCall Wooldridge Nitzky & George A. Nitzky

(Written on the photo is: "Mr. & Mrs. Geo. A. Nitzky, Sr. 1865" They did not marry until 1866, so either this was taken before their marriage, or the date is wrong.)

DAR Lineage Form - 1922
Anna Wooldridge McFarlin

LINEAGE

I _Anna W. McFarlin_ being of the age of eighteen years and upwards, hereby apply for membership in the Society by right of lineal descent in the following line from _Captain Philip Strubing_ who was born in _Geneva Switzerland_ on the day of _before 1758_ and died in _Reading Pa last place_ on the day of _after 1799 after 1799 child twin 1794_

His place of residence during the Revolution was _Reading Berks Co_

I was born in _Cincinnati_ County of _Pennsylvania_

State of _Ohio_

1. I am the daughter of

Wm M Wooldridge	born _July 18 1838_ _1836_	died _Mar 2 1909_ _1863_	and his ( ) wife*
Anna McCall	born _July 13 1838_	died _Mar 22 1909_	married _Feb 5 1856_ nov 29 1857 July 5 1866

2. The said _Anna McCall_ was the _dau_ of

Charles Bukman McCall	born _Feb 5 1817_	died _Dec 4 1896_	and his ( ) wife
Margaret Strubing	born _Oct 4 1815_	died _July 30 1882_	married _Sep 5 1836_

3. The said _Margaret Strubing_ was the _dau_ of

James Strubing	born _Mar 9 1792_	died _Sep 20 1845_	and his ( ) wife
Catharine Kromel	born _Jan 22 1796_	died	married

4. The said _James Strubing_ was the _son_ of

Philip Strubing	born _before 1758_	died _after 1799_ after 1799 child two	and his ( ) wife
Sarah Leamer	born	died	married

5. The said _____ was the _____ of

	born	died	and his ( ) wife
	born	died	married

6. The said _Philip Strubing_ was the _____ of

	born	died	and his ( ) wife

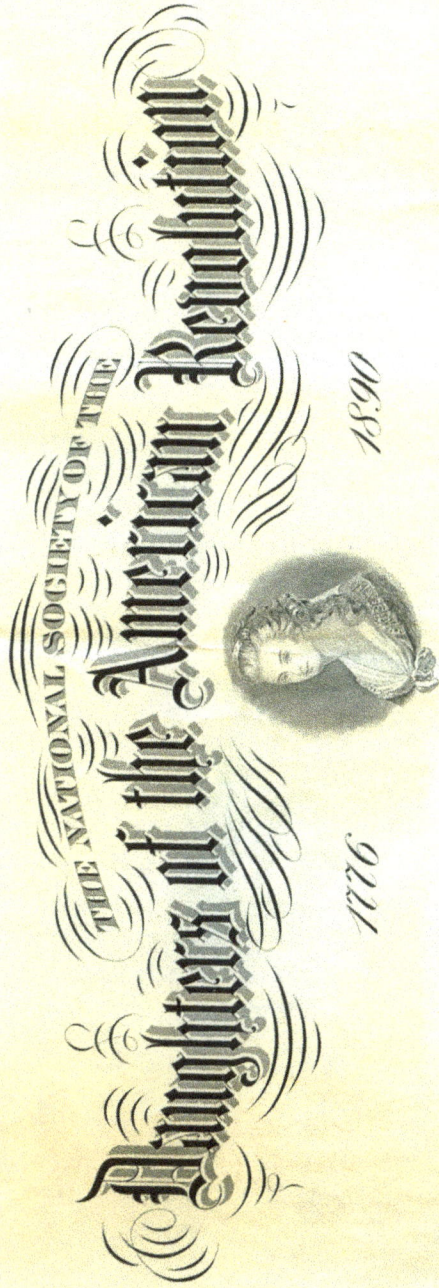

Daughters of the American Revolution

THE NATIONAL SOCIETY OF THE

1776   1890

This Certifies that

Mrs. Anna Wooldridge McFarlin

is a regularly approved member of the National Society of the Daughters of the
American Revolution, in connection with the _____ Quaker City _____ Chapter,
having been admitted by the National Board of Management by virtue of her
descent from _____ Philip Rodney _____ who with
unfailing loyalty rendered material aid to the cause of American Independence
as a _____ Lieutenant _____ during the Revolutionary War.

Given under our hands and the seal of the National Society
this _____ twentieth _____ day of _____ January _____ 1923

National No. 18 42 44
Admitted December 6 1922

Anne Rogers Minor
President General

Nita M. Langles
Recording Secretary General

Emma T. Strider
Registrar General

The Gans Lineage

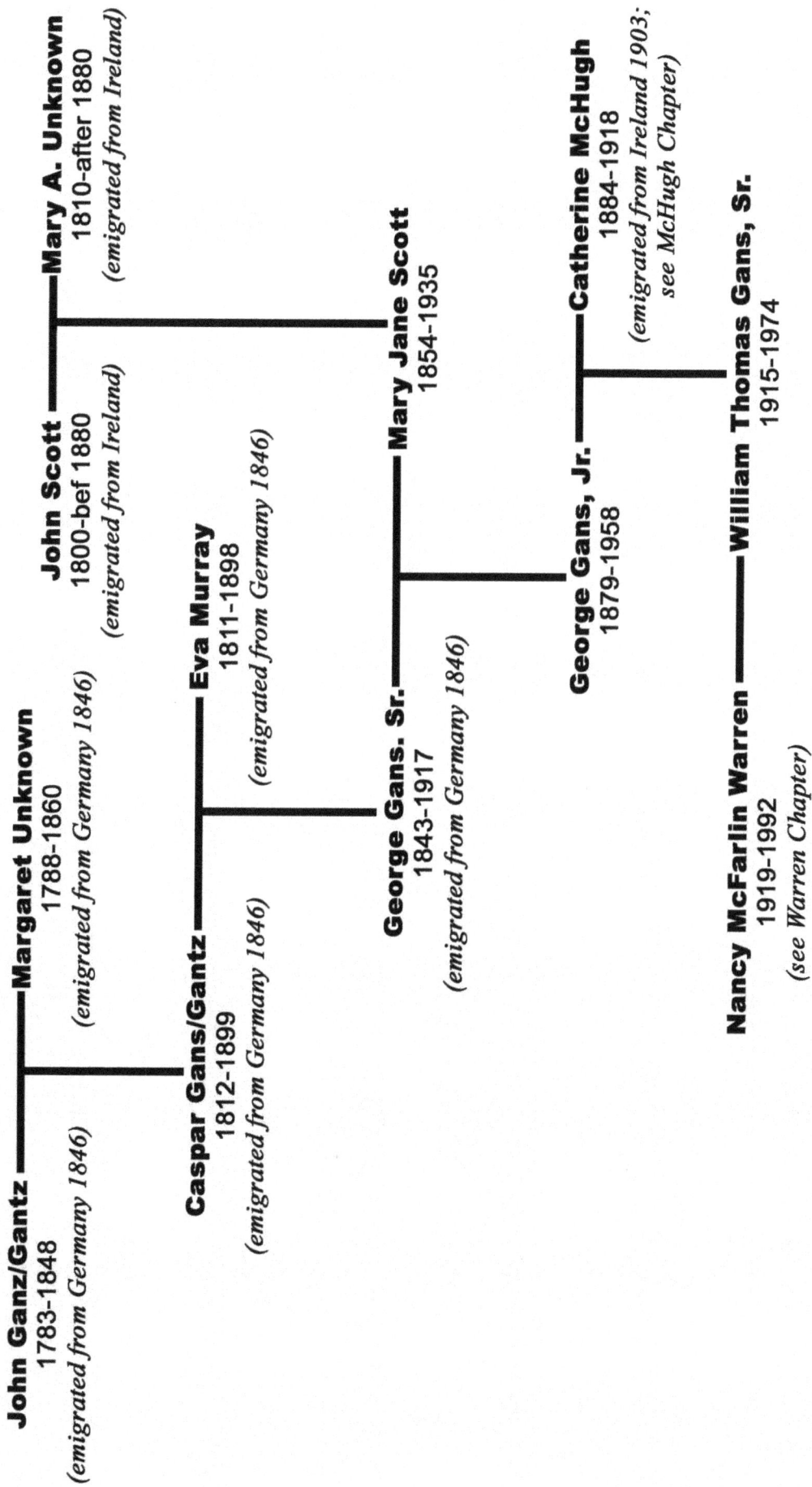

John Ganz/Gantz
1783-1848
(emigrated from Germany 1846)

Margaret Unknown
1788-1860
(emigrated from Germany 1846)

John Scott
1800-bef 1880
(emigrated from Ireland)

Mary A. Unknown
1810-after 1880
(emigrated from Ireland)

Caspar Gans/Gantz
1812-1899
(emigrated from Germany 1846)

Eva Murray
1811-1898
(emigrated from Germany 1846)

George Gans. Sr.
1843-1917
(emigrated from Germany 1846)

Mary Jane Scott
1854-1935

George Gans, Jr.
1879-1958

Catherine McHugh
1884-1918
(emigrated from Ireland 1903; see McHugh Chapter)

Nancy McFarlin Warren
1919-1992
(see Warren Chapter)

William Thomas Gans, Sr.
1915-1974

The Gans Lineage

The Gans lineage originated in the Hesse–Darmstadt region of Germany.[1] Why they left Germany is unknown, although failures of harvests in 1846 caused famine and may have played a role, as well as poor economic conditions in cities. Whatever their reason, on 19 September 1846, the ship *Sardinia of New York* arrived in New York bearing 3 generations of Ganses…[2]

John Gans (c. 1783–bef 1850) and Margaret Unknown (1788–1860)

Aboard the *Sardinia* was John Gans (63), with his wife, Margaret (58). With them on board were 3 other Gans couples, some with children.[3] From the ages of the younger generation, I believe the 3 couples to be the sons of John and Margaret. I am certain the youngest, Caspar, is their son, and believe the other 2 to be as well.

John and Margaret's proposed family looks like this:

John, Jr. (b.c. 1808) – *married Mary Unknown.*
Jacob (b.c. 1810) – *married Mary Unknown.*
Caspar (1812–1899) – *married Eva Murray.*

There was also a girl, Valentine Gans (b.c. 1828), listed with John and Margaret. She is too young to be their daughter. I'm guessing she is a daughter of John, Jr., as she fits with the dates his children were born (sons Joseph, b.c. 1832, and Steven, b.c. 1841).[4] Or she could be a cousin or grandchild from another son who did not make the journey.

John and Margaret arrived in New York in 1846. By 1850, Margaret was a widow living with her son Caspar in Philadelphia, PA.[5] John Gans died sometime between 1846 and 1850, place unknown. I have not found him listed in any New York or Philadelphia City Directory for those years.

Widowed Margaret Gans lived with her son Caspar and his family in 1850. The family lived in the 2nd Ward, Southwark, Philadelphia, PA. Caspar (36) was the head with wife Eva (37), mother Margaret (62), and children Clara (11), George (8), Mary (5), Margaret (3), and Joseph (5 months).[6]

Margaret Gans, age 72, died 10 January 1860 of apoplexy, and resided at 118 Catharine St., Philadelphia, PA.[7] This address is next door to Caspar's residence, 116 Catharine, and in 1859 had been occupied by John Ganz—likely Caspar's brother.[8] (The Gans name was variously spelled Gans, Ganz, and Gantz.)

Margaret is buried at Holy Trinity Church at 5th and Locust in Philadelphia, PA.[9] The cemetery still exists, but the headstones are too worn to read. I will need to find the actual records to find out where she is buried in the cemetery, and if her husband, John, is there as well. I suspect he might be, because otherwise I would have expected her to be buried in the Gans family plot where Caspar's family is buried, in a different cemetery.

Caspar Gantz (1812–1899) and Eva Murray (1811–1898)

First, a word about the last name. Caspar seemed to consistently use the Gantz spelling, but his mother used both Gantz and Gans, and his son George seems to have Americanized it to Gans consistently. Caspar's 2 other sons, Joseph and John, kept the Gantz spelling. I suppose it was a matter of personal preference.

Caspar Gantz was born in 1812 in Hesse–Darmstadt, Germany.[10] He immigrated to New York on 19 September 1846 on the *Sardinia*. With Caspar (34) were wife Eva (35) and children Clara (listed as Laura) (7), George (3), and Mary (listed as Anna Maria) (2). The ship had last sailed from Liverpool, England, and the captain was C.K. Crocker.[11]

Caspar and Eva had 7 known children, the first 3 born in Germany:[12] [13]

Clara (c. 1839–1915) – *married Unknown Bellwoar.*
George Joseph (1843–1917) – *married Mary Jane Scott.*
Anna Maria (Mary) (1844–1925) – *married Frederick A. Arleth.*
Margaret (c. 1847–1851)
Joseph J. (1850–1904)
Louisa (b.c. 1852)
John F. (b. 1855) – *married Mary Unknown.*

Caspar is not noted in the Philadelphia Directory until 1850,[14] indicating that he came no earlier than 1849 (sometimes it took a year for the Directories to catch up to people). His father (deceased by then) is obviously not in it, and there is no indication of John, Jr., or Jacob. I suspect they all stayed in New York from 1846 until 1850, which might indicate that father John died there.

In 1850, the family was in the 2nd Ward, Southwark, Philadelphia, PA. Caspar (36) lived there with wife Eva (37), mother Margaret (62), and children Clara (11), George (8), Mary (5), Margaret (3), and Joseph (5 months). Caspar's occupation was "carter."[15]

Their 1850 residence was the rear of 62 Catharine St., and Caspar (listed as Caspar Gang) was a laborer.[16] By 1852, Caspar lived at 6 Spragg Ave., but then in 1853 the family is listed as rear 62 Catharine St. again, so perhaps 1852 was where Caspar worked rather than lived.[17] 1855 finds them at 60 Catharine St.[18] Caspar was a laborer for all of those years.

In 1858 they had relocated to the rear of 116 Catharine St.[19] Caspar was a waiter. They remain at 116 Catharine at least until 1861.[20] Caspar was a laborer mostly, except in 1861 when he worked in a shop.

The 1860 Census found the family in the East Division of the 3rd Ward of Philadelphia, PA. Kaspar (Caspar) (48) and Eva (49) live with children George (18), Mary (16), Joseph (9), Louisa (7), and John (5). Caspar was a laborer.[21]

From 1863 on, Caspar was a stonemason. In 1863 he lived at 2307 Jefferson;[22] in 1864 he resided at rear 917 North 9th.[23]

In 1870, he lived on 19th Street, in the 20th Ward, 62nd District of Philadelphia, PA. While the first Census enumeration[24] in July only had daughter Louisa living with them, the second enumeration[25] in November showed Caspar (58) living there with wife Eva (60) and children Joseph (21), Louisa (18), and John (16).

By 1880, they lived at Poplar above 47th. Caspar (66) and Eva (68) lived there with son John (26).[26] The 1881 City Directory had their address as 4715 Poplar, which is likely the same address as during the 1880 Census.[27]

Eva Murray Gans died 28 November 1898, at the age of 87. She lived at 926 Markoe St., 34 Ward, at the time of her death. Eva died of old age and debility. It is worth mentioning that Eva's maiden name is listed as

Kramer on her daughter Clara's death certificate, but is listed as Murray on her own. Eva was buried 30 November 1898 in Old Cathedral Cemetery, Philadelphia, PA.[28]

Caspar Gantz died a little over a year later, on 16 December 1899, at age 87. At the time of his death, he resided at 926 N. Markoe Street. He died of Bright's disease, a historical name for what are now known to be separate kidney–related diseases. Caspar was a member of the Lafayette Beneficial Society. He was buried out of St. Ignatius Church, interred on 20 December 1899 in Old Cathedral Cemetery, located at 48th and Lancaster Avenue, Philadelphia, PA.[29][30]

George Joseph Gans, Sr., (1843–1917) and Mary Jane Scott (1854–1935)

George Joseph Gans, Sr., was born in Germany in November 1843. He was 3 when he arrived with his family in New York aboard the *Sardinia*.[31]

George was listed in the 1860 Census as being an apprentice ship carpenter.[32] However, in the Pennsylvania Tax Roll of December 1862–May 1863, George was listed as a butcher, at West King Street, Philadelphia. This may have been his place of business, rather than his residence. He was being taxed for having 29 horned cattle.[33]

In 1865, there was a George Gans listed at 2417 Martha St.[34] At 22, George may have been out on his own, however, this George is not a butcher, but a laborer. So while it may be him, I am not 100% certain.

He was naturalized in Philadelphia, PA, on 22 September 1866.[35]

In the 1870 Census, George (27) was living with a group of other young men who all seem to be learning the trade of victualler (grocer) in the 4th Precinct, 24th Ward, 77th District of Philadelphia, PA.[36]

He married Mary Jane Scott about 1871. She was born on 4 October 1854 in New York City. She was the daughter of John Scott (1800–bef 1880) and Mary A. Unknown (1810–aft. 1880), both born in Ireland.[37][38]

George, Sr., and Mary Jane had 9 children, but I have only found 8:[39][40]

Clara (c. 1872–1882)
Louise L. (b. 1874) – *married George Bradley.*
Mary E. (b. May 1876) – *married Unknown Regan.*
George Joseph, Jr. (1879–1958) – *married Catherine McHugh, then Helen A. Donovan.*
William T. (b. 1881)
Agness (1888–1888)
Catherine P. (b. 1889) – *married Charles E. Oates.*
Lawrence (c. 1891–1893)

In 1880, George (38) and Mary Jane (28) lived with children Clara (8), Louisa (7), Mary E. (4), and George, Jr. (1), at 3915 Warren St., Philadelphia, PA. George was a butcher.[41]

In 1900, George (56) and Mary Jane (45) lived at 628 Preston St., Philadelphia, PA. They had been married for 29 years. George's occupation was fireman. I have contacted the Philadelphia Fireman's Hall Museum, and our George is not listed among them during that time. The man from the museum suggested that perhaps George was a stoker, as they were also called firemen.

In 1900, young Mary (24) was a laundress; young George (21) was a driver; William (19) was a meter maker, and Catherine (10) was presumably still in school.

Also in 1900, 2 boarders lived with the Gans family – Sallie and John A. Devlin. They appear to be siblings, as they are not married, and were born 3 years apart. They were both born in Pennsylvania, but their parents were from Ireland. Sallie (25) was a laundress, and John (18) was a meter maker. They worked in the same line of work as 2 of the Gans children, so either one of them could have been friends of the Ganses.[42]

In 1910, George (67) and Mary Jane (56) lived with children Mary (32) and Catherine (20). They still rented their house at 628 Preston St., and George was listed as a "stationary fireman"—a boiler stoker, as the museum worker had suggested.[43]

George Joseph Gans, Sr., died 25 July 1917 at age 73 in Philadelphia, PA, at their residence of 139 55th St. Daughter Catherine Gans signed his death certificate, and she apparently knew very little about her father, since she wrote that he was from Ireland. He died of cerebral apoplexy with pulmonary edema.[44] There was a Requiem Mass at Our Lady of Victory Church, 54th and Vine. George was a member of St. Agatha's Holy Name Society.[45]

George was buried in St. Denis Cemetery in Haverford, PA, Section 4, Range 7, Lot 84 – the Gans plot. His brother Joseph and sister Anna Maria (Mary) are also buried there, with their spouses, and a number of George's children and their spouses.[46]

In 1920, widowed Mary Jane (61) lived at 139 55th St. (which she rented) in Philadelphia, with 2 of her children and a boarder. Young Mary (42) was working as a hairdresser in a dressing shop, and Catherine (29) is an operator in the phone company. Their boarder, George Ragan (43), was born in Pennsylvania of Irish parents, and owned his own cigar store.[47]

In 1930, Mary Jane (75) lived with her daughter at 5445 Irving St., Philadelphia, PA. Her daughter Kathryn P. Gans (42) was married to Charles E. Oates (48). They married in 1924. Charles rented the house where they lived for $38 a month, and they had a radio set. Charles was born in Pennsylvania, but both his parents were from Ireland. He was a bricklayer in the contracting business, and Kathryn worked as an office clerk with the telephone company.[48]

Mary Jane Scott Gans (81) died on 5 September 1935. At the time, she lived in Collingdale, Delaware County, PA, at 819 Walnut St., apparently still with Kathryn. Her cause of death is listed as uremic coma brought on by chronic hepatitis.[49] She was buried in St. Denis Cemetery in Haverford, PA, Section 4, Range 7, Lot 84, on 9 September 1935.[50]

George Joseph Gans, Jr., (1879–1958) and Catherine McHugh (1884–1918)
(see McHugh Lineage chapter)

George Joseph Gans, Jr., was born in Pennsylvania on 26 January 1879.[51] He married Catherine McHugh in September 1905.[52] Catherine McHugh was one of 4 siblings who emigrated from Ireland – Mary (20), Catherine/Kate (18), Thomas (10), and Charlie (8). They sailed from Londonderry, Ireland, on 22 February 1903 aboard the SS *Ethiopia*. They arrived in New York on 11 March 1903.[53]

George and Catherine had 4 children:[54]

George Franklin (1906–1907)[55]
Charles B. (1908–1984) – *married Ethel Gegan.*
Helen C. (1910–1945)
William Thomas (1915–1974) – *married Nancy McFarlin Warren.*

George, Jr., lived at his parents' house at 628 Preston St., Philadelphia, PA, until he married in 1905.[56]

In 1910, George (31) and Catherine (25) lived in Philadelphia's 24th Ward. George was a teamster working in the wholesale liquor industry. They had a 2–year–old son, Charles, and Catherine's brother Thomas McHugh (20) also lived with them. He was a clerk in a liquor store, a job probably gotten through George's connections.[57]

From 1915 to 1918 the family lived at 4238 Powell Ave., Philadelphia, PA.[58]

Catherine McHugh Gans (34) died of pneumonia during the great flu pandemic of 1918, when William Thomas was only 3 years old.[59] She contracted the flu October 8, got pneumonia October 14, and died October 18.[60] Catherine is buried in St. Denis Cemetery in Haverford, PA, with her husband and daughter (Section 2, Range 5, Lot 40), although she was originally buried in a plot owned by her sister's husband (Gallagher plot: Section K, Range 8, Lot 92). There is some confusion over whether she was actually moved or if her name was simply added to George's headstone when it went up.[61]

In 1920, George (40) and family lived at 5625 Pine St., Philadelphia, PA, in a house George owned on a mortgage. He was still a teamster, but now in the contractor industry. He had remarried very soon after Catherine's death to Helen A. Donovan (29). George's three children with Catherine lived with them – Charles B. (11), Helen C. (9), and William (4).[62]

George and Helen had 3 children:

Margaret (Peg) M. (1920–1999) – *married Andrew Kaiser.*
Mary Jane (1923–2002) – *married Arthur Guest.*
George Joseph, III (1928–2009) – *married Lorraine Orr.*

In 1930, George (51) and family lived at 20 E. Langhorne St., Haverford, PA. George owned his house (worth $1,500), and they had a radio set. Living with him were wife Helen A. (39), and children Charles B. (22), Helen C. (19), William T. (14), Margaret M. (9), Mary J. (7), and George J. (2 months). The eldest 3 children were from his first marriage to Catherine McHugh, and the younger 3 belonged to Helen A. George and Helen had been married for about 10 years. George was a proprietor of a garage, while Charles was a plumber. The other children were all in school.[63]

In 1940, the family was at 20 East Measea Ave., Haverford, PA. George (61) lived there with second wife Helen A. (48) and children Helen (27), Mary (20), Margaret (16), and George (13). Helen was a secretary at an architectural office, making $780 a year, and Mary was a clerk at a department store, making $884 a year. George was a laborer on the highway, making $198 a year.[64]

George Joseph Gans, Jr. (79), died on 12 June 1958 at Hahnemann Hospital in Philadelphia, PA. At the time of his death, he lived at 34 Darby Rd., Llanerch, Delaware County, PA. His job at the time was doorman at the local movie theatre, Suburban Square. His cause of death was gastrointestinal hemorrhage due to carcinomatosis.[65] He was buried 16 June 1958 in St. Denis Cemetery in Haverford, PA, Section 2, Range 5, Lot 40.[66]

William Thomas Gans, Sr., (1915–1974) and Nancy Warren (1919–1992)
(see Warren Lineage chapter)

William Thomas Gans was born 27 August 1915 at 4238 Powlton Ave., Philadelphia, PA.[67] He married Nancy Warren in Chestertown, MD, on 25 August 1939. William was 25; Nancy was 19. William was a truck driver from Llanerch, PA, and Nancy was a secretary from Brookline, PA.[68]

William and Nancy had 5 children.[69] Because they are living, I am respecting their privacy by not placing their information here.

In 1940, newlyweds William (23) and Nancy (20) lived at 88 State St., Upper Darby, Delware County, PA. Both his and Nancy's information stated that their places of residence in 1935 were "rural" in Delaware County. William was a soft drink salesman making $1,768 a year.[70]

From 1943 until his enlistment in the Navy in 1944, William (26) was a salesman for Clymers Distributors.[71]

William (27–28) served in the United States Navy during World War II, stationed at Naval Training Center Bainbridge in Maryland. He entered active service 2 August 1944, and was honorably discharged on 11 October 1945. At this time, he lived at 1811 Robinson Ave., Upper Darby, PA.[72]

William Gans and family lived in Haverford until the summer of 1956, when they moved to Ocean City, New Jersey. William bought a paint store, William T. Gans and Sons, at 653 Asbury Ave. While William ran the paint store, Nancy worked first at women's retailer K. Averil Dolaway at 827 Asbury Ave.,[73] then at the National Aviation Facilities Experimental Center (NAFEC) military installation outside Atlantic City, NJ, where she was in charge of the secretarial staff.[74]

The Gans family moved a few times while in Ocean City, NJ. First the family lived over the paint store, but in 1962 they moved to 266 Bayshore Drive; in 1965, moved to 732 Central Ave., and in 1967, moved to 1907 Glenwood Drive. In August/September 1973, William and Nancy moved out of Ocean City to Schnecksville, PA.[75]

William Thomas Gans, Sr., died 28 March 1974 at age 58. At the time of his death, he was a vocational school instructor. He died in Allentown Hospital, and resided at the Sand Spring Apartments, G5, in Schnecksville, PA. He is buried in West Laurel Hill Cemetery in Philadelphia, PA, Everglade 516.[76] [77]

After William's death, Nancy moved in 1974 to Old Forge Crossing in Wayne, PA. Her health declined and when her children could no longer care for her at home, she moved into the Ocean Point nursing home in Somers Point, NJ, where she lived until her death.[78]

Nancy Warren Gans died at age 72 on 26 July 1992 at the nursing home in New Jersey. She is buried in West Laurel Hill Cemetery in Philadelphia, PA, Everglade 516.[79]

---

[1] *1850 United States Census*, Philadelphia, PA. Year: 1850; Census Place: Southwark Ward 2, Philadelphia, Pennsylvania; Roll: M432_821; Page: 104B; Image: 214.

[2] *New York, Passenger and Immigration Lists, 1820-1850*, [database online] *Sardinia*'s list into NYC. Found on Ancestry.com - surname misspelled as Gneis.

---

[3] *New York, Passenger and Immigration Lists, 1820-1850*, [database online] *Sardinia*'s list into NYC. Found on Ancestry.com - surname misspelled as Gneis.

[4] *New York, Passenger and Immigration Lists, 1820-1850*, [database online] *Sardinia*'s list into NYC. Found on Ancestry.com - surname misspelled as Gneis.

[5] *1850 United States Census*, Philadelphia, PA. Year: 1850; Census Place: Southwark Ward 2, Philadelphia, Pennsylvania; Roll: M432_821; Page: 104B; Image: 214.

[6] *1850 United States Census*, Philadelphia, PA. Year: 1850; Census Place: Southwark Ward 2, Philadelphia, Pennsylvania; Roll: M432_821; Page: 104B; Image: 214.

[7] Margaret Gans' Coroner's Report, Film 1977062, digital folder 4009944, image 703. Philadelphia, PA. Original housed at Philadelphia City Archives, 3101 Market Street, Philadelphia, PA 19104.

[8] *McElroy's Philadelphia City Directory 1859*. Philadelphia: A. McElroy & Co., 1859; p 246.

[9] Margaret Gans' Coroner's Report, Film 1977062, digital folder 4009944, image 703. Philadelphia, PA. Original housed at Philadelphia City Archives, 3101 Market Street, Philadelphia, PA 19104.

[10] *1850 United States Census*, Philadelphia, PA. Year: 1850; Census Place: Southwark Ward 2, Philadelphia, Pennsylvania; Roll: M432_821; Page: 104B; Image: 214.

[11] *New York, Passenger and Immigration Lists, 1820-1850*. [database online] *Sardinia*'s list into NYC. Found on Ancestry.com - surname misspelled as Gneis.

[12] *1850 United States Census*, Philadelphia, PA. Year: 1850; Census Place: Southwark Ward 2, Philadelphia, Pennsylvania; Roll: M432_821; Page: 104B; Image: 214.

[13] *1860 United States Census*, Philadelphia, PA. Year: 1860; Census Place: Philadelphia Ward 3, Philadelphia, Pennsylvania; Roll: M653_1153; Page: 81; Image: 85; Family History Library Film: 805153.

[14] Philadelphia City Directory, 1850 McElroy's p 145.

[15] *1850 United States Census*, Philadelphia, PA. Year: 1850; Census Place: Southwark Ward 2, Philadelphia, Pennsylvania; Roll: M432_821; Page: 104B; Image: 214.

[16] *McElroy's Philadelphia City Directory 1850*. Philadelphia: A. McElroy & Co., 1850; p 145.

[17] *McElroy's Philadelphia City Directory 1853*. Philadelphia: A. McElroy & Co., 1853; p. 143.

[18] *McElroy's Philadelphia City Directory 1855*. Philadelphia: A. McElroy & Co., 1855; p 189.

[19] *McElroy's Philadelphia City Directory 1858*. Philadelphia: A. McElroy & Co., 1858; p 235.

[20] *McElroy's Philadelphia City Directory 1861*. Philadelphia: A. McElroy & Co., 1861; p 339.

[21] *1860 United States Census*, Philadelphia, PA. Year: 1860; Census Place: Philadelphia Ward 3, Philadelphia, Pennsylvania; Roll: M653_1153; Page: 81; Image: 85; Family History Library Film: 805153.

[22] *McElroy's Philadelphia City Directory 1863*. Philadelphia: A. McElroy & Co., 1863; p 276.

[23] *McElroy's Philadelphia City Directory 1864*. Philadelphia: A. McElroy & Co., 1864; p 256.

[24] *1870 United States Census*, Philadelphia, PA. Year: 1870; Census Place: Philadelphia Ward 20 District 62, Philadelphia, Pennsylvania; Roll: M593_1406; Page: 111A; Image: 225; Family History Library Film: 552905.

[25] *1870 United States Census*, Philadelphia, PA. Year: 1870; Census Place: Philadelphia Ward 20 Dist 62 (2nd Enum), Philadelphia, Pennsylvania; Roll: M593_1435; Page: 662A; Image: 563; Family History Library Film: 552934.

[26] *1880 United States Census*, Philadelphia, PA. Year: 1880; Census Place: Philadelphia, Philadelphia, Pennsylvania; Roll: 1183; Family History Film: 1255183; Page: 322D; Enumeration District: 505; Image: 0472.

[27] *Gopsill's Philadelphia City Directory 1881*. Philadelphia: Gopsill, 1881, p. 604.

[28] Death Return of Eva Murray Gans, City of Philadelphia, # 11191. Original housed at Philadelphia City Archives, 3101 Market Street, Philadelphia, PA 19104.

[29] Death Return of Caspar Gans, City of Philadelphia, # 11690. Original housed at Philadelphia City Archives, 3101 Market Street, Philadelphia, PA 19104.

[30] Obituary of Caspar Gans. *Philadephia Inquirer*, 1899-12-20.

[31] *New York, Passenger and Immigration Lists, 1820-1850*. [database online] *Sardinia*'s list into NYC. Found on Ancestry.com - surname misspelled as Gneis.

[32] *1860 United States Census*, Philadelphia, PA. Year: 1860; Census Place: Philadelphia Ward 3, Philadelphia, Pennsylvania; Roll: M653_1153; Page: 81; Image: 85; Family History Library Film: 805153.

[33] *Pennsylvania Tax Rolls,* Dec 1862-May 1863. Original housed at Philadelphia City Archives, 3101 Market Street, Philadelphia, PA 19104.

[34] *McElroy's Philadelphia City Directory 1865*. Philadelphia: A. McElroy & Co., 1865; p 254.

[35] George Gans, Sr.'s Naturalization Papers. Originals housed at Historical Society of Pennsylvania, 1300 Locust Street Philadelphia, PA 19107.

[36] *1870 United States Census*, Philadelphia, PA. Year: 1870; Census Place: Philadelphia Ward 24 District 77, Philadelphia, Pennsylvania; Roll: M593_1411; Page: 329B; Image: 140; Family History Library Film: 552910.

[37] *1910 United States Census*, Philadelphia, PA. Year: 1910; Census Place: Philadelphia Ward 24, Philadelphia, Pennsylvania; Roll: T624_1398; Page: 6A; Enumeration District: 0515; Image: 110; FHL microfilm: 1375411.

[38] Death Certificate of Mary Jane Scott Gans. File # 80101, Registered #: 26. Original housed at PA Department of Health, Division of Vital records, PO Box 1528, New Castle, PA 16103.

[39] *1880 United States Census*, Philadelphia, PA. Year: 1880; Census Place: Philadelphia, Philadelphia, Pennsylvania; Roll: 1183; Family History Film: 1255183; Page: 148D; Enumeration District: 493; Image: 0119.

[40] *1900 United States Census*, Philadelphia, PA. Year: 1900; Census Place: Philadelphia Ward 24, Philadelphia, Pennsylvania; Roll: 1466; Page: 3A; Enumeration District: 563; FHL microfilm: 1241466.

[41] *1880 United States Census*, Philadelphia, PA. Year: 1880; Census Place: Philadelphia, Philadelphia, Pennsylvania; Roll: 1183; Family History Film: 1255183; Page: 148D; Enumeration District: 493; Image: 0119.

[42] *1900 United States Census*, Philadelphia, PA. Year: 1900; Census Place: Philadelphia Ward 24, Philadelphia, Pennsylvania; Roll: 1466; Page: 3A; Enumeration District: 563; FHL microfilm: 1241466.

[43] *1910 United States Census*, Philadelphia, PA. Year: 1910; Census Place: Philadelphia Ward 24, Philadelphia, Pennsylvania; Roll: T624_1398; Page: 6A; Enumeration District: 0515; Image: 110; FHL microfilm: 1375411.

[44] Death Certificate of George Gans, Sr. File # 81526, Registered # 18964. Original housed at PA Department of Health, Division of Vital records, PO Box 1528, New Castle, PA 16103.

[45] Obituary of George Gans Sr. *Philadelphia Inquirer*, 26 July 1917.

[46] St. Denis Cemetery Records. Originals located at St. Denis Church, 2401 Saint Denis Lane, Havertown, PA 19083.

[47] *1920 United States Census*, Philadelphia, PA. Year: 1920; Census Place: Philadelphia Ward 34, Philadelphia, Pennsylvania; Roll: T625_1630; Page: 3B; Enumeration District: 1180; Image: 662.

[48] *1930 United States Census*, Philadelphia, PA. Year: 1930; Census Place: Philadelphia, Philadelphia, Pennsylvania; Roll: 2140; Page: 15B; Enumeration District: 502; Image: 148.0; FHL microfilm: 2341874.

[49] Death Certificate of Mary Jane Scott Gans. File # 80101, Registered #: 26. Original housed at PA Department of Health, Division of Vital records, PO Box 1528, New Castle, PA 16103.

[50] St. Denis Cemetery Records. Originals located at St. Denis Church, 2401 Saint Denis Lane, Havertown, PA 19083.

[51] Marriage application for George Gans, Jr. and Catherine McHugh, 8 Sept 1905. Original housed at Philadelphia City Archives, 3101 Market Street, Philadelphia, PA 19104.

[52] Philadelphia Marriage Index 1885-1951, #190124. Original housed at Philadelphia City Archives, 3101 Market Street, Philadelphia, PA 19104.

[53] *New York, Passenger and Immigration Lists, 1820-1850*, [database online] Ship's manifest - *SS Ethiopia*. Found on Ancestry.com.

[54] *1920 United States Census*, Philadelphia, PA. Year: 1920; Census Place: Philadelphia Ward 46, Philadelphia, Pennsylvania; Roll: T625_1647; Page: 3B; Enumeration District: 1762; Image: 498.

[55] St. Denis Cemetery Records. Originals located at St. Denis Church, 2401 Saint Denis Lane, Havertown, PA 19083.

[56] Marriage application for George Gans, Jr. and Catherine McHugh, 8 Sept 1905. Original housed at Philadelphia City Archives, 3101 Market Street, Philadelphia, PA 19104.

[57] *1910 United States Census*, Philadelphia, PA. Year: 1910; Census Place: Philadelphia Ward 24, Philadelphia, Pennsylvania; Roll: T624_1397; Page: 8A; Enumeration District: 0496; Image: 816; FHL microfilm: 1375410.

[58] Birth Certificate of William Thomas Gans, Sr. Registered # 29846. Original housed at PA Department of Health, Division of Vital records, PO Box 1528, New Castle, PA 16103.

[59] Death Notice of Catherine McHugh Gans. *Philadelphia Public Ledger*, 23 Oct 1918.

[60] Death Certificate of Catherine McHugh Gans. File #: 144152; Registered #: 36715. Original housed at PA Department of Health, Division of Vital records, PO Box 1528, New Castle, PA 16103.

[61] St. Denis Cemetery Records. Originals located at St. Denis Church, 2401 Saint Denis Lane, Havertown, PA 19083.

[62] *1920 United States Census*, Philadelphia, PA. Year: 1920; Census Place: Philadelphia Ward 46, Philadelphia, Pennsylvania; Roll: T625_1647; Page: 3B; Enumeration District: 1762; Image: 498.

[63] *1930 United States Census*, Haverford, PA. Year: 1930; Census Place: Haverford, Delaware, Pennsylvania; Roll: 2031; Page: 33B; Enumeration District: 74; Image: 839.0; FHL microfilm: 2341765.

[64] *1940 United States Census*, Haverford, PA. Year: 1940; Census Place: Haverford, Delaware, Pennsylvania; Roll: T627_3492; Page: 4B; Enumeration District: 23-96.

[65] Death Certificate of George Gans Sr. Registered # 12144. Original housed at PA Department of Health, Division of Vital records, PO Box 1528, New Castle, PA 16103.

[66] St. Denis Cemetery Records. Originals located at St. Denis Church, 2401 Saint Denis Lane, Havertown, PA 19083.

[67] William Thomas Gans, Sr.'s Birth Certificate, Registered # 29846. Original housed at PA Department of Health, Division of Vital records, PO Box 1528, New Castle, PA 16103.

[68] Marriage Certificate of WT Gans & Nancy Warren, Kent County, MD #982. Original in possession of Kerry Gans Douglas.

[69] Personal witness by author Kerry Gans Douglas

[70] *1940 United States Census*, Upper Darby, PA. Year: 1940; Census Place: Upper Darby, Delaware, Pennsylvania; Roll: T627_3497; Page: 63A; Enumeration District: 23-191.

[71] William T. Gans, Sr.'s Navy Discharge Papers. Original in possession of Kerry Gans Douglas.

[72] William T. Gans, Sr.'s Navy Discharge Papers. Original in possession of Kerry Gans Douglas.

[73] Address from the *Ocean City Sentinel-Ledger*, February 1971.

[74] Personal Witness: told to author Kerry Gans Douglas by 4 children of William and Nancy.

[75] Personal Witness: told to author Kerry Gans Douglas by 4 children of William and Nancy.

[76] Death Certificate of William T. Gans Sr. #2682074 Pennsylvania. Original housed at PA Department of Health, Division of Vital records, PO Box 1528, New Castle, PA 16103.

[77] Record of Burial Place of a Veteran, Commonwealth of Pennsylvania Department of Military Affairs. Original in possession of Kerry Gans Douglas.

[78] Personal Witness: told to author Kerry Gans Douglas by 4 children of William and Nancy.

[79] Social Security Death Index. [database online]

PASSENGER LIST OF SARDINIA OF NEW YORK, 1846

CASPAR GANS, WIFE EVA, CHILDREN CLARA, GEORGE, & MARY
CASPAR'S PARENTS, JOHN & MARGARET GANS, ARE ALSO ON BOARD
UNKNOWN HOW THE GIRL VALENTINE GANS IS RELATED

Name	Age		
Caspar Gans	34	Brick	
Eva do	30	Female	
Clara do	8	do	
George do	4	Maple	
Eva of America	2	Female	

Clara Gans	65	do
Margaret Gans do	52	Female
Valentine do	13	do

CATHERINE McHUGH GANS &
GEORGE J. GANS, JR. (WITH SON CHARLES)
c. 1910

GEORGE J. GANS, JR., AND
2ND WIFE, HELEN DONOVAN
21 OCTOBER 1950

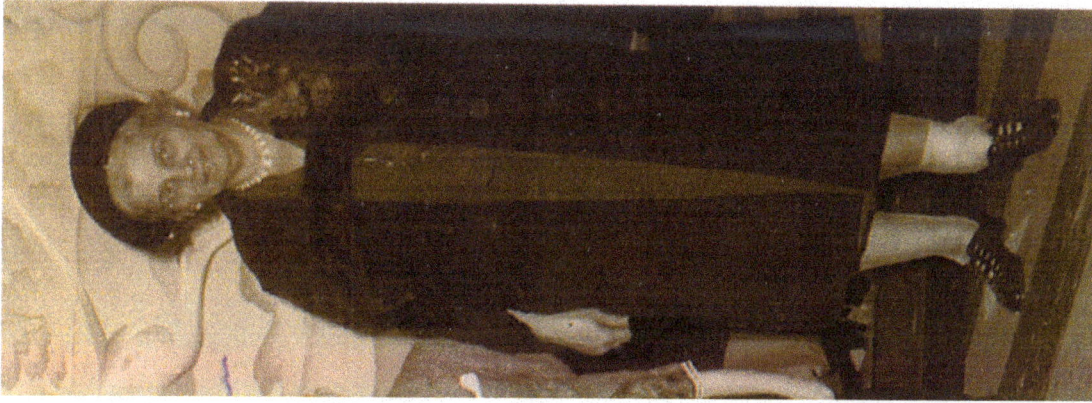

GEORGE J. GANS, JR., AND
1ST WIFE, CATHERINE MCHUGH
SEPTEMBER 1905

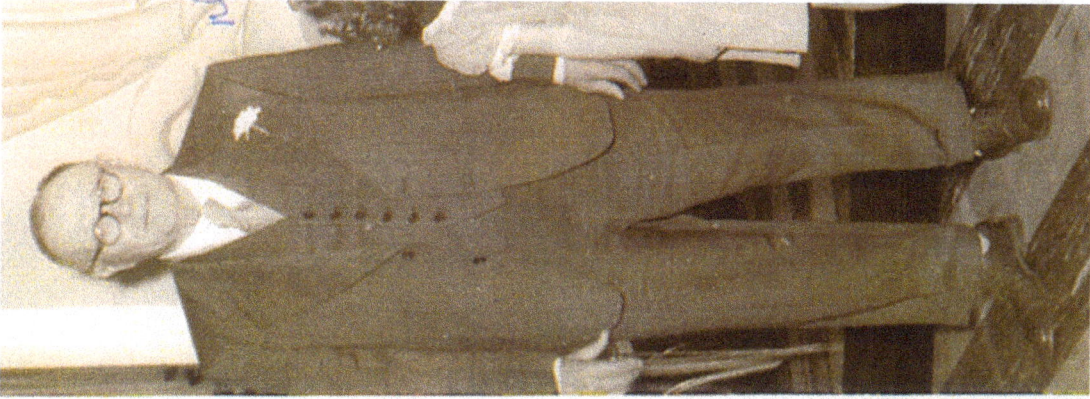

GRANDCHILDREN OF GEORGE J. GANS, JR.
21 OCTOBER 1950

GEORGE J. GANS, JR.

DOLORES   KATHY   CHRIS   BILL, JR.   CHARLES   JOHN   HELEN DONOVAN GANS

NANCY

LARRY   CAROLEE   RON   HELEN   DONALD   JERRY

Gans Headstone in St. Denis Cemetery Havertown, PA

George J. Gans
Catharine Gans (first Wife, William's Mother)
Helen A. Gans (Second Wife)
Helen C. Gans (Catharine & George's Daughter)

(photos: January 2006)

WILLIAM T. GANS, SR.'S CHILDHOOD HOME
20 E. LANGHORNE AVE., HAVERTOWN, PA
(PHOTOS: JANUARY 2006)

WILLIAM T. GANS & NANCY WARREN
1939 - MARRIAGE CERTIFICATE

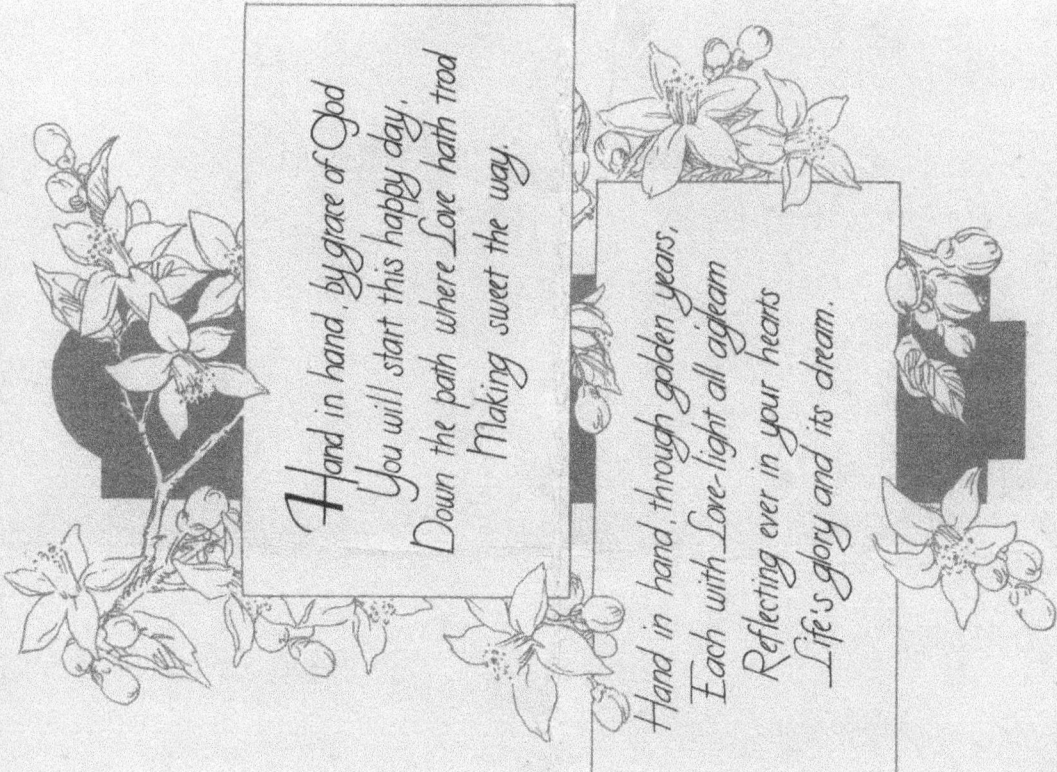

This Certifies that

William T. Gans

of Klarener, Pa

and

Nancy Warren

of Brookline, Pa

were by me united in

Holy Patrimony

at Chestertown

According to the Ordinance of God
and the laws of Maryland
on the 25th day of August
in the year of Our Lord 1939

J. M. Roberts
Minister

Witnesses

Hand in hand, by grace of God
You will start this happy day.
Down the path where Love hath trod
Making sweet the way.

Hand in hand, through golden years,
Each with Love-light all agleam
Reflecting ever in your hearts
Life's glory and its dream.

WILLIAM T. GANS & NANCY WARREN
AUGUST 25, 1939 - MARRIAGE LICENSE

GOOD ONLY IN COUNTY
WHERE ISSUED

Marriage License
STATE OF MARYLAND
KENT COUNTY

No. 982

I Hereby Certify, That on this 25th day of August Nineteen hundred and thirty nine the below, were by me united in marriage at Chestertown in accordance with the License issued by the Clerk of the Circuit Court of the County herein indicated.

William T. Gans
(Name of Groom)

and

Nancy Warren
(Name of Bride)

Residence of Groom Llanerch, Pa.   Age 23   Color W.   Nativity Pa
(State or Country)

Occupation Truck Driver   and who is single
(State here whether single, widower or divorced as the case may be)

Residence of Bride Brookline, Pa.   Age 19   Color W.   Nativity Pa.
(State or Country)

Occupation Secretary   and who is single
(State here whether single, widow or divorced as the case may be)

Name of Person consenting if Groom is a Minor
(Parent or Guardian)

Name of Person consenting if Bride is a Minor
(Parent or Guardian)

not related
(State here whether the contracting parties are in any way related)

W. P. Roberts
Signature of Officiating Clergyman

Minister
Official Character

Chestertown, Md
Address

☞ This Certificate to be given to the Contracting Parties.

WILLIAM THOMAS, SR.
& NANCY WARREN GANS

C. 1945

The McHugh Lineage

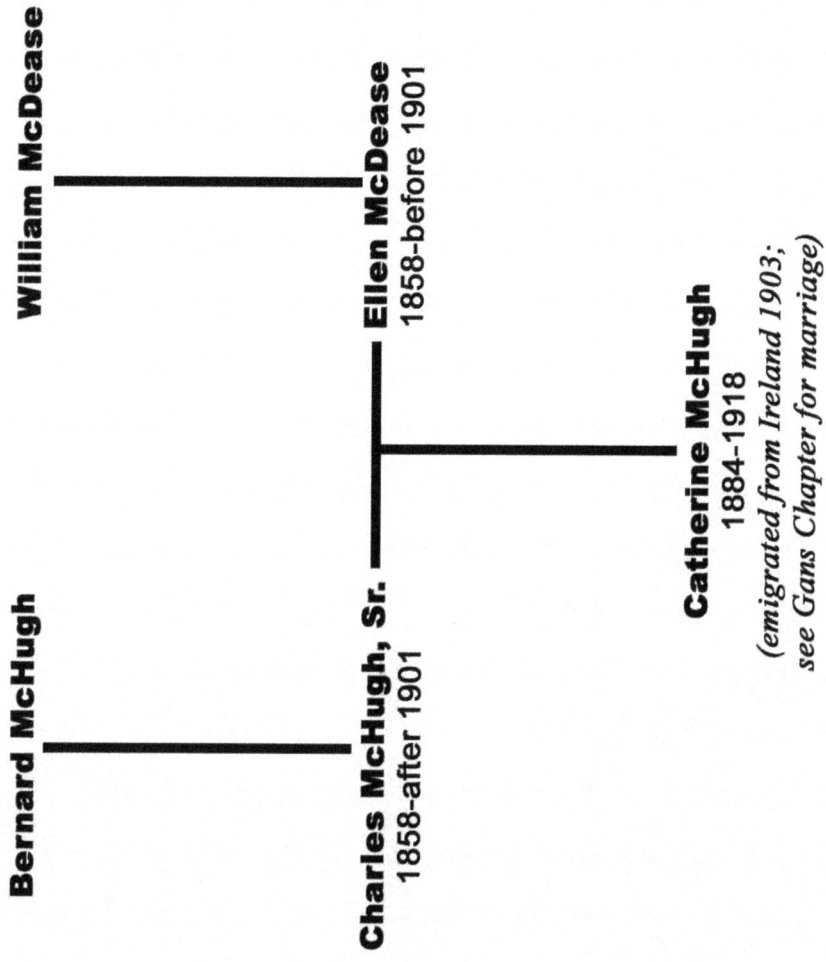

William McDease

Ellen McDease
1858–before 1901

Bernard McHugh

Charles McHugh, Sr.
1858–after 1901

Catherine McHugh
1884–1918
(emigrated from Ireland 1903;
see Gans Chapter for marriage)

McHugh

The McHugh Lineage

Charles McHugh, Sr., (1858–after 1901) and Ellen McDease (1858–before 1901)

Charles McHugh, Sr., and Ellen "Helen" McDease are the parents of the 4 McHugh siblings who came to America in 1903. Catherine McHugh, the younger daughter, married George Joseph Gans, Jr.[1] (*See The Gans Lineage chapter.*)

Charles and Ellen married 25 November 1880, at Enniskillen, Pettigo Parish, County Fermanagh, Ireland. They both were 22, and listed as farmers. Ellen lived at Kilmore, Pettigo, County Donegal. Charles lived at Kilgarnan, Pettigo, County Donegal. They were married in the Bannagh Roman Catholic Chapel in Pettigo Parish. Their witnesses were William Robinson and Mary McKestry.[2]

Charles' father was Bernard McHugh, and Ellen's was William McDease.[3]

- There are only 2 Bernard McHughs found in the 1857 Griffiths Valuation. The Bernard of interest to us is Lot 9 in Carn, Templecarn parish, Donegal union, Tirhugh barony. He rented a house, office, and land from John Leslie. Since he lives in Carn, in Templecarn parish, which is where our Charles spent his adult life, and probably grew up, this is almost certainly the correct Bernard.[4]

- Ellen's father, William McDease, was not found in the 1857 Griffiths Valuation. In fact, the ONLY McDease of this spelling ANYWHERE in Ireland in this Valuation is Patrick McDease, who lived in Billary, Templecarn, Donegal.[5] It is possible that William was living with him – perhaps Patrick was William's father (or brother). Ellen was not born until about 1858, so perhaps William had not married and moved out yet. This connection to Templecarn could explain how Ellen met Charles McHugh, whose father, Bernard, lived in Carn, Templecarn, Donegal at this same time.

All of Charles and Ellen's children were born in Carn. Carn is in the barony of Tirhugh and the parish of Templecarn.[6]

In the 1901 Ireland Census, Charles was a widow. Ellen McDease McHugh died sometime between 1893 (when their youngest child was born) and the 1901 census. The census found Charles, Sr. (43), as head of household, with children Mary (20), Catherine (17), Thomas (13), and Charles, Jr. (8). The family was Roman Catholic, and lived in Carn, Pettigo, County Donegal.[7]

Charles McHugh, Sr., died sometime after 1901. Since his children left Ireland en masse in 1903, it is almost certain he had died by that date.

The McHugh Family History
As Told by Clare Gallagher to Kerry Gans
January 22, 2006

Clare Gallagher is the daughter of Mary "Minnie" McHugh Gallagher and Edward Gallagher. I am the great–granddaughter of Catherine "Kate" McHugh Gans—Mary's sister. Clare and I met 22 January 2006 in Wynnewood, PA, and she told me what she knew of the McHugh family's history. She was 85 years old at the time.

McHugh

The McHugh family is from Pettigo, in County Donegal in Ireland. The mother McHugh passed away, and the father fell ill. He knew he was dying, so he saved as much money as possible to send his children to live with his brother in Philadelphia. On 22 February 1903, Mary, Kate, Thomas, and Charlie McHugh boarded the *SS Ethiopia* in Londonderry, Ireland. Mary was 22, Kate 19, Thomas 15, and Charlie 10. Their final destination was their cousin John McHugh's house at 545 Eiry (Eire) Ave., Trenton, NJ. They arrived in NY on 11 March 1903.[8]

The story goes that their uncle from Philadelphia went to New York to meet them. The ship was late in arriving – so late that he was told the ship had hit an iceberg and sunk. He returned to Philadelphia. Then the ship arrived, and the McHugh siblings stepped onto U.S. soil with no one to meet them, and no one they knew in New York. Somehow, they got word to their uncle, who came up to get them. The uncle already had 10 children of his own, and the McHugh siblings made 14. But the girls immediately went to work, so they contributed to the family.

Kate McHugh married George Joseph Gans, Jr., in 1905. Mary McHugh married Edward Gallagher in 1906. As was to be expected, they each had many children, some who died early, some who survived to adulthood.

Kate and George had 3 children – Charles, Helen, and William. Kate died in October 1918, in the flu pandemic. She was buried in the Gallagher family plot. There was quite a stir made when George showed up to Kate's viewing with his girlfriend, Helen Donovan, on his arm. They married 6 months later. Clare was not born at the time, but she knew Helen well and said she remembers her as a nice woman. Helen and George had 3 children of their own, and Clare was very close to the oldest girl, Peg, in this second family.

Mary's children and the Gans children were quite close growing up. The second 3 Gans children did not know that the older 3 were not their full siblings. That is, not until Clare dropped the bomb. As children do, Clare and Peg were fighting over something stupid, and Peg said she didn't like Clare anymore. Clare responded with, "I don't care, because we're not related anyway!" And the secret came out. As Clare said, how was she supposed to know that the kids didn't know?

Of Kate and George's children, Helen died in her 30s of a brain tumor. Charles married and had 4 boys. Bill married Nancy Warren and was blackballed by the family for not marrying in the Catholic Church. He lost touch with Charles' family after that. He and Nancy had 5 children. Clare says she does not understand what the big problem was about, since George was not a very devout Catholic himself! Clare feels that it had more to do with stepmother Helen. Helen had not taken to Kate's boys, and particularly picked on Bill. Both Charles and Bill had to quit school for work, neither completing high school. Bill later got his GED.

Mary McHugh and Edward Gallagher also had numerous children, several of whom died young (Dorothy, 15 months; Catherine, 4 years). Four survived to adulthood – Thomas, Helen, Eddie, and Clare. Helen died at age 24. Edward died in 1939; Mary in 1951. [*Clare Gallagher died in November 2010, age 89.*]

As for the McHugh boys who came over with their sisters, they lived with their sisters after the girls got married – Charlie with Mary and Thomas with Kate. They both married. Charlie and his wife, Anna, could not have children, as Charlie had caught chickenpox as an adult and become sterile.

Thomas' wife ran off with the neighbor, leaving 3–year–old Edith McHugh home alone. The wife took another girl with her, claiming she was the daughter of the neighbor, not of Thomas. Thomas could not raise Edith on his own, so she was mostly raised by Charlie and Anna. She stayed with her father on weekends, but they spent most weekends at Mary's house. It got to the point where Edith insisted that Charlie was her father, and Thomas was not. This caused a great deal of pain in the family. Edith did ask Thomas to give her away at her wedding, but only because Charlie was very ill. Even then, she denied to the priest that Thomas was her father, only to later admit in confession that he was! Poor Edith obviously had some unresolved issues. The rift was never mended, and Edith drifted away from the rest of the Gallagher family.

Quite suddenly, around 20 years ago, a woman contacted Clare – and it was the other girl from Thomas' marriage! It turned out that she was NOT the neighbor's daughter, but Thomas' and she was looking for her family. She had only found out the truth after her mother died. She met Clare, and Clare sent her on to Roslyn, PA, where Charlie, Anna, and Edith had lived. Edith and Anna had run a hairdressers shop in their home across the street from Roslyn train station, and this woman found the old sign, even though the shop was long closed! So, she reunited with her sister, although Thomas and Charlie were long dead by then.

And so closes the McHugh family story. Charlie never had any descendants. If Thomas' girls had any children, we do not know them. The Gallaghers are into their 4th generation, and number about 14 people. The Ganses are all over the place – Charles' four boys had numerous offspring, many of whom have children now. Bill's 5 had 10 children among them, and there are 4 children to those as of this writing.

[1] *Philadelphia Marriage Index 1885-1951*, #190124. Original housed at Philadelphia City Archives, 3101 Market Street, Philadelphia, PA 19104.
[2] Marriage License of Charles McHugh and Ellen McDease. Found on RootsIreland.ie http://www.rootsireland.ie/
[3] Marriage License of Charles McHugh and Ellen McDease. Found on RootsIreland.ie http://www.rootsireland.ie/
[4] *1857 Griffiths Valuation of Ireland.* http://freepages.genealogy.rootsweb.ancestry.com/~donegal/templecarngv.htm
[5] *1857 Griffiths Valuation of Ireland.* http://freepages.genealogy.rootsweb.ancestry.com/~donegal/templecarngv.htm
[6] *1901 Ireland Census*, Carn, Pettigo.
[7] *1901 Ireland Census*, Carn, Pettigo.
[8] Ship's manifest - *SS Ethiopia. New York Passenger Lists, 1820-1957* [database online] NARA document found on Ancestry.com.

McHugh Family Farm
Pettigo, Donegal, Ireland

(PHOTOS COURTESY
JOHN A. GANS)

LIST OR MANIFEST OF ALIEN (SECOND CABIN) IMMIGRANTS FOR THE COMMISSIONER OF IMMIGRATION.

Required by the Regulations of the Secretary of the Treasury of the United States, under Act of Congress approved March 3, 1893, to be delivered to the Commissioner of Immigration by the Commanding Officer of any Vessel having such Passengers on board upon arrival at a Port in the United States.

S.S. ETHIOPIA — sailing from LONDONDERRY — 22d Feby 1903 — Arriving at Port of NEW YORK

Catherine McHugh & Siblings
Ship Manifest: The Ethiopia

Departed: Londonderry, Ireland, 22 February 1903
Arrived: New York, United States, 11 March 1903

(Enlargement)

No.	Name	Age	Sex	Calling	Read	Write	Nationality	Last Residence	Destination	Relationship	Ever in US
4	Mary McHugh	20	F	Servant	Yes	Yes	Irish	Donegal	New York	self / Trenton N.J.	no
5	Kate McHugh	18	F	Servant	Yes	Yes	Irish	Donegal	New York	self / Trenton N.J.	no
6	Thomas McHugh	10	M	none	Yes	Yes	Irish	Donegal	New York	sister / Trenton N.J.	over 30 — no
7	Charlie McHugh	8	M	none	no	no	Irish	Donegal	New York	sister / Trenton N.J.	over 30 — no

Cousins — John o'Hugh, 345 Eirny Ave, Trenton N.J.

THE McHUGH SIBLINGS
THOMAS (SEATED), MARY (WHITE DRESS), CATHERINE & CHARLES

Nationality Charts

WARREN SISTERS NATIONALITY GRAPH
This version of the graph uses only nationalities I was able to trace in full.
You can see the amount of uncertainty this leaves as to our heritage.

■ German ■ English ■ Swiss ■ Welsh ■ Scottish ■ Irish ■ Canadian ■ Unknown

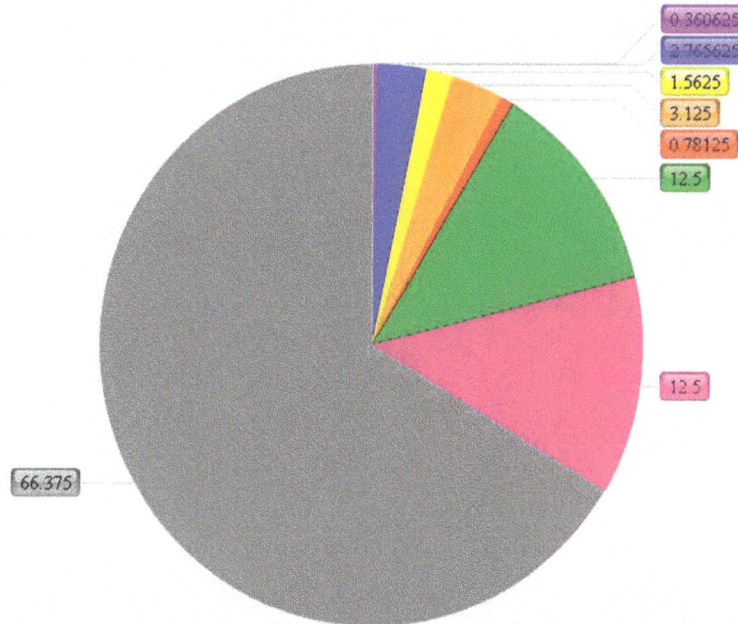

0.360625
0.765625
1.5625
3.125
0.78125
12.5

12.5

66.375

For the graph below, I researched the origins of names and hypothesized on probable
nationalities. When a name had more than one derivation, I used both. For
example Godshall can be English or German, so I made the first Godshall in line
half English and half German. When a wife had no last name, I made the
assumption that the men married within their dominant nationality community, such as
a German man marrying a woman of German extract, since that was the tradition in colonial
times. Using those assumptions, the Warren sisters' heritage looks like this:

■ German ■ English ■ Swiss ■ Welsh ■ Scottish ■ Irish ■ Canadian ■ French

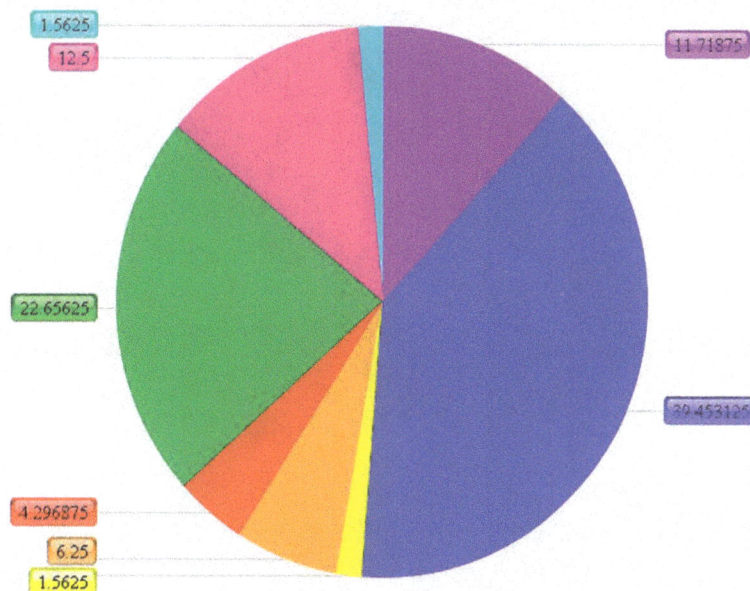

1.5625
12.5
11.71875

22.65625

39.453125

4.296875
6.25
1.5625

GANS NATIONALITY CHART

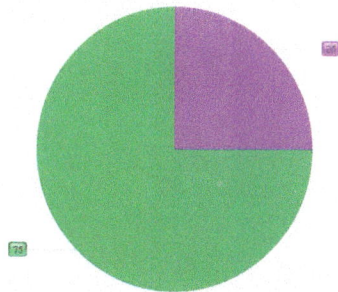

■ German ■ Irish

This is William Thomas Gans, Sr.'s nationality chart.
He was simple: 25% German, 75% Irish. When you add his
chart to the Warren Chart, you get the following:

■ German ■ English ■ Swiss ■ Welsh ■ Scottish ■ Irish ■ Canadian ■ French ■ Unknown

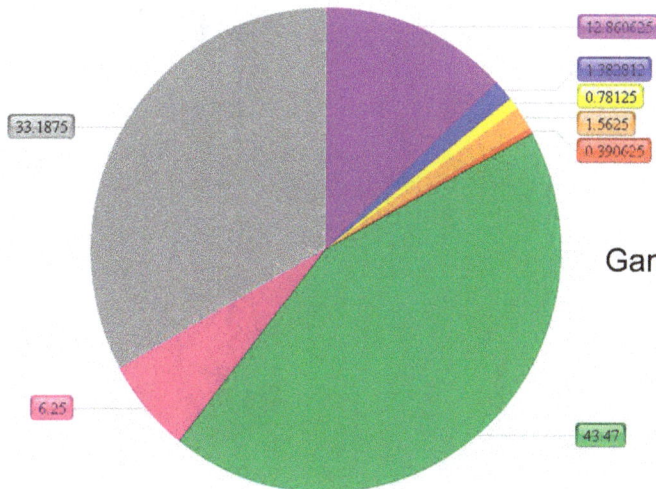

Gans Nationality Chart Proven

12.860625
1.382812
0.78125
1.5625
0.390625
33.1875
6.25
43.47

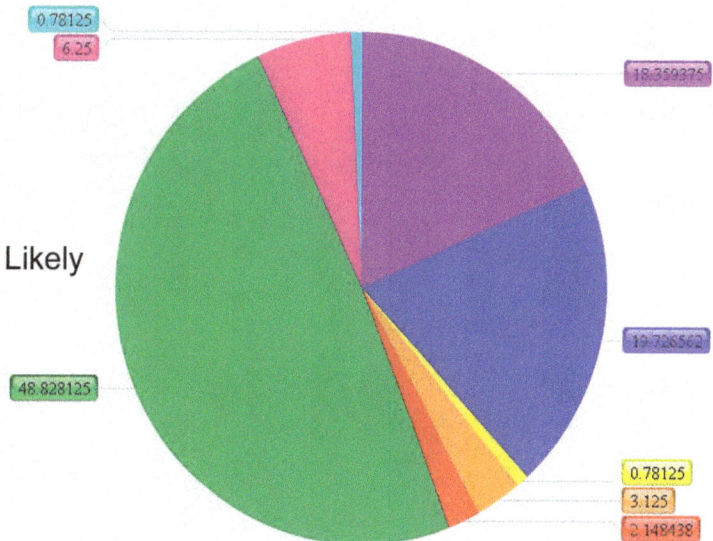

Gans Nationality Chart Likely

0.78125
6.25
18.359375
19.726562
0.78125
3.125
2.148438
48.828125

Name Index

Name Index

Friend
Elizabeth (servant), 2
Gallagher
Catherine, 111
Clare, 110, 111
Dorothy, 111
Edward, 110, 111
Edward, Jr., 111
Helen, 111
Thomas, 111
Gallaut/Garwood
John, 32
Gallop
Gideon, 83
Gans
Agness, 102
Caspar (Gantz), 100, 101, 102
Catherine P., 102, 103
Charles B., 104, 111
Clara, 100, 101, 102
Clara (b. 1872), 102
George Franklin, 104
George, III, 104
George, Jr., 102, 103, 104, 110, 111
George, Sr., 100, 101, 102, 103
Helen, 104, 111
Jacob, 100, 101
John, 100, 101
John F., 101
John, Jr., 100, 101
Joseph, 100, 101, 103
Joseph (b. 1832), 100
Lawrence, 102
Louisa, 101
Louise L., 102
Margaret, 100, 101
Margaret M., 104, 111
Mary, 100, 101, 103
Mary E., 102, 103
Mary J., 104
Steven, 100
Valentine, 100
William T., 102, 103
William Thomas, Sr., 4, 104, 105, 111

Garlick
Abigail, 57
Hannah, 57
Gegan
Ethel, 104
Gibbon
Ruth, 49
Godshall
Andrew, 17, 18
Andrew (Mennonite preacher), 18
Charles F., 19, 20
Clara C., 1, 3, 19, 20, 21
Frederick, 17, 18, 58
Frederick (b. 1869), 20
Frederick, III, 18, 19
Frederick, Jr., 17, 18, 19, 58
George, 19
Henry "Harry", 20
Henry Stites, 18, 19, 20, 85, 86, 87
Kate A., 19, 20, 21
Lilly H., 20, 21
Louis, 20
Mary L., 20, 21
Norwell/Howell, 19, 20
Prudence Sophia, 18, 19
Samuel, 18, 19
Gondolf
Edward, 4
Goodwin
Elizabeth, 83
Samuel, 83
Grant
(Reverend), 1
Gray
Sophia (servant), 25
Griffith
Ann, 64
Guest
Arthur, 104
Guitteau
Francis, 36
Hall
Francis, 57
Mary, 57
Unknown (2nd wife of Humphrey Underhill, Jr.), 56

Place Index

Place Index

Cemetery and Church Index

Cemetery & Church Index

www.ingramcontent.com/pod-product-compliance
Lightning Source LLC
Chambersburg PA
CBHW080242030426
42334CB00023BA/2672